Corridor city: travel on horizontal motion

The city is an endless corridor. Land or passage, the corridor is the horizontal link between places. It materialises as a linear transitional space, or an enclosed passageway opening onto new possible worlds. In other words, the corridor is the back bone for any interior spatial organisation. It is the route, the light, the access, and a door to another destination. The inhabitants spend most of their time in corridors. In a group or alone, they move horizontally into a space that projects itself toward an infinite vanishing point. A horizontal journey, *Corridor city* does not lack perspectives.

If a city can be considered a place, one has to imagine a city, not an ordinary one, but a linear city, a transitional place. *Corridor city* is composed of an infinite number of passages. Those do not only give access to a place to stay, such as a room, but they open onto other linear spaces. Together, they form a complex geometry of corridors - a perfect maze.

As one of the most public spaces among the others, the corridor is often the attractor to a high density of activities and serves them as connector. When this happens, it transforms into linear space lined with continuous shop windows displaying all kind of new products. Each window competes with the others for maximum diversity, the brightest colours and attractive prices. The linearity is emphasised by low ceilings and smooth surfaces with uniform marble or tiled floors.

Protected from the exterior environment, the enclosed linear space is essentially animated by mechanical openings and people. As a result, the city grows as the inhabitants open and close its doors, moving from one corridor to another. From the train to the residence, the office, airport or hotel, the corridor frames the inhabitants' daily routine.

In *Corridor city* no one pays much attention to the aesthetic but to the fluidity of the continuous zone. Its economy is reduced to one word: efficiency. So that its aesthetic is reduced to a form of advertisement, some codified elements of decoration, or to nothing but the rough material of its enclosure.

Here the climate fully ignores exterior meteorological elements: 16-19 degrees, dry. As a matter of fact, the inhabitants are dressed to respond to a corridor condition.

Corridor city is codified by an extensive set of rules. These are posted at each intersection along with an orientation map and the corridor name, in a way that no one can be lost, nor ignore the law. They illustrate a perfect codification of personal behaviours under permanent control. Standard sets of digital devises plus a police patrol ensure the transitional character of *Corridor city*.

A moving walkway is often more than welcome to accelerate the flux. Walking is the only type of authorised movement, as running would appear extremely suspicious. Therefore, the inhabitants are the antithesis of the stroller as they never divert from their routes nor can they be lost. As one crosses various sectors, it is not recommended to stop, or to break the flow. An encounter in a linear architecture does not last long. Therefore, social exchanges can only happen while walking in the same direction, and at the same speed. In *Corridor city*, the individual is dissolved in the anonymous flux of the masses.

The city is no longer understood as a distinct structure defined by the presence of spaces, but becomes a dynamic system generated by the interstitial spaces in-between: the corridors. Together they produce the most extraordinary form of assemblage, an accumulation of potential usable spaces but also an increase in physical mobility. Everybody here enjoys moving from one place to another with the possibility of discovering new shops and facilities. Spatial mobility and continuous human migration create a chequered motion, providing these artificial lines with a prime functional space between the apartment and the territory.

OUR PAST

HK LAB

香港實驗室

MAP BOOK PUBLISHERS

Many aspects of Hong Kong show positive forms of development, and particularly ones that have failed to succeed elsewhere. Geographical limits and economic tensions have produced a dynamic process, one which paradoxically combines both specific and ever changing demands mapped onto a re-convertible environment. One of the major challenges is how to absorb new layers – physical but also demographic, cultural, economic, political – that are complex and stratified in both horizontal and vertical structures running over the territory. The continual fluctuation of people, goods, data and services as transitory entities forms a condition where the whole system is in movement, a temporal process where the course of experimentation can take place.

laurent gutierrez, ezio manzini, valérie portefaix, editors / foreword by dejan sudjic / with contributions by ackbar abbas, tak chi lee, stewart clegg, norman jackson ford, judith hollows, doreen heng liu, alice ming wai jim, laura ruggeri, alfred yeung

---

HK LAB is the first volume of the *HK LAB Trilogy*.

Many aspects of Hong Kong show positive forms of development, and particularly ones that have failed to succeed elsewhere. Geographical limits and economical tensions have produced a dynamic process matching with a specific demand, to ever-changing demand, to re-convertible environment. One of the major challenges, is in effect that of absorbing new layers – physical but also demographic, cultural, economic, political – complex and stratified in both horizontal and vertical structures running over the territory. A continual fluctuation of people, goods, data and services, as moving entities, is forming a condition where the whole system is in movement, a temporal process where the course of experimentation can take place.

Laurent Gutierrez, Ezio Manzini, Valérie Portefaix, editors / foreword by Dejan Sudjic / with contributions by Ackbar Abbas, Tak Chi Lee, Stewart Clegg, Norman Jackson Ford, Judith Hollows, Doreen Heng Liu, Alice Ming Wai Jim, Laura Ruggeri, Alfred Yeung / ISBN 962860403 – 9 / MAP Book 2002

HK LAB 3 presents a fictional history of Hong Kong, a do-it-yourself history · observing Hong Kong from china, reading future in the past. HK LAB 3 is reinvestigating historical moment/spaces to construct an experience in which some mythological invention explore the way we live, speak, exchange and represent. Here, the constant mutation, characteristic of Hong Kong condition has contributed to build an utopian world. HK LAB 3 is reflecting on this archaeology of contemporary living.

Laurent Gutierrez, Valérie Portefaix, editors · Forthcoming Map Book 2006

HK LAB 3
香港實驗室三
MAP BOOK

HK LAB 3
香港實驗室三 MAP BOOK PUBLISHERS

HK LAB 3 is the third volume of the *HK LAB Trilogy*. The original setting and new strategic ways of living in the first volume, *HK LAB*: A geography of living, was extended in the second – *HK LAB 2*: An exploration of Hong Kong paradigmatic interior spaces. The third volume moves from spatial conditions - interior or exterior – to the consideration of the fourth dimension by sur-imposing additional layers of time and history.

HK LAB 3 will present a 'fictional' history of Hong Kong, a do-it-yourself history - observing Hong Kong from China – reading the future in the past. *HK LAB 3* will reinvestigate historical moments/spaces to construct an experience in which past and future narrative and mythological inventions reveal the ways we live, speak, exchange and re-present. Here, the constant mutations and systemic stasis characteristic of the Hong Kong condition are seen to contribute to the building of a 'utopian' world.

HK LAB 3 turns to reflect upon this archaeology of contemporary living.

Norman Jackson Ford, Laurent Gutierrez, Valérie Portefaix, editors / Forthcoming ISBN 962860400 - 7 / MAP Book 2006

HK LAB 2
An exploration of Hong Kong interior spaces

Editors: Laurent Gutierrez - Valerie Portefaix - Laura Ruggeri

Cover and graphic design: MAP OFFICE

English editing: Judith Hollows

English proof reading: Norman Jackson Ford

Chinese translation: Tian Hong (except "2046")

First published 2005 by
MAP BOOK PUBLISHERS
5th Floor, 231, Wing Lok Street
Sheung Wan, Hong Kong
(852) 2546 3016
mapoff@netvigator.com
www.map-office.com

Available in Europe through IDEA BOOKS
Nieuwe Herengracht 11, 1011 RK Amsterdam, The Netherlands
Tel: +31 20 6226154 Fax: +31 20 6209299

Available in North, South and Central America through D.A.P./Distributed Art Publishers Inc
155 Sixth Avenue, 2nd Floor, N.Y. 10013
Tel: (212) 627-1999 Fax: (212) 627-9484

ISBN 962-86040-8-2
Printed in Hong Kong, 2005

Supported by

香港藝術發展局
Hong Kong Arts Development Council

HK LAB 2

香港實驗室二

Laurent Gutierrez - Valérie Portefaix - Laura Ruggeri (eds.)

An Exploration of Hong Kong Interior Spaces

香港內部空間的探險

MAP BOOK PUBLISHERS

GUTIERREZ + PORTEFAIX

HOU HANRU

GUTIERREZ + PORTEFAIX / LAURA RUGGERI

CONTENTS

GUTIERREZ + PORTEFAIX

Booth city - 089

GUTIERREZ + PORTEFAIX / LAURENT MALONE

Underneath the highway - 141

GUTIERREZ + PORTEFAIX

Light city - 109

MARY BUNEO

GUTIERREZ + PORTEFAIX / LAURENT MALONE

HSBC stories - 163

KATHY LO PUI-YING

Upstairs shops - 117

RENE CHEN

See-fong choi - 129

CONTENTS

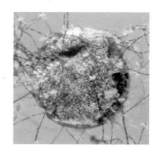

CONTENTS

Ackbar Abbas, professor at Department of Comparative Literature, and director of the Centre for the Study of Globalisation and Cultures at The University of Hong Kong. He is the author of, among other works, "The New Hong Kong Cinema and the *Déjà Disparu*" in *Discourse* (1994), *Hong Kong: Culture and the Politics of Disappearance* (1997), and "The Erotics of Disappointment", in *Wong Kar-wai* (1997).

Mary Buneo, has been working as a domestic helper in Hong Kong since 1994.

Gary Chang, graduated from the Department of Architecture, The University of Hong Kong in 1987, and founded EDGE in 1994. He was among the first group of representatives from Hong Kong to be invited to participate in the International Biennial Exhibition of Architecture, Venice, in 2000, and again 2002. His first solo exhibition was held at the Hong Kong Art Centre in 2000. His work has received many awards and has been extensively published internationally, including a monograph, *Gary Chang - Edge Works* (MCCM, 2005).

Laurent Gutierrez, architect, and assistant professor at the School of Design, The Hong Kong Polytechnic University. In 1997, he co-founded MAP OFFICE (with Valérie Portefaix). His research details both the physical and dynamic transformations taking place in Hong Kong, China and the US. Current research focuses on 'lean planning', which explores the impact of economic production and distribution mapped onto a reconvertible environment and the specific 'Made in China' condition of the Pearl River Delta region.

Rene Chen, holds a master of arts in design from The Hong Kong Polytechnic University. Starting as a graphic designer in Toronto, she has solidly worked her way up until to become an art director in several well established graphic design companies in Hong Kong. She recently started her own business in the design and creative area.

Cecilia Chu, designer and educator. She has been a visiting lecturer for the MA Design program at The Hong Kong Polytechnic University and the SPACE Environmental Design program at The University of Hong Kong since 2002. Actively involved with local design and conservation issues, she has played a major role in several campaigns on urban development in Hong Kong. She is currently pursuing a Ph.D in architecture at The University of California, Berkeley.

Hou Hanru, has lived and worked in Paris as an independent critic and curator since 1990. Known for ground-breaking exhibitions such as *Cities on the Move* (co-curated with Hans-Ulrich Obrist), *Out of the Center, Parisien(ne)s* and the Kwangju Biennial in Korea, his work addresses questions of globalisation and identity, understanding contemporary art practice as it exists beyond geographical and regional boundaries.

Mishko Hansen, visiting lecturer for the MA & MDES programs at The Hong Kong Polytechnic University. He previously worked as an investment manager with several Asia based hedge-funds and is currently pursuing multi-disciplinary research on the process of value creation. He has also been an activist on urban development issues and contributed to several NGO projects.

Ho Sui-kee, is a visual artist. He holds a Ph.D in fine art from RMIT, and a master of fine art from Cranbrook Academy. His video installations and projects develop a space whose proportions are oriented on those of the artist's body. His artwork has been exhibited in leading Biennials, museums and galleries, including the 49th Venice Biennial. He is a senior lecturer at The Art School, Hong Kong Art Centre.

Eric Howeler, is an architect and author practising in New York. He is principal of Howeler + Yoon, an interdisciplinary design studio co-founded with J. Meejin Yoon. He is a senior designer with Diller + Scofidio and formerly with Kohn Pedersen Fox. He holds a bachelor and a master of Architecture from Cornell University. He has published in a number of journals including *Praxis*, *Archis*, and *Loud Paper*. He is author of *Skyscraper: Vertical Now* (Rizzoli/Universe 2003), and *1,001 Skyscrapers* (Princeton Architectural Press, 2001), with J. Meejin Yoon.

Pierre Larauza, is a cross-disciplinary artist involved in individual and collective projects in several fields - visual arts, architecture, performing art. He is conducting research and experiments on space/non-place and movement of the subjective body and has participated in numerous group exhibitions. He has just finished a dance-drama *Over the game* with the dancer Emmanuelle Vincent and is currently working on an architectural project, *paysages rhizomatiques*.

James Law, is chief cybertect and chairman of James Law Cybertecture International, a global consultancy specialising in the design and strategy formation of cybertecture projects. These include futuristic architecture, infrastructure and city planning, strategic planning of new business and communication models, advance research and production of custom software applications that power cybertecture projects. He is the author of *Cybertecture* (MCCM, 2005).

Neil Leach, is an architect and theorist. He has been visiting professor at the Architectural Association in London and the Dessau Institute of Architecture in Germany, Columbia University, New York; professor of architectural theory at the University of Bath; and reader in architecture and critical theory at the University of Nottingham. He is the author of *China* (Map, 2004), *The Anaesthetics of Architecture* (MIT, 1999), *Millennium Culture* (Elipsis, 1999), *Camouflage* (MIT, 2005); editor of *Rethinking Architecture* (Routledge, 1997), *Architecture and Revolution* (Routledge, 1999).

Leung Chi-wo, is an artist and a founding member of Para/Site Art Space in Hong Kong. He holds a master of fine art from The Chinese University of Hong Kong. He has exhibited in New York, Melbourne, Tokyo, Oslo, Vienna, Hamburg and Toronto. His site specific project *Would you like a piece of sky?*, in collaboration with Sara Wong Chi-hang, was exhibited in the Hong Kong pavilion at the the 49th Venice Biennial.

Leung Kam-ping, has been a marriage and family counsellor in Hong Kong for thirteen years, and is now working as a training consultant at The University of Hong Kong, Hong Kong Jockey Club Centre for Suicide Research and Prevention. Based on her research on the relationship between household arrangements and family relationships, she published a book *The wings of dreams-stories of searching household space* (2004).

Kathy Lo Pui-ying, holds a master of arts in design from The Hong Kong Polytechnic University. She has a cross-disciplinary background in design and communication. Her professional experience includes multimedia design, website design, graphic design and business communications. Her research interests range from lifestyle, popular culture to design and technology.

Laurent Malone, is a photographer based in Marseilles. He is principal of LMX, a research and production laboratory focusing on collaborative public projects and publications that address the urban context. In collaboration with Denis Adams, he published *JFK* (LMX, 1997), a photographic dialogue along a 11-km walk across New York City.

Valerie Portefaix, director of MAP Office, a collaborative studio based in Hong Kong involved in cross-disciplinary projects that incorporate architecture and the visual arts. An architect with a Ph.D in Urbanism, her research and projects detail both the physical and dynamic transformations taking place in Hong Kong and China. In conjunction with the 7th Architecture Venice Biennial, she published *mapping HK*, with Laurent Gutierrez (Map, 2000), and co-edited *HK LAB* (Map, 2002), *Yung Ho Chang/Atelier FCJZ* (Map, 2003), *Learning from Antipodes* (map, 2003), *Gary Chang: Suitcase House* (MCCM, 2004).

Laura Ruggeri, born in Milan, since 1997 she has been living in Hong Kong where she teaches theory and research methods at The Hong Kong Polytechnic University. For the past ten years she has been realising videos, installations, and urban scale art projects across Europe, investigating the relationship between spatial theory and critical practice, body and architecture and promoting attention to meaning construction and its articulations, focusing in particular on the role of metaphor. She is now devoting her time to the exploration of Hong Kong infraspaces.

Ziteng, was formed in 1996 by a group of local women activists who shared the common goal of assisting and empowering Hong Kong sex workers through direct services, legal advocacy, and raising public awareness on sex workers' issues. It aims to empower these workers by providing services for them in Hong Kong and Mainland China.

VISUAL CREDITS

Photography

All photographs in *HK LAB 2* by Laurent Gutierrez and Valérie Portefaix except:

Domestica invisibile , Leung Chi-wo, 56-63.

XS property shops, Pierre Larauza, 78-84.

Underneath the highway, Laurent Malone, 141, 148, 152, 160.

HSBC stories, Laurent Malone, 166-171.

Urban dynamics, ©EDGE Design Institute Ltd, Gary Chang, 186-195.

Chungking city, Unknown, 200.

Moulding time, ©Centre de recherches sur les céréales, Agriculture et Agroalimentaire Canada, 228-235.

My life, ©Ziteng, 258-269.

"2046", ©James Law, 271, 275-276, 290; from Wong Kar-wai "2046", 272, 283-284, 289.

Maps / Graphics

All maps and graphics in *HK LAB 2* were created by Laurent Gutierrez and Valérie Portefaix except:

Sit, stand, lie, Ho Sui-kee, 42-47.

Domestica invisibile , Leung Chi-wo, 56-62.

XS property shops, Pierre Larauza, 76-85. (Including graphic design)

Urban dynamics, ©EDGE Design Institute Ltd, Gary Chang, 196.

We would like to thank:

All the contributors involved, a special thank you, without your brilliant work there simply would have been no *HK LAB 2*.

We are particularly grateful to Judith Hollows for her infinite patience during the editing of all these texts.

Tian Hong, for her Chinese translation.
Additional thanks to Norman Jackson Ford and Roger Ball for their careful readings.
Hong Kong Arts Development Council, for their generous subsidy.

We extend our gratitude to a number of people and institutions:
School of Design, The Hong Kong Polytechnic University, The Fringe Club, Mary Chang.

HOU HANRU

HK LAB 2 – a city of real life

Hong Kong, what a wonderful city! It's one of the most dynamic centres of a global economy. However, its particular geopolitical and cultural position forces a constant negotiation between Chinese influences and an integrated international identity, between post-colonial conditions and the contradictory stature of 'one country, two systems'. This context creates an exciting but complicated battlefield for innovation in terms of political, social, cultural and everyday life. Simultaneously, the official slogan, 'Hong Kong, Asia's World City', attempts to re-create the city as a 'regional hub'. All this makes Hong Kong a most unique site for experiments in urban invention.

In a phrase, Hong Kong is a life-size laboratory for urbanism. Laurent Gutierrez and Valérie Portefaix fell in love with this exciting and mysterious laboratory 9 years ago. They decided to turn themselves into real Hong Kong-ese, having now lived in the city for almost a decade. Coming from France, they admit they cannot imagine living anywhere else. As architects, they have the most natural and convincing reason to stay and create work, and thus, their new life. Almost all Hong Kong inhabitants are in fact eternal exiles and help to incessantly reinvent the city.

This sounds like a perfectly common and banal story for many settlers from outside in this fantastic city. However, Gutierrez and Portefaix story is remarkably different and singular. They not only enjoy the experiences in such an urban lab, but also critically explore it, proposing equally inventive readings and visions of the city life and its urbanistic future. One such experiment is a series of projects called simply *HK LAB*. It's not only a pioneering project in the manifestation of Hong Kong's unique position as a global city, but also a fruitful collaboration between different specialists from diverse backgrounds. This invaluable result of collective intelligence, of those who share the same desire and courage, navigates the extreme urban conditions of such a city: density, speed, constantly shifting, hybrid and contradictory – a typical case of 'post-planning'.

In the first *HK LAB*, Gutierrez and Portefaix, with Ezio Manzini and their collaborators, provided us with a broad picture of the urban conditions of the city. They have also successfully shown the close link between Hong Kong and its neighbours in the Pearl River Delta. In fact, Hong Kong is not only a laboratory for urban development in general but, more specifically, is a laboratory for China's recent urban expansion, that turns out to be even more radical and explosive than previously thought.

In *HK LAB 2*, the couple, with Laura Ruggeri, carry on this research from a more specific perspective, guiding us through aspects beyond the concerns of conventional urban and architectural studies. With the contributions of different specialists, they bring us to the space of the everyday, the vernacular, the self-organised, the bottom-ups...

This second *HK LAB* clearly scrutinises the 'dark side' of a brilliant, spectacular and prosperous city. It reveals, in its XS spaces and popular inventions, the very secrets that have made Hong Kong so fantastic. As the dynamic and innovative ways of using and transforming urban areas emerge, the spontaneous, intelligent investments and interventions of its people become even more evident – especially in those surviving under the poverty line and in those who create a 'real' street life. We now have a chance to travel through Chungking Mansion, booth city, lift city, sex city, light city, HSBC stories, etc. Clearly, it's not only the official forms of skyscrapers that make Hong Kong's skyline so unique. In fact, it is primarily because of the lower parts of the street level architectural and urban solutions – solutions which deal with everyday emergencies – that Hong Kong is rendered with such incredible energy and innovativeness. They are veritable anti-monuments. Yet, it's also because of these quotidian conditions that life in this totally air-conditioned city can still generate real fresh air... And this is monumental!

Gutierrez and Portefaix, with friends who share their spirit of adventure, not only understand and but 'touch' a critical 'acupoint' on the nervous system of this urban jungle. And this makes the book much more 'useful' than any official city guide. It's a city in itself, and it's a city of real life...

9 March 2005, on arrival in Paris from Hong Kong, with AF 185

An exploration of HK interior spaces

I
HK LAB 2 picks up where *HK LAB* left off, and extends it.

The *HK LAB Trilogy* was conceived as a new type of city monograph, an experimental publishing project that is responding to new and specific urban, economic, social, political conditions. The focus is set between the physical structure of the city and the different systems that run through it, between a collection of hard data and their sensible interpretation, between the local urban-architectural production and the global forces that impact upon it. External fluctuations are visible in the making of the series itself. With different centres or geography of living, working, living, transporting, entertaining, *HK LAB* explores a number of themes that are distinct and yet connected with each other. The logic of late capitalism is dispersive, does not tend toward wholes of whatever kind. It marks a loosening of the modern construction such that its elements and components float at a certain distance from each other, and yet generate formations that are under constant mutation, morphing into new topographies as we write.

Correspondingly, the present volume, *HK LAB 2* pushes the exploration forward. Here the editors' approach is to move from the concept of city-scape to urban practices. From a macro to a micro approach, it brings together artists' projects and a number of theoretical and critical viewpoints on Hong

Kong infra-spaces. Therefore, the changing nature of urban experience and inhabitation calls for new critical paradigms and interdisciplinary approaches.

HK LAB 2 is conceived as a polycentric book where a number of themes come together: private-public, use-exchange, space-time, local-global, prescribed-interim use, control-deviation, surface-structure. These are to be regarded as both paradigmatic and/or dialectical oppositions. These oppositions are mostly experienced in forms of contact / conflict, social rhythms, hybridisation, re-appropriation of space and the body.

Instead of trying to impose order on material that resists classification and constantly spills over the borders of any taxonomic approach to space, this edition, like its predecessor, aims to retain the palpable flux and fluidity of a heterogeneous collection - inherently dialogical with the potential to resonate in unpredictable ways. It will deliberately erase the finely etched line between the academic and the artistic, arguing that the labyrinthine and contaminated quality of metropolitan life leads to something more than simply new cultural connections. It also undermines the presumed purity of thought. If critical thought can entertain this encounter, then it is projected into the more extensive regimes of the everyday world.

We believe that understanding the city must involve both the micro and the macro. Neither is inherently privileged, but there is always the accompanying recognition that no city - indeed no 'lived' space - is ever completely known no matter what perspective is taken. The appropriate response to the micro versus macro scenario is thus an assertive and creative rejection of the either/or in favour of the more open ended.

Artists' projects and reflections on the city interior spaces deal with the mutations at work today, whether they are expressed in extreme and spectacular ways or in a gradual and less visible fashion.

The acts of building, decorating, furnishing, using, transforming and representing interiors are laden with meanings, implied or explicit. These meanings can inform us about the interiors' creators, owners and users; about political, social and familial aspirations and attitudes; and about the reciprocal relationships between people and interiors. Our editorial project explores the tactics which people use to articulate some of these meanings through their relationships with the spaces they inhabit, occupy temporarily or represent.

It offers a drift, a search for untried representations of Hong Kong's liminal spaces, an examination and elaboration of possible multiple systems of mapping. *HK LAB 2* is informed by the spatial practices of its contributors and every act of mapping or projecting them inherently contains distortions. Yet, we believe that generating an authentically productive field of tensions amidst the vast array of materials offered by the city enables a new configuration to arise out of the disruption of habitual modes of thinking and seeing.

The organic structure proposed here reflects the urban practices and experiences that we set out to map. Moving along the lines of distinctive entities one can recognise specific patterns and follow them at will.

The underlying structure of the book is given by the first and last stories - *Corridor city* and *Lift city*. Each contribution opens on a specific area of research that can be isolated or linked to other parts of the book. One can choose to read it from A to Z or personalise his/her own reading, ignoring some contributions and reading others 10 times. The 4 spheres - domestic, commercial, strategic and fictional - suggest another possible organisation of the textual and visual material offered.

II
Along the lines of *HK LAB 2...*
The distinction between the inside and the outside, public and private is constantly being renegotiated; a blurred, soft zone, where boundaries open and surfaces unfold, a *pli* that allows for slippage, leakage, dis-placements and re-placements. The soft zone accommodates both the urban landscape (hard space) as well the private domain (soft space), disseminating the soft in the hard and the hard in the soft. Here the complex exigencies of contemporary urbanism combine the requirements of the urban and the individual leading to a reconsideration of often dichotomous relationships. The individual is inserted into multidimensional sets of radically discontinuous realities, a world where differences are juxtaposed and coexist within non-stable networks that cannot be easily mediated or synthesised.

Ho Siu-kee, one of Hong Kong's leading artists, explores the spatial relationship between the body and the environment. Taking his cue from a Chinese folk idiom "Bend at three months, sit at six months and stand with help at nine months" Ho Siu-kee looks at the way the human body adjusts to space, and the perceptual changes that naturally accompany such an adaptive process. Hong Kong is a place that seems to put unlimited demands on the human body, the *homo urbanus* that inhabits this space is an extremely plastic one, one without fixed dimensions, whose extraordinary resilience is often compared to that of the city itself. In *Ellie's story* **Kathy Leung Kamping** describes the tactics deployed by single, working class women who live with their parents and relatives in small flats in public estates. They try to cope with insufficient space and lack of privacy by using personal objects to demarcate 'their territory', or appropriating public spaces such as libraries and restaurants. Another Hong Kong leading artist, **Leung Chiwo** bases his work on the memory of a space and explores the possibilities to perceive and represent it. With this new series of photographs and drawings, the artist presents a mapping of the left-over space under the furniture - a desk, an armchair, a cabinet - extruding optional space for further storage. *Domestica invisibile* is a homage to the knowledge of the housewife (his mother) and her capacity to compact and conceal daily life objects.

In the readings, interior design erects an intriguing sign system that indexes the individual as well as the collective psyche. It stages, in material forms and relations, a certain conception of home – a given notion of belonging and selfhood. Parallel to the signifying operation of all languages, the sign value of objects enforces a logic of differentiation and establishes, through display and conspicuous consumption, a distinctive hierarchy of taste, status, and identity. Indeed, all commodities, participate in an ingenious "social discourse of objects" that contributes to what Jean Baudrillard once described as a general "mechanism of discrimination and prestige."

The ancestral house once served as a means of integrating thought, memory and dreams. When the past is routinely erased, emotional investment is pinned on the future, and the present has to be artificially re-enchanted. In their essay *Constructing the 'real' dream home* **Cecilia Chu** and **Mishko Hansen** explore the particularities of Hong Kong's property market and role of interior design. The ordered spaces of show-flats, while representing an ideal vision of living, are also real spaces themselves where people interact and construct their own (different) versions of home according to their imaginations. If Hong Kong residents have learned the tricks of high-density living and can make the most of limited space, real estate agents who deal with low-cost properties in the old and most crowded districts of Wanchai and Mongkok have adopted a similar approach. Their extra small shops consist of little else than a computer, a desk and a couple of stools that can be unfolded on the pavement if necessary. They occupy small recesses in the wall, often less than a meter deep. **Pierre Larauza** turns his camera to these street level offices where the valorisation of capital and the maximisation of space come together, and where the office and the properties rented or sold reflect the same logic. **Gutierrez + Portefaix**'s *Booth city* and *Light city* further explore this maximisation; the ability of Hong Kong to invent systems and spaces in order to develop business. The small structures are detailed methodically by groups of students for *Booth city*. These structures demonstrate this amazing capacity to adapt very small spaces to whatever configuration with minimum budget. Drawings and photos document basic movements: rotation, sliding, folding to increase the surface and therefore the business opportunities. A similar logic is explored in *Light city*, where a new scenario for business in the jungle is presented.

Consumption forms an essential part of Hong Kong life but, as in most developed countries, it is not merely a matter of consuming goods but rather of constructing identity, relating to people and groups, marking social differences, and pursuing emotional and aesthetic pleasures. **Kathy Lo Pui-ying**'s text *Upstairs shops: resistance against mundanity* investigates the burgeoning phenomenon of shops that are usually located on the first or second floors of buildings, sandwiched between ground level shops below and residential flats above. They offer not only a different, more adventurous type of shopping experience, they can also be read as a kind of heterotopia of compensation. Dog and cat themed cafés where patrons can play with someone else's pets fulfil the frustrated desire of owning a pet in hyper-dense Hong Kong where the public housing authority bans animals. Retail outlets that provide a home feeling are patronised especially because that feeling is missing from overcrowded flats where personal space must be constantly negotiated. **Rene Chen**'s *See-fong choi* (private upstairs dining) or home made cooking restaurant, is a niche for new consumer behaviour. This contribution explores the phenomenon through the perspectives of traditional Chinese eating culture, social class distinction, community, singularity and lifestyle. With no more distinction between spaces, the private flat is transformed, enlarging the kitchen and dining room. The private sphere is invaded by the public.

From upstairs to underneath, it is a question of perspective and territorial definition. Appropriation by occupation and transformation seems to be the major logic of an under condition. *Underneath the highway* by **Maeva Aubert / Gutierrez + Portefaix / Laurent Malone**, explores the space under an elevated infrastructure through a photo/audio report that articulates major sequences along a line from Kennedy Town to North Point. If juxtaposition of elements and programs tend to ignore both context and surrounding, here the 'underneath' is definitely a space of opportunity. A similar logic applies to HSBC stories. Visually illustrated by the previous authors, the chapter is a compilation of stories collected by **Mary Buneo**. Meeting almost every Sunday under the glass belly of the world famous headquarters of The Hong Kong and Shanghai Bank, the Philippine domestic helper community appropriates the space every Sunday, almost as a form of revenge against capital. There, they meet friends, eat, share shopping, get or give fresh news from their native village/region and endlessly chat. The world famous bank becomes the one-day theatre for a swarm of domestic rumours.

Neil Leach's essay *Drag space* posits Hong Kong as the quintessential site of spatial appropriation, a laboratory where a theory about the performativity of space can be tested. By transforming the nature of the space through a method of activation, the function of the space is rewritten and reinvented. This might accommodate an alternation between prescribed use and event, the transformation of a conference venue into a wedding banquet hall, and back into conference room in less than 24 hours, temporary shops opening for a few days between two leases, or the residual space between buildings used by hawkers and food stalls owners.

Similarly, **Gary Chang**'s '4C' theory identifies Connection, Choice, Change and Coexistence, as the major characteristics of Hong Kong spaces. Through his own projects and the reading of various visible phenomena, the architect proposes flexible and reversible design for a continuous exploration of possible spaces.

Paradigmatic of this peculiar condition, Chungking Mansions is one of the most famous buildings in Hong Kong, yet no-one has told its story. Unlike the Kowloon Walled City which once demolished became the subject of a number of publications, *Chungking city* by **Gutierrez + Portefaix** picks up the left over building to transform it into a monument, and ultimately into a possible game to navigate the complex interior spaces. *Re-city* by the same authors looks at the city from the angle of material consumption, looking at product waste instead of space. Questioning the object after life and Hong Kong's recycling strategy, this photographic work promptly exposes the unseen and dark side of our daily consumption.

In her writing experiment *Moulding time*, **Laura Ruggeri** follows the premises of *HK LAB* to their most extreme conclusion, putting Hong Kong mould under the microscope and observing the interplay of organic and inorganic matter. Yet the closer she looks, the more metaphorical her observations become. Wandering through a network of associations and connections, she creates new relationships by transferring or deferring meaning from the realm of familiar experience into the realm of the unfamiliar. She sets off a process that is analogous to that set off by fungi, most of which are recyclers, 'process engineers', change agents.

Thermal city by **Eric Howeler** presents a multi-faceted space design for a specific climate - air-conditioning. The atmospherical projection of Hong Kong's reflective facades is, according to the author, creating an interiority with a climatic negation of the outside. **Laura Ruggeri** engages in (s)mall deviations with *The erotics of the shopping mall*. In shopping malls we find the implicated shadows of self, desire, and consumption in amongst the goods on display and the crowds of people. Cruising, stalking, soliciting, voyeurism, fetishism make up a large and often neglected aspect of the shopping mall experience. On the backstage, behind glittering shops and marble-clad walls, one can navigate the soft belly of the mall. There are no security cameras, floors and stairs are concreted and pipes hung overhead. Shop assistants and cleaners congregate, eat or rest on the steps-smokers join them for a puff, and lovers exchange languid caresses.

For the 2004 exhibition *My life* curated by the non-profit organisation **Ziteng**, 30 sex workers were given disposable cameras and invited to represent themselves and their working environment, subverting the usual fetishistic and voyeuristic economy that makes them the object of the male gaze. The pictures they chose to contribute to *HK LAB 2* reveal their efforts to create a domestic space of self-expression in the one-woman brothels where they work. '1-lau-1' are small apartments rented by one woman at a time – she might work the day shift and then go home to take care of her family, while another one takes her place at night. One woman might work only on weekends while another uses all the time allowed by her tourist visa to see as many clients as possible. The '1-lau-1' arrangement dodges the legal provision that keeping a place where two or more persons engage in prostitution is punishable as keeping a vice establishment. '1-lau-1' reflect specific relations of power in society. It is therefore not surprising that most of the sex workers in Hong Kong are from Mainland China, Thailand, the Philippines and other Asian countries.

The *2046* guide book by **James Law** follows the structure of classic tourist guide books. Facts, getting around, things to see and do, places to stay, places to eat, etc. are all combined to build up information about a space/city to come. Invited by the Hong Kong film director Wong Kar-wai, the author has developed a complete stage design for fiction to take place. Surprisingly, *2046* is described here as a super dense vertical city, covered by a gigantic dome that creates the biggest interior space ever.

Finally, **Ackbar Abbas** concludes *HK LAB 2* with the *Asian phantasmagorias of the interior*. Referring directly to Walter Benjamin, his essay goes back to the premises of *HK LAB*, extending "Hong Kong as a phantasmagoria." Here the desire and disappointment found in the bourgeois interior, is in turn reflected in the recent films of Wong Kar-wai.

Proposing a second strategic vision of Hong Kong, and to follow the idea of approaching the city/territory from a laboratory perspective, *HK LAB 2* navigates in-between spaces. Using the 'interior' as foundation, we continue the experiment initiated in *HK LAB*, observing and interpreting what we see, hear and smell through this framework. Specific issues arise from this perspective, in turn provoking a variety of responses, some harsh and dark while others emerge as seductive and energetic. As an image, a life style, or an urban atmosphere, our understanding of the city first passes through our experience of it. This explains why either real or fictional, *HK LAB 2* stories enable the exposure of primarily interior spaces, but never its inhabitants. By putting things downside-up, outside-in, macro-micro, the city itself becomes an animated hybrid of flesh and metal. From the test tube of the mad scientist to his android creation, new organic life begins to emerge...

坐
sit

Sit, stand, lie

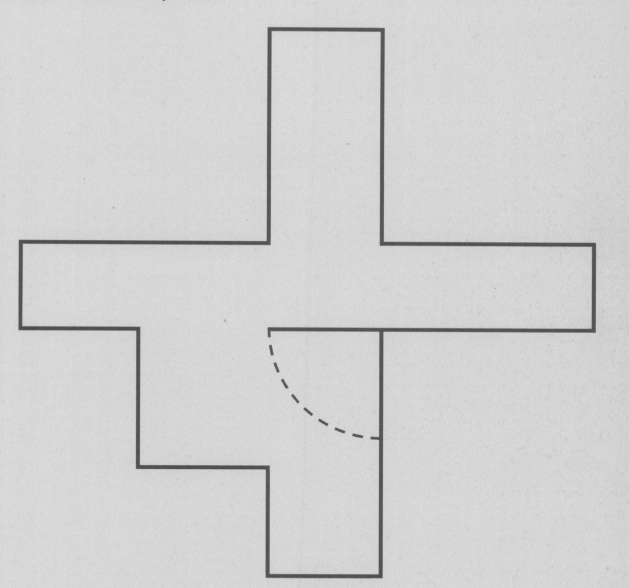

立
stand

臥
lie

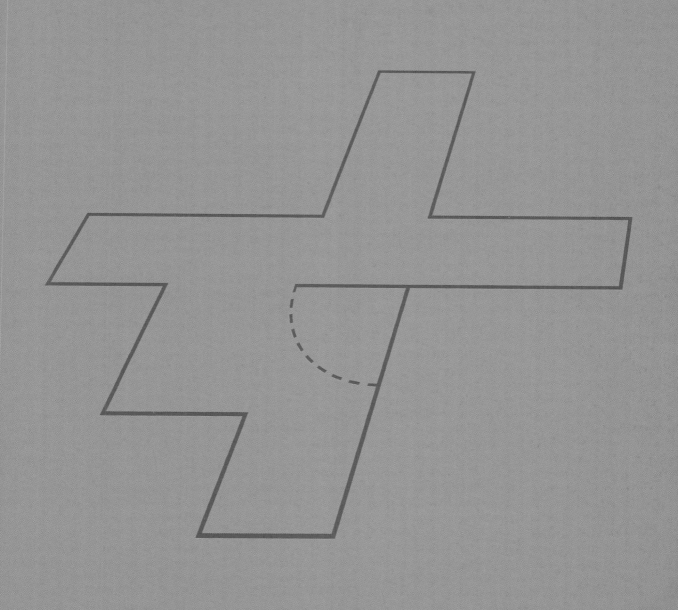

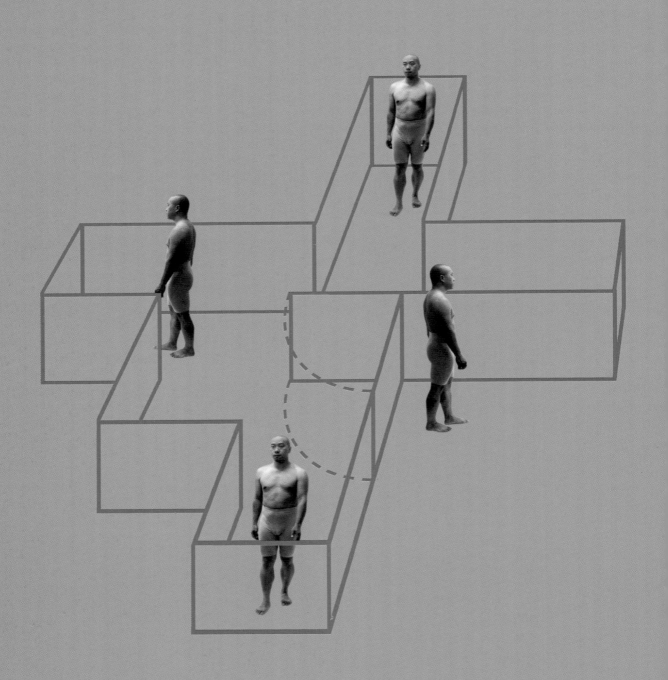

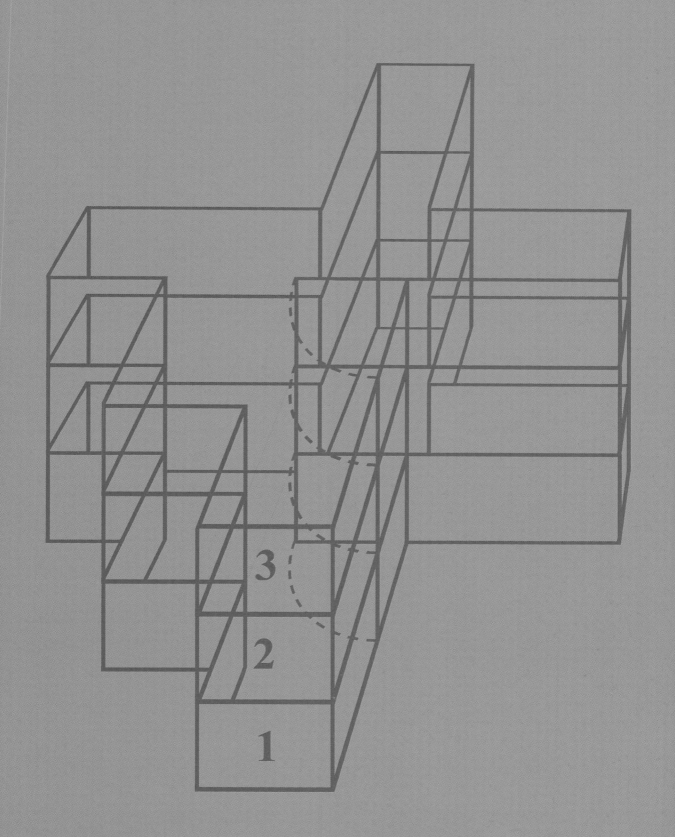

Ellie's story
From spatial arrangement to personal stress and family relationships

Conditions

This is an inside story about an unmarried woman living at home in Hong Kong's high-density environment. To reveal the interplay between these private conditions and external pressures this chapter looks at one woman's struggle with her personal space and sense of self.

Ellie's Parental Home Space = Six Family Members Living in an 18.6 sq. m. Unit.

She has shared this public housing unit with her family all her life.
Ellie = a 34-year-old unmarried daughter, living with her father (65), mother (60) and a younger sister (22). Her older brother and sister have already moved out after getting married.
Interior = a private toilet, a kitchen, but the kitchen is also the corridor leading to the toilet. There is a small balcony in front of the toilet. There are no rooms or partitions in the flat.

The following description shows the floor plan of her parental home. Although there are no partitions, her parents and two siblings (previously four) all possess their own, assumed domains. Inside, there are no locks or doors. Personal belongings and clothing are stored according to habitual use and none of the family members transgress his or her boundaries. Through experience, Ellie thoroughly learned the rules behind the use of space at home. Personalised objects = a way to create personal space.

Ellie's space = 1.2 x 1.8 m bed, her domain since childhood.

Her personal objects transcend spatial distance and create an individual space, like bricks for building a little kingdom.

Reflection

More than an attempt to express territory or uniqueness, personal belongings also are extensions of inner feelings and thoughts. We record our significant events in photo albums, mark our achievements by displaying trophies and recollect our affection for deceased relatives through the objects they leave behind. Through the different stages of our lives we discard or collect personal objects and these objects contain personal meanings. Similar to most of us, Ellie has certain connections with different personal objects. For example, her rattan basket, her schoolbag from the early ROC (Republic of China) years, a souvenir book, her 'smart kid' and 'smart pins', a watch case. There are not simply Ellie's treasure, but a personal museum that records her history of personal growth.

In a tiny home, family members lived in close proximity with each other. They build up intimate and close family relationships at the cost of losing their own identities. Though Ellie is able to keep a physical and psychological distance within the family, her ability to achieve a sense of autonomy was still clearly hindered by the arrangement of space in the home.

According to Ellie "the home was too small. People are too close to one another. My ego seems to be vanishing bit by bit." The "umbilical cord relationship" with her mother could be seen as a product of the non-partitioned home. Her mother's comments were Ellie's comments. Her mother's likes and dislikes were Ellie's likes and dislikes. Ellie's first love fell through because her mother thought her boyfriend unsuitable due to his low income and poor education.

Upset with her mother's comments on her appearance, using her clothes, spending her money and reading her diary, Ellie finds it difficult to retain any personal sense of self. In the name of filial piety, she tolerates her mother's intrusion into her thoughts and ideas, interpretation of her feelings, influences on her choices and decisions, forcing her keep secrets she does not want to keep.

Ellie is of course aware of her mother's excessive interference. Although she wants to "cut the cord", it is not easy to do. This is partly because her mother does not want it to change and partly because "the home is too small, so it is simply impossible to avoid mum." In the cramped home without any partitions, the mother's worries and unpleasant feelings are easily passed on to Ellie. They influenced Ellie's moods, making it hard for her to enjoy any peace of mind. "(I) felt that there might be no place at home, well, no space, I couldn't find myself. Apart from feeling crowded, (I) could not focus on my work. This was also crucial, i.e., I couldn't concentrate on my work myself."

Transition

"Nice to see each other, hard to live together" (相见容易相处难) is a Chinese idiom accurately reflecting the interaction between one's physical and psychological space within the home – especially a home like Ellie's. On the one hand, a constricted living space cultivates intimate family relationships. On the other, it interferes in a negative sense since it's too restricted to keep one's boundary without intrusion. Faced with a competitive job market, Ellie worked hard for a master's degree, yet her intrusive mother and cramped home became an obstacle.

Not surprisingly, Ellie decides to move out, causing a serious quarrel with her parents. They insist that unmarried daughters cannot be allowed to move out alone. Facing constant attacks and unable to deal with the situation Ellie considers suicide. Afraid that she might indeed go through with it, her parents finally agree with her plans to find a flat near her place of employment. Even then, her parents keep it a secret from all their relatives, for fear of shame. And she does miss the intimacy of her old home. Ellie's parents cherished their relationship with her, as did she. Yet despite the shame her parents feel, Ellie enjoys her new-found freedom. More importantly, now that Ellie is out of the house, her parents show their concern for her in small but explicit ways – little affections not openly displayed before. When they see each other today, there is simply less tension and more enjoyment. Keeping geographical distance has resulted in emotional closeness.

Results and Considerations

Ellie looks back, ambivalently... "The time when I lived in our old home... it was the family relationship... it's not that they didn't love me, but it seemed like it's not good... well, (I) couldn't say it's not a nice family! They would love me; when I was in trouble, (they) were willing to cry with me, (they) would share my (worries) and support me... The place was really very small, so small that we didn't even have a place to stand. Thus, when there's a person less, there's a person less to compete with. Ah... they have more space to move around." We can "borrow" from public places, i.e. restaurants, libraries, fast food shops, parks, shopping malls; we might nurture ourselves in country parks; but we need a place called home as a haven for our body and soul.

The interior spatial arrangement of the home is a mirror reflecting the observers' stories in the narratives of its inhabitants. A messy bedroom might reflect the teenager's anger; a big picture prepared for a funeral facing the son's bedroom might convey an elderly mother's unspoken anger; a collection of photos of friends speaks to the child's relationships outside the home, and so on. This list could be extended, but the point is to show how negotiations in, and for a home space are connected to one's own sense of place and self.

Closeness and freedom, space and connection, autonomy and interrelatedness – these are the constant oppositions that begin from the home space we share with our family members. How we negotiate these oppositions and contradictions determines both the future of our familial relations as well as how well our own stories turn out.

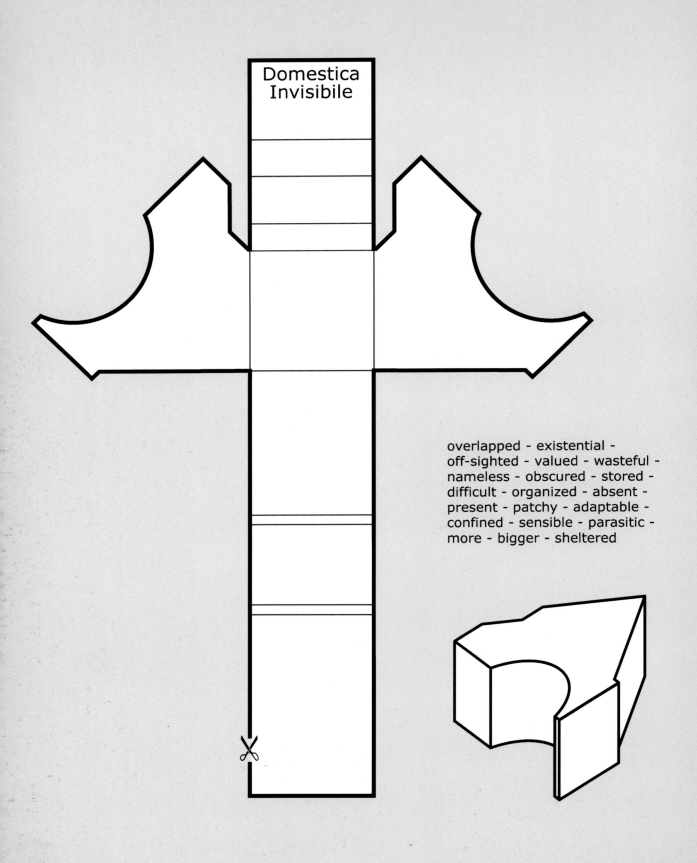

Domestica
Invisibile

overlapped - existential -
off-sighted - valued - wasteful -
nameless - obscured - stored -
difficult - organized - absent -
present - patchy - adaptable -
confined - sensible - parasitic -
more - bigger - sheltered

Domestica invisibile

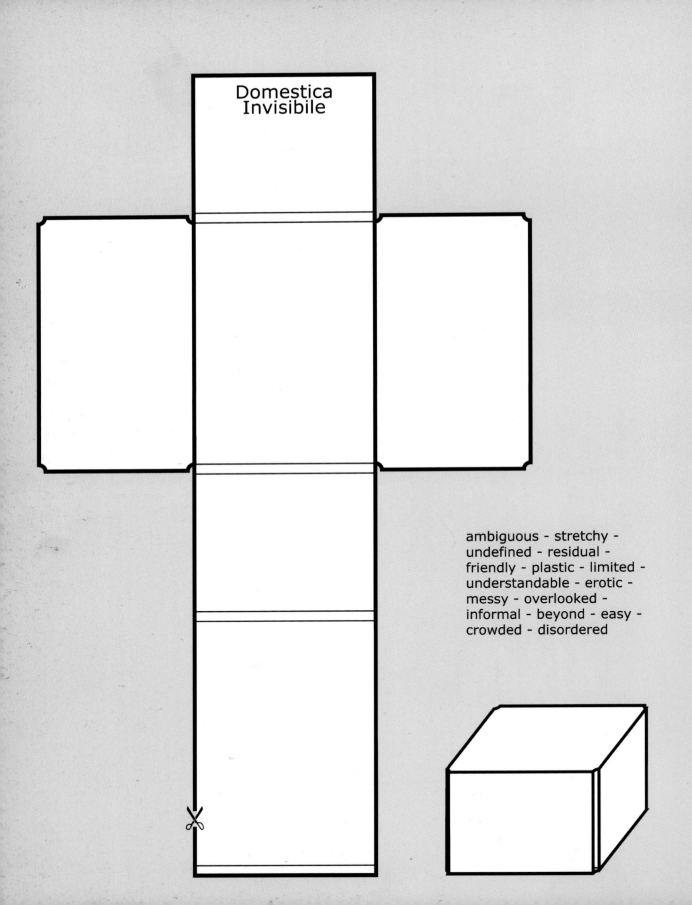

Domestica
Invisibile

ambiguous - stretchy -
undefined - residual -
friendly - plastic - limited -
understandable - erotic -
messy - overlooked -
informal - beyond - easy -
crowded - disordered

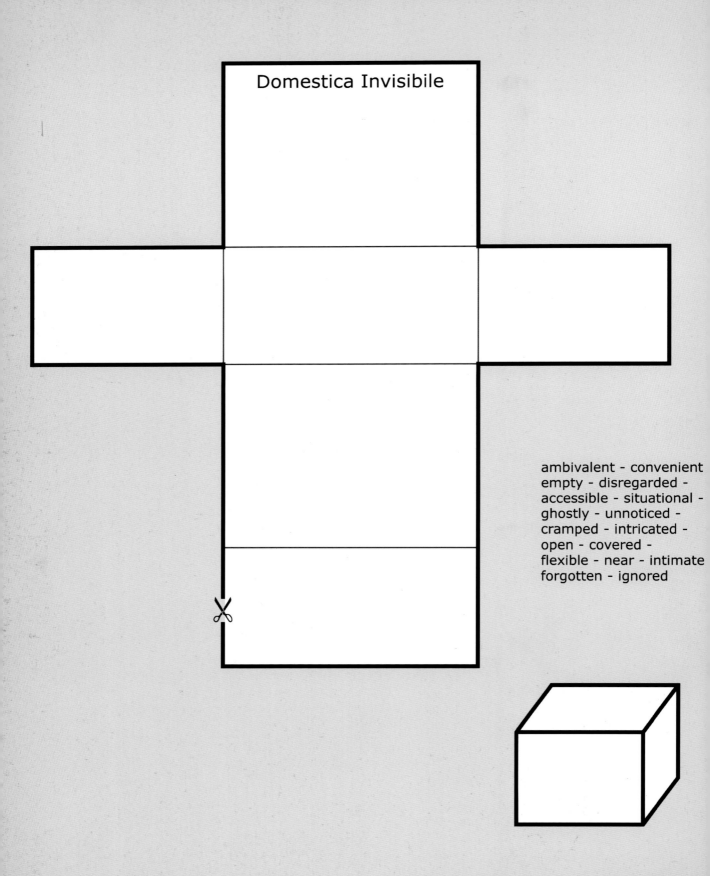

Domestica Invisibile

ambivalent - convenient
empty - disregarded -
- accessible - situational -
ghostly - unnoticed -
cramped - intricated -
open - covered -
flexible - near - intimate
forgotten - ignored

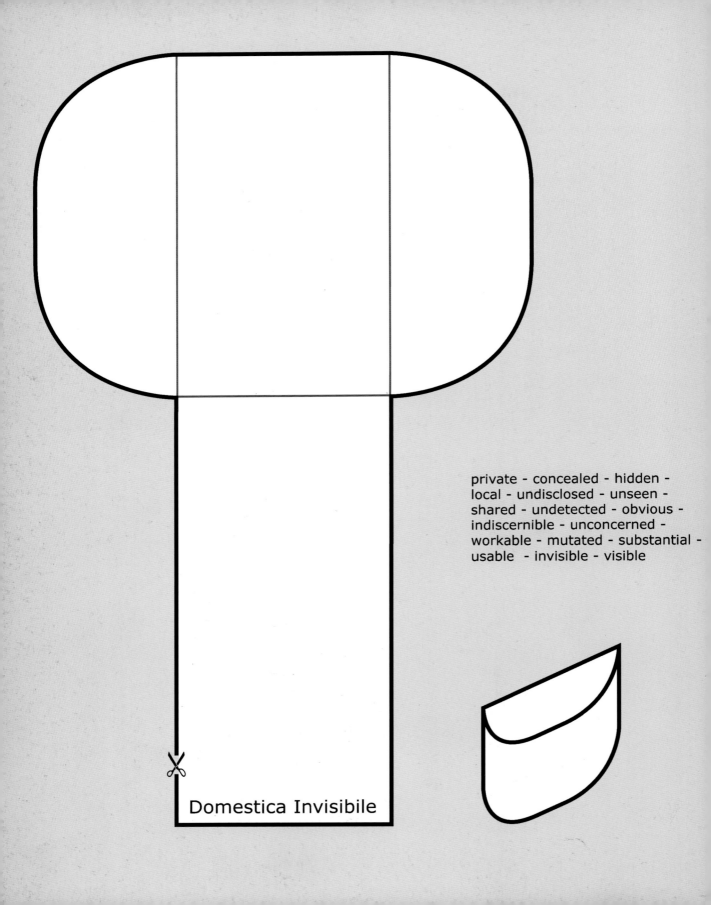

private - concealed - hidden -
local - undisclosed - unseen -
shared - undetected - obvious -
indiscernible - unconcerned -
workable - mutated - substantial -
usable - invisible - visible

Domestica Invisibile

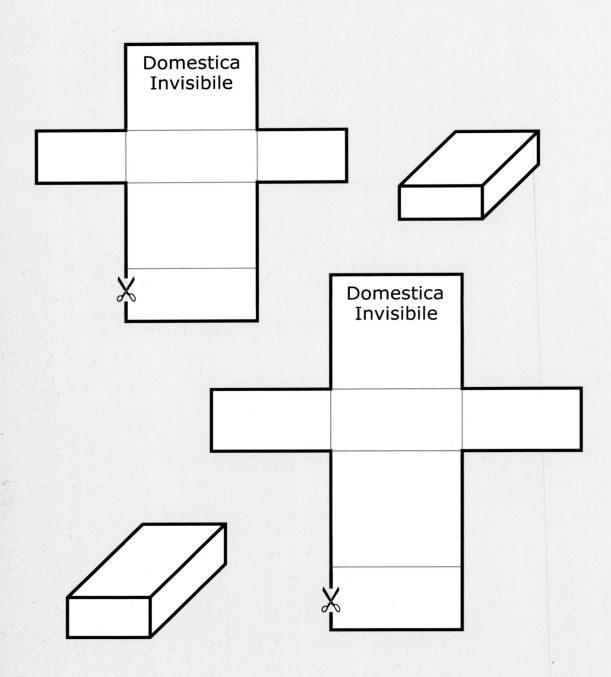

Domestica
Invisibile

Domestica
Invisibile

CECILIA CHU & MISHKO HANSEN

Constructing the 'real' dream home
Interior design and consumption practice in Hong Kong

For those who have never been to the sales centre for a new residential development in Hong Kong, a visit to one is quite a spectacle. This is especially true if you go on the launch day, which never fails to attract thousands of people. Many come with the entire family, old and young, as if on a family holiday outing. People enthusiastically wander from one show-flat to another, looking, chatting and commenting on the design of the flats from their layout to colour schemes to outside views, comparing one with another and proclaiming which one they like and why. Invariably, a courteous salesperson stands by the exit with a stack of brochures, trying to persuade some of these potential buyers to make a deposit for a flat.

One might think the phenomenon just described is the natural result of a booming real estate market. However, the truth is that the Hong Kong market has been relatively weak for much of the past seven years. Despite boasting of record-breaking numbers of show-flat visitors – something which has become an almost routine statement in the news releases following the launch of each high profile project - most of the people who visit the show-flats do not end up making a purchase.[1] According to many visitors who were at a recent sales launch, they came not so much with the intention to buy, but more for the enjoyment of seeing the show-flats. Some people even admitted that they treat visiting show-flats as a regular leisure activity. When asked what they liked about the visit, many said that they came out of curiosity for how 'others' design their flats. Some also remarked that it is simply enjoyable to see 'nicely-designed' homes, and that they were looking forward to another launch.

Of course, using show-flats as a means to promote new real estate developments is nothing new and is common in many parts of the world. But in Hong Kong, a city where property looms large in the collective psyche, the design and marketing of show-flats takes on a special significance. One peculiar phenomenon is that almost all of the new flats here are sold long before their construction, meaning that the show-flats are often located at another place away from the site itself. However, in order to convey a sense of 'realness' to potential buyers, care has been taken in the design to enable visitors to imagine the 'actual' context, so to speak. One method is to project images of the city skyline, usually a view 'seen' from the top floor unit, onto the window panes of the show-flat in the form of a lightbox. This allows visitors to 'see' the outside scenery, an important attribute affecting purchase decisions, as having a nice view, especially a harbour view, is often equated with higher status and standard of living in Hong Kong.[2]

The interiors of most show-flats are meticulously designed, usually organised into a set of themes with different styles of furnishing, each applied to a unit of particular size (often a more 'high-end' look is applied to the larger, more expensive units). If one looks at the floor plans of these units, however, there is actually very little difference between their basic layouts. In fact, the floor plans of most new developments are almost exactly the same as those of existing buildings dating back a decade or more.[3] One reason for providing these close-to identical units is, obviously, that they allow developers to save substantial costs when compared to providing more novel architectural designs. More important, however, is that their shape and features are calculated to offer the maximum allowable interior space based on the idiosyncratic rules governing building and redevelopment in Hong Kong.[4] It should be noted that this familiarity with what already exists is also attractive for many visitors, who contend that these familiar spaces allow them to relate to their own living environment, while the interior decoration enables them to envision a 'better' version of it. The excitement in viewing show-flats can thus in part be related to a process in which imagination, not only on the part of the designer but also of everyone of the show-flat visitors, plays a central role.

It might be difficult for people from outside Hong Kong to understand the high level of enthusiasm attributed to the make-believe world(s) conveyed by these show-flats which, after all, are made up of furnishings and other details which do not come with the purchase of the flats anyway.[5] It is not surprising then, that ubiquitous advertising for property projects and the coverage of the 'show-flat frenzy' in the media has led some cultural commentators to conclude that show-flats epitomise consumerism run amok in Hong Kong, where endless desires are fuelled by manufactured dreams of 'better' living. However, while there is no doubt that show-flats as mediators of imagination are important for consumption practices, the process is by no means a simple one. First, most of the visitors, including those who actually purchase a flat, are not wholly

unaware that what they see is an unreal, ideal portrayal of an imagined context set up to persuade them to buy. Moreover, many visitors, as mentioned, are not prepared to make a purchase, but come to see these designed spaces for their personal enjoyment. This reflects the discrepancy between what is being consumed (in a wide sense) and what is being sold, and reveals that there are complex, multiple processes at work. This leads us to question what designed imagined homes mean to people in Hong Kong, and what, as a practice of consumption, does visiting a show-flat enable them to do?

Many critics of consumption have long lamented that interior design, which is sometimes seen as the trivial pursuit of styles, is used almost exclusively to promote commodified space. In the case of show-flats in Hong Kong, the commodities are the flats which property developers aim to sell for as much money and as quickly as possible in order to generate maximum profits. As a sign signifying 'ideal' living, such designed spaces can be seen as components of the social discourse of objects which, according to Baudrillard, are part of the general mechanism of discrimination and prestige central to consumption.[6] And indeed, advertising for showflats and the lifestyles associated with the designed interiors in Hong Kong are almost invariably aimed at invoking and reinforcing the potential residents' class and status, their imagined 'exclusivity' versus the rest in a society.[7] Clearly then, the meaning of a designed home in Hong Kong is, to a large degree wrapped up with social prestige and accomplishment.

While prestige and status matter not only in Hong Kong but almost everywhere else, and while property ownership is no doubt among the most significant discriminatory 'commodities' (and certainly among the most expensive), it would be overly simplistic, to equate interior designs with static displays of status and exclusivity. Interpreting designs in this way in a sense reduces them to mere 'tools' for developers to seduce consumers, who are seen as passive subjects that have no choice but to 'buy' into the constructed images of dream homes. As Penelope Harvey argues, consumption is not merely a top down stratagem, but rather a dynamic process which involves the active participation of the consumers.[8] Addressing de Certeau's emphasis on the practices of everyday life, Harvey points out that consumption practice, which is about the signification of objects, also involves a re-signification process where consumers constantly reinterpret the meanings and values of products from their own perspective. In other words, the design of show-flats, no matter how calculated and 'perfectly' arranged, can never direct the visitors to see them in one 'perfect' way. Rather, their meanings always remain indeterminate, depending on what the visitors bring to the interaction.

This is everywhere evident if one listens closely to the conversations of people viewing the show-flats. Despite the high level of enthusiasm, not all the comments on the design are complementary.

In fact, many viewers seem to be rather critical of what they see. Even while appreciating the interior design as beautiful, many remark that if they had this flat they would change the layout and decoration to their own liking in quite specific ways. Indeed, part of their enjoyment of the experience seems to derive from expressing these opinions themselves. The show-flats, in this respect, offer not only a space for imagining an ideal home but also a space for communicating what they know and desire.

To follow this line of thinking, it can be said that the practice of reinterpretation entails the accumulation of knowledge, and thus also the potential growth of the power of choice, which in turn can impact upon the production and marketing of the products themselves. It also implies that the products – the showflats in our case – are always dialogically enacted. Their values are not fixed but subject to constant negotiations between the consumers and producers. This partly explains why real estate developers have to actively come up with new marketing strategies and new designs to elicit enthusiasm of potential buyers who will not be satisfied by being presented with the same flat over again.

The recognition of the active participation of the consumers in the production process points to a more positive way to understand consumption. However, this does not imply that the commodification of space and objects is altogether unproblematic. In fact, the counter-discourse of consumer-sovereignty, which celebrates atomistic market relations and the ever-expanding 'choices' available to consumers, is misleading as it tends to play down the producers' ultimate interests in maximising profits (often with little regard to social and environmental impacts), and their constant efforts in repositioning and adapting themselves in order to achieve this goal.[9] It should also be noted that peoples' imagination and interpretation of what they consume are still to a large degree contingent on what is available to them through packaged presentations. In the case of the show-flats, developers who are no doubt highly aware of these processes have continued to step up efforts in providing more lavish new interiors, attempting to engage their consumers' interests and elicit stronger desires to buy these imagined homes.

From Harvey's exploration of visitors' experience at the World Expo, it is clear that how people interpret a designed environment depends very much on their own backgrounds.[10] It also shows that the meanings of interior design and consumption practice can vary widely from one place to another. This suggests the need to resist making generalisations without considering the particular historical and cultural contexts of a place in more detail. As pointed out by Tony Fry, there always exists a reciprocal relationship between how design is produced and consumed, learnt and thought - one which inevitably continues to shape perceptions and expectations in particular ways.[11] In other words, the designed environment continues to 'design' peoples thinking of design and the values and meanings it carries. To follow this indication, it might be helpful then to further examine some of the salient features that connect design, the property market, and consumption practice in Hong Kong.

Ironically, despite the tremendous growth of interest in design, which is evident in daily conversation and popular media in Hong Kong, interior design is, still seen as a form of superficial packaging which is more or less 'trivial' and 'non-essential' and does not engage with other (more serious) disciplines which are supposed to contribute more to the 'larger culture'. This perception is reinforced by the view that interior designs, like Hong Kong itself, are transient.[12] A constant impetus to renew, refurbish and renovate, has been shaped by rapid population growth and economic and land policies that have rendered Hong Kong's built environment impermanent.[13] Continual demolition has come to be a way of life and rarely is the design of an interior expected to last over a long period.[14] A frequently speculative property market also encourages the population to move home fairly regularly.[15] This reinforces the view that designed interiors are primarily casual exercises in style that are quickly used up then shed like a skin to be replaced with a new and unrecognisable updated versions. For a population with a strong group psychology, this tendency to pick up a trend and then discard it only further reinforces the view that interior designs are cosmetic, transferable and disposable.

The high prices and frequent speculation in Hong Kong property market can partially be attributed to the political economy of the territory which has resulted in deliberate policies to restrain the amount of land available for housing, and thus drive up living density and flat values. Contrary to the 'free market' image which Hong Kong enjoys internationally, the property market is split into two main sectors: public housing in which the government provides low cost accommodation for about half of the population, and the private sector which is largely in the hands of a small number of dominant players. Some of these developers have also expanded extensively into other industries including telecommunications, logistics, retail and utilities. Their powerful market presences place them in a strong position to influence the political environment as well as to orchestrate large, comprehensive sales campaigns and design efforts that shape the popular imagination and meanings of home.

The clear social division between those living in their own private flats and those living in government low-cost housing estates is of particular importance in assessing the meanings of designed flats. The property market boom from the 70's to mid 90's helped to create a kind of 'myth' which linked upward mobility and wealth with flat ownership in the popular consciousness. Design, which is seen to be a part of the investment in a flat, is associated almost entirely with the private sector, and thus has also acquired connotations of aspirations for a better future. As indicated in Helen Cheng's study, the purchase of a flat is almost always imagined as a door to independence and establishing a family and as a step towards a higher quality of life.[16] To put this in another way, a designed home signifies the potential realisation of these dreams - dreams which could dramatically transform the lifestyle and social status of the owner.

The particularities of Hong Kong's property market, government policies, and role of interior design obviously entails complexities which could be further contextualised within the political and cultural domains of Hong Kong, its colonial history, its economic trajectory and its changing relations to Mainland China. Nevertheless, the issues outlined in this paper point to the dialectic process of design and consumption practices, and how they are shaped by the local political economy and socio-cultural context. The ordered spaces of the show-flats, while representing an ideal vision of living, are also real spaces themselves where people interact and construct their own (different) versions of home according to their imaginations. It is here where its multiple meanings are constituted, all the while embedded in a wider social world and its shared values. Viewing a show-flat can then be seen as a social ritual above and beyond the specifics of 'this' flat. Participating in this ritual by, for example, visiting as part of a family outing, also entails the appropriation of existing social meanings and/or creation of new ones. This openness of interpretation indicates that people do not necessarily 'buy in' to what is being shown. Collectively, however, they do tend to 'buy in' to the values and aspirations shaped by the larger social context.

Therefore, consumption practice in relation to home is partially a product, as well as a determinant, of show-flat design. It is important, however, in observing the current role and manifestations of interior design, to remember that the so-called 'Hong Kong context' is not a single fixed entity,

but dynamic and constantly shifting. It is comprised of concrete spaces where people continue to reinterpret and remake meanings, participate in as well as redirect practices. The designed interiors can be seen as moments where people individually and collectively construct a dream. Each iteration of home, each design made or reflected upon are steps on the road towards an indeterminate future. Design, as an act of making meanings and new relations, plays a crucial role in this process, intentionally, derivatively, inevitably.

Notes

1. Some people do end up making a purchase at the sales centre, of course. But the proportion is low.

2. Most of these "views" of outside scenery are wildly optimistic. For example, a brilliant sea view in the show-flat may omit the highway, container port, buildings, etc. that take up most of what would really be seen. For a sympathetic reading of the the role of "sea views" and other notable features in promoting Hong Kong property developments see Helen Hau-ling Cheng's article "Consuming a Dream: Homes in Advertisements and Imagination in Contemporary Hong Kong" in, *Consuming Hong Kong*, Hong Kong: Hong Kong University Press, 2001.

3. Ibid.

4. An even more striking example of the way government regulation in Hong Kong shapes the built environment is in the New Territories and outlying islands where the so-called "Small House Policy", originally intended to allow for the building of traditional rural homes, has led to building vast numbers of identical modern three story units which perfectly maximise the space allowed in the Policy.

5. While this is generally true flats usually come with some of the fixtures and occasionally even some of the furniture featured in the show-flats.

6. See Jean Baudrillard, *The System of Objects*, London: Verso, 1968.

7. See for example the discussion in Gutierrez + Portefaix, "Homes for China" in, *Design Issues*, Volume 19, No.3, Summer 2003.

8. See Penelope Harvey, *Hybrids of Modernity*, New York and London: Routledge, 1996.

9. For an amusing and illuminating analysis of the discourse of "consumer-sovereignty" see Thomas Frank, *One Market Under God*, New York: Doubleday, 2000.

10. See Penelop Harvey, "Hybrid Subjects: Citizens as Consumers" in, *Hybrids of Modernity*, New York and London: Routledge, 1996.

11. See Tony Fry, "The Placement, Displacement and Replacement of Design" in, *Form/Work*, Sydney: University of Technology, No.1, Vol.1, October 1997.

12. See Ackbar Abbas, *Hong Kong: Culture and the Politics of Disappearance*, Hong Kong: The University of Hong Kong Press, 1997.

13. See Cecilia Chu and Kylie Ubergang, "Saving Hong Kong's Cultural Heritage" in, *Conservation in Hong Kong*, Hong Kong: Civic Exchange, 2002.

14. The Hilton Hotel in the Central district was a notable example of a building that was completely and expensively refurbished in the 1990s only to be torn down shortly after its completion when the site was sold and redeveloped as a high-rise office building.

15. See Helen Hau-Ling Cheng, "Consuming a Dream: Homes in Advertisements and Imagination in Contemporary Hong Kong" in, *Consuming Hong Kong*, op.cit., pp.206-208.

16. Ibid.

PIERRE LARAUZA

XS
Property
Shops

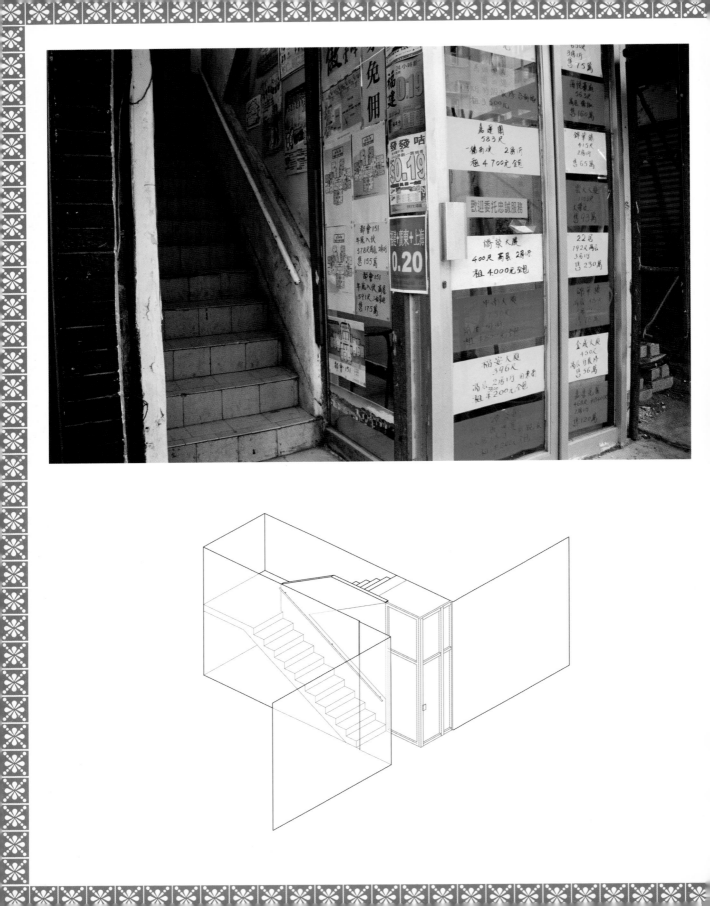
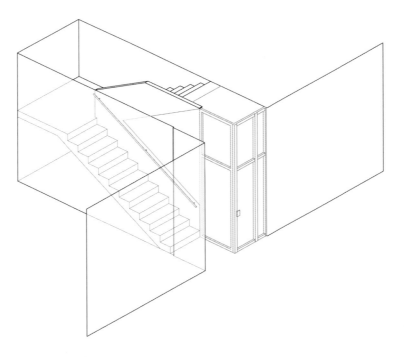

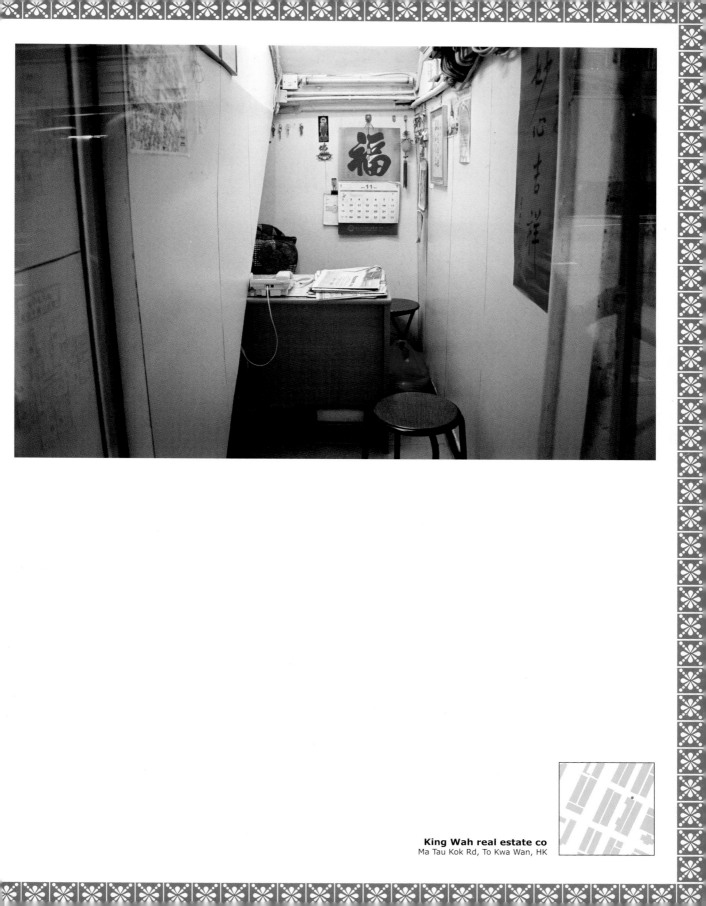

King Wah real estate co
Ma Tau Kok Rd, To Kwa Wan, HK

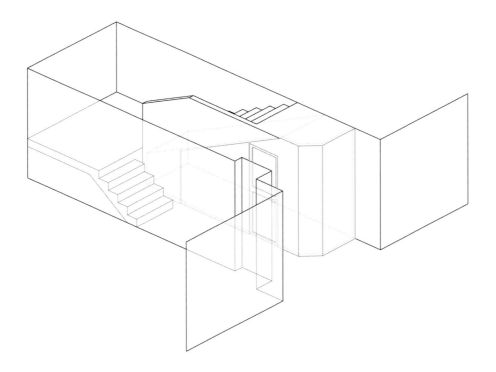

Wai Hing Property Agency
Shanghai St, Mongkok, HK

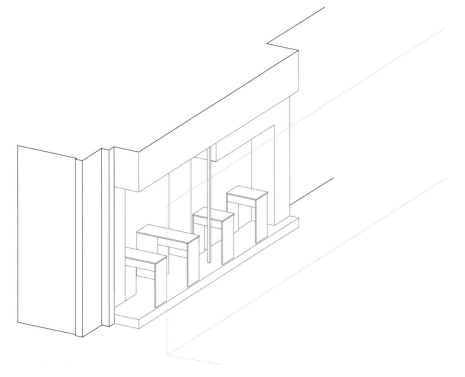

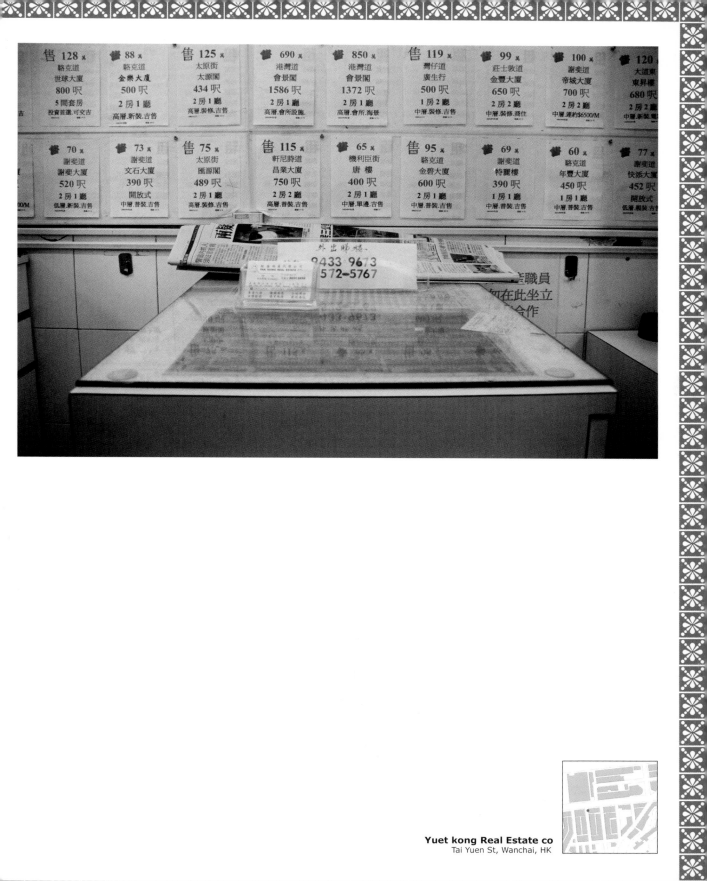

Yuet kong Real Estate co
Tai Yuen St, Wanchai, HK

Gold Dragon Property Agency
Stone Nullah L, Wanchai, HK

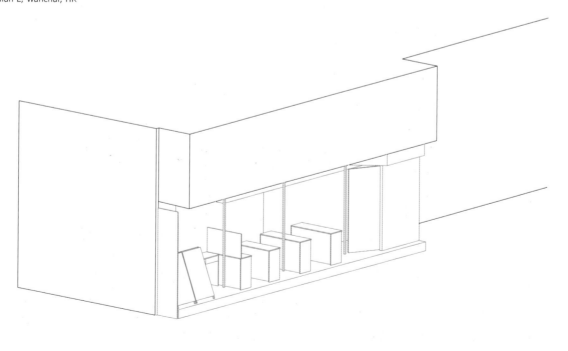

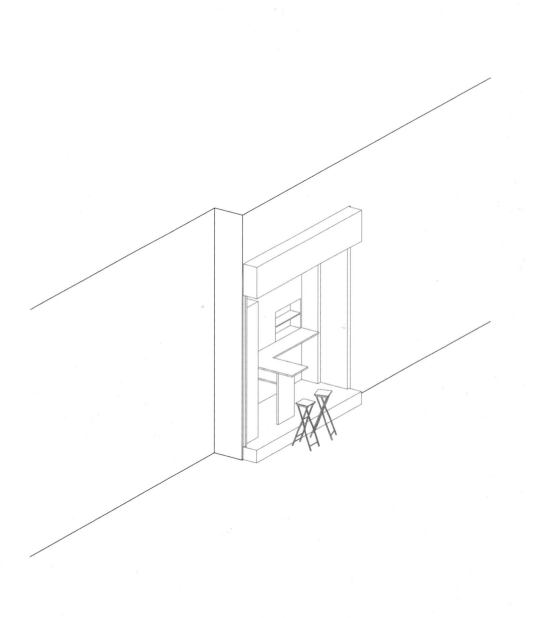

Golden Hill Properties co
Lockhart Rd, Wanchai, HK

Booth city

A booth! What is it? A kiosk, a stall, a cubicle..., a small dark green structure, a couple of steel bars rooted in the cement, a thin timber sheet used as a platform? An anonymous vernacular form, a makeshift construction somewhere between architecture and furniture? A booth is a minimum working space - three by four feet - serving a large group of people - some 10 000 according to a recent official survey. They usually come in series, forming a line, parallel to the traditional rooted shops. They were set up by the government at the beginning of the last century to extend the range of commercial activities and spaces. By 1970, more than 50 000 licensed or unlicensed hawkers provided a specific character to the streets of Hong Kong.

A simple metal structure defined by some government standard or custom made by the owner with the help of a carpenter, a booth costs some HK$ 7 000 to 10 000 to construct. Although very light, cheap, and exposed to the difficult climate, they easily last for 20 years or more. Each part is simple but strong enough to resist strong winds during the typhoon season. The booth can be navigated like a sailing boat. It will catch the wind to help natural ventilation. In case of heavy rain, the shopkeeper rolls a sheet of plastic from the edge of the roof. Otherwise, timber or steel panels can form an umbrella to block sunlight and keep the booth cool in summer.

It takes usually an average of 20 to 30 minutes for the shopkeeper to set up/close his booth. Minimum security is required for a perfect enclosure. The booth owners are part of the neighbourhood community who are also most of their clients. Recently, the government took action against booth owners and started a campaign to remove them entirely in order to 'clean up Hong Kong'. Most of the booths in this survey have already disappeared to make space for developers and their 'beautification' of 'Asia's World City'.

A survey, interviews and measurement drawings were conducted separately by Laurent Gutierrez and Valerie Portefaix with two groups of students in 2003:
- First year students of The School of Design, The Hong Kong Polytechnic University:
Chau Sau-man, Chan Tsz-wai, Chan Hei Chelsea, Yeung Lai-sheung, Stephanie Lai, Mak Hin-shing, Liem Lai-man, Kwok Wai-chi, Cheung Hoi-mei, Wong Hang-wa, Ting Yik-lai, Chan Ka-shun
- First year students of The Department of Architecture, The Hong Kong University:
Chan Kin-cheong, Chan Wing-pui, Cheung Sze-wai, Lau Ying, Leung Lok-kei, Li Ka-man, Mok Wai-ming, Mung Kit-man, Sin Chi-kei, Tse King-tong, Yu Hoi-ting.

Chee Loy-heung egg-roll booth is one of the small retailing hawker booths located for almost two decades in upper Centre Street in Sai Ying Pun district. Chee is a family business which sells home made cookies, biscuits and egg-rolls. The booth was made by a carpenter when the father first started the business. It is made out of steel bars of various lengths rooted in the cement. Chee's opening hours are from 0900-1930. It usually takes 30 minutes for the owner to open/close the booth.

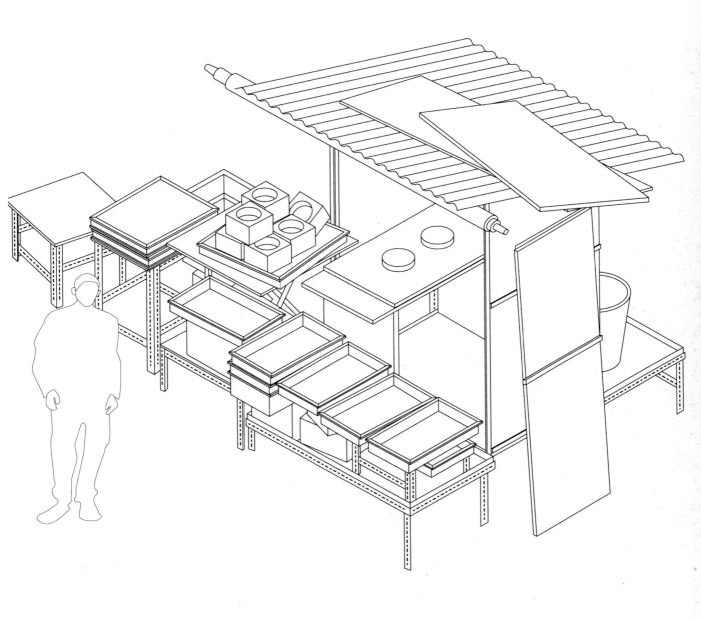

Eggroll Booth

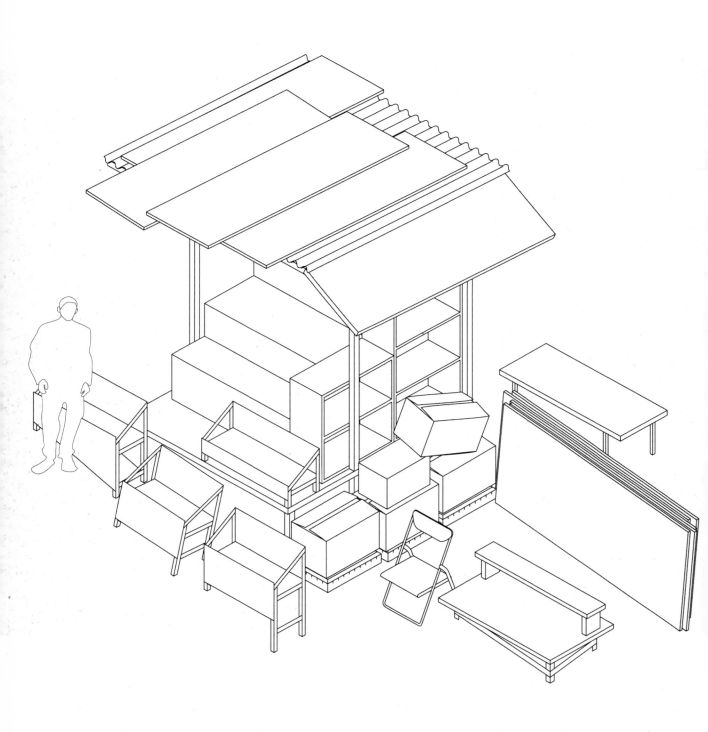

Shoes Booth

The shoes booth is located in Peel Street next to Central market. Mr T. has run the business for over 40 years in the same location changing booths only once in his career. A tailor-made structure designed by the owner, this stainless steel and wood booth is the second version built in 1985. It usually takes 10 minutes for Mr T. to open or close the booth.

Sum Kei tailor booth in Mercer Street in Sheung Wan district, opened more than 10 years ago. It was designed by its owner according to the government regulations. Sewing remains the main activity during opening hours - 1000 to 1800. The steel structure can be opened/closed in 2 to 3 minutes.

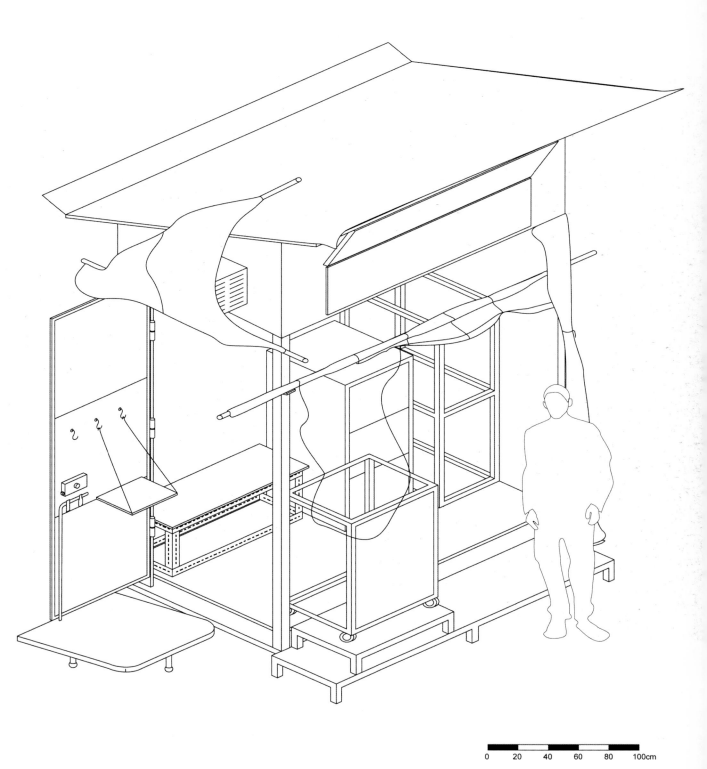

0 20 40 60 80 100cm

Tailor Booth

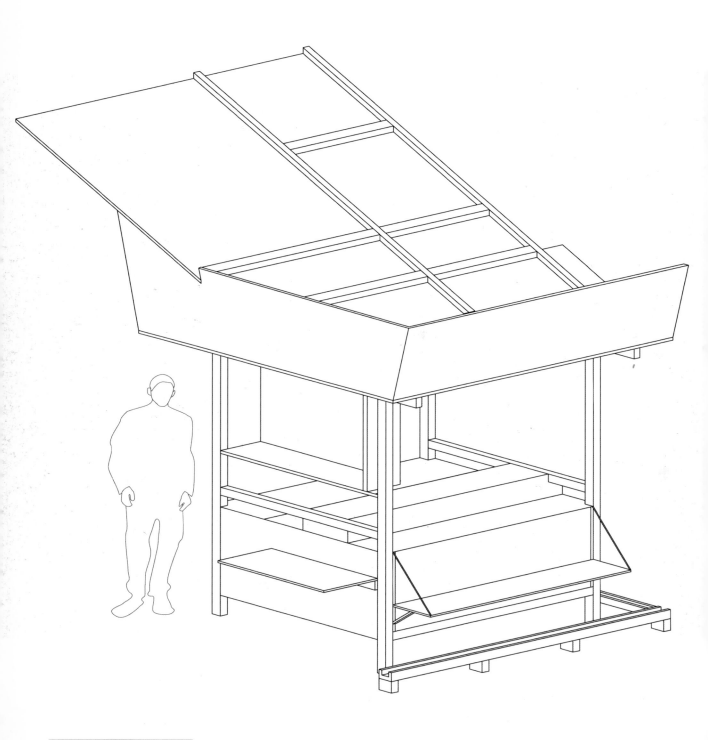

0   20   40   60   80   100cm

Flower Booth

The flower booth stands at the intersection of Jervois and Mercer streets in Sheung Wan. Its main façade is made of flower pots protected by a bamboo screen during the summer. A small workshop to prepare wreathes is located on the side while several materials are stored in the thick roof.

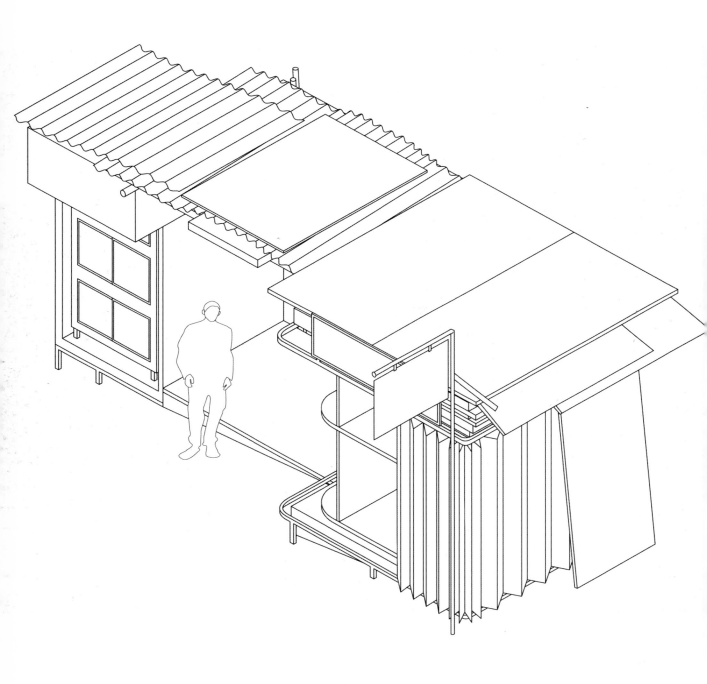

0 20 40 60 80 100cm

Copper & Iron Utensil Booth

Cheung Kee Copper & Iron business of Mr. Y. is located in Pottinger Street, Central district. He has been in the neighbourhood for 40 years, and is open from 0930 to 1700 every day. Built and developed gradually over the years by the owner, the booth consists of a series of metallic fragments combined together.

In operation since 1943, Mr. W.'s fish booth is located in Mercer Street, Sheung Wan district. Since specialising 10 years ago in breeding *Qi Cai Shen Xian* fish, Mr. W. has won many prizes in Mainland competitions. The steel structure is open at the front and there is a cover for the aquarium. Business starts at 0730 every day.

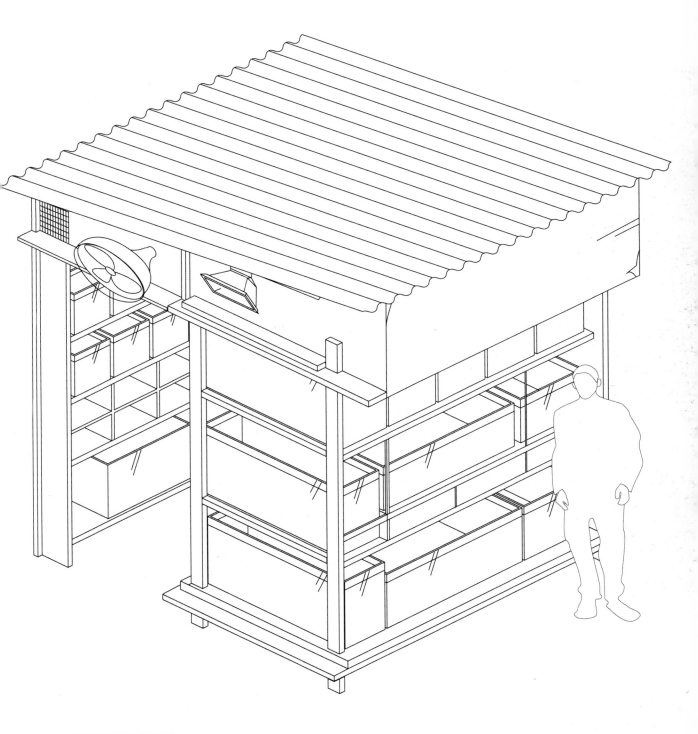

0 20 40 60 80 100cm

Fish Booth

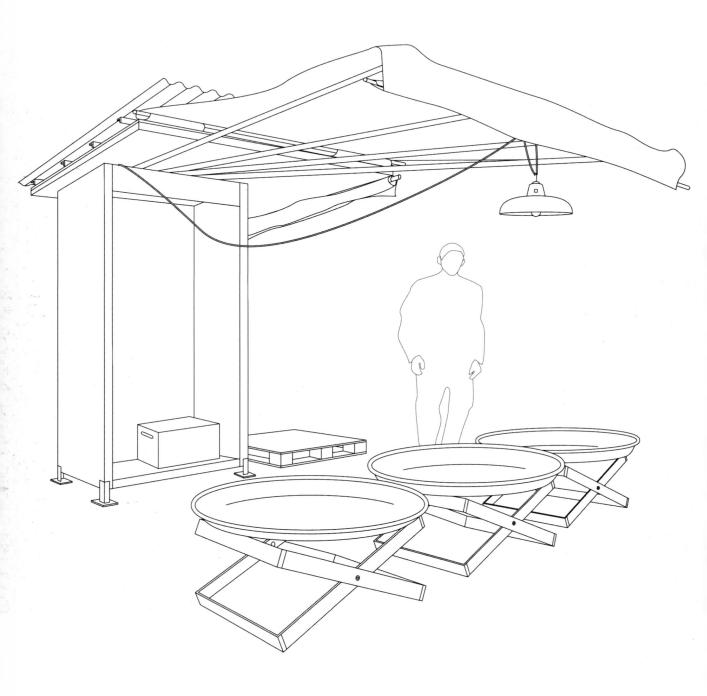

0   20   40   60   80   100cm

Fruit Booth

This fruit booth in Mong Kok mainly sells oranges. Its huge cantilevered canopy protects the fruit sellers from the sun and rain, and supports light bulbs. There are always a few boxes of oranges stored in a small cabinet in order to stabilise the structure. Sometimes, the other side of the booth houses another small business.

In operation since 1988, this fruit booth is located in Pottinger Street in Central. Standardised and assigned by the government, the booth can expand up to four times its enclosed volume. It takes around twenty minutes to open/close the booth. It is transformed into a flower booth during Chinese New Year.

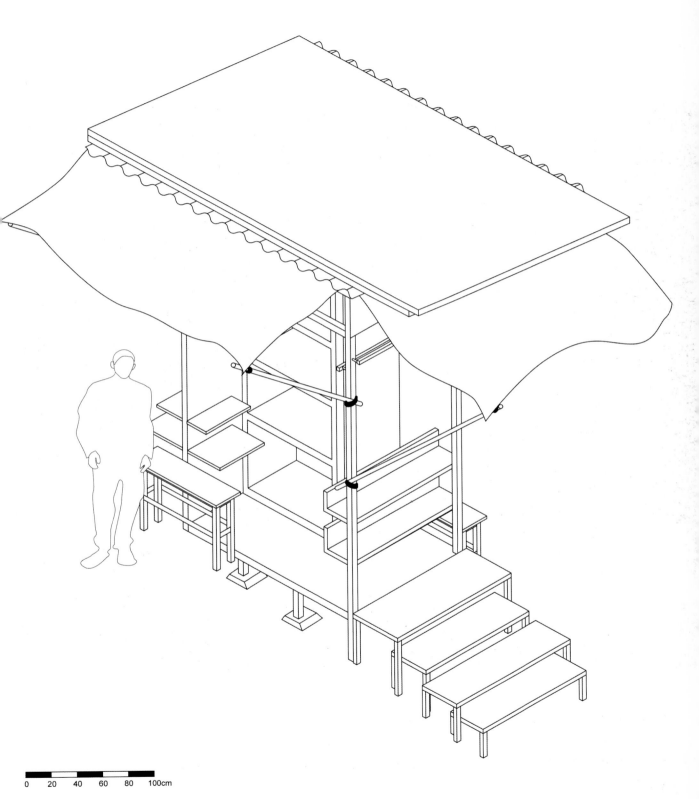

0 20 40 60 80 100cm

Fruit Booth

Light city

We first thought they were there to shoot a film. There were small groups of people working with computers and cameras in the jungle, running around with frenetic energy. Only cinema and TV create such an atmosphere, an environment constantly under flourescent lighting and in constant movement. But one month later they were still there. Obviously, something else was going on.

Hong Kong is famous for its capacity to respond to new demands and therefore to develop new business. This is one. It started with the booming industry of tourists from the Mainland, and located at a strategic point - a public toilet with a panoramic view of the Hong Kong skyline. Everyday from 6 to 9pm, a continuous line of tourist buses move down from the Peak and stop for about 10 minutes at Stubbs Road's look-out area for a last glimpse of the 'City of Light'.

A public space served by thousands of tourists. A beautiful moment to take home and show your friends. An opportunity for 6 groups of photographers to develop a business: an average of 250 photos per evening. HK$ 20 per photo. Some HK$ 5000 shared between 4 main characters - the 'advertiser', the 'cameraman', the 'printer', and the 'roadrunner'.

The business scenario is fairly simple. The 'advertiser' catches tourists getting out of the bus and takes them to the panorama while the 'cameraman' is waiting to immortalize the moment and the view. "I was there!" will be claimed back home. The latest digital camera model equipped with a small additional plasma screen shows instantly the result to the client. A simple formality is undertaken before the 'roadrunner' takes charge of the compact flash or similar devise to the 'printer'. Located 100 metres further down in the middle of the jungle, the 'base' is over equipped with one or two powerful laptop computers, two to three colour printers and multiple accessories including printing paper and a ready made flyer to insert the printed result. Finally, the 'roadrunner' rushes back to find his clients among the average of 10 000 Mainland Chinese tourists stopping here every night.

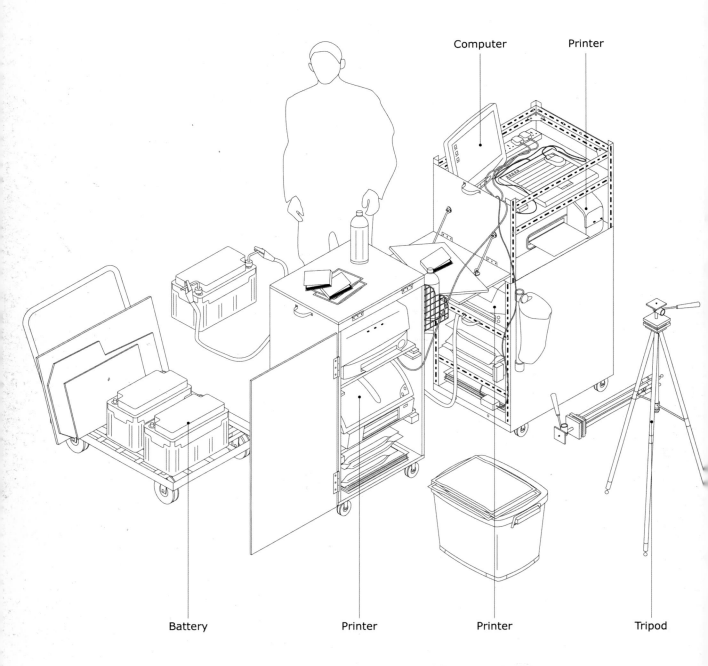

Computer

Printer

Battery

Printer

Printer

Tripod

0   20   40   60   80   100cm

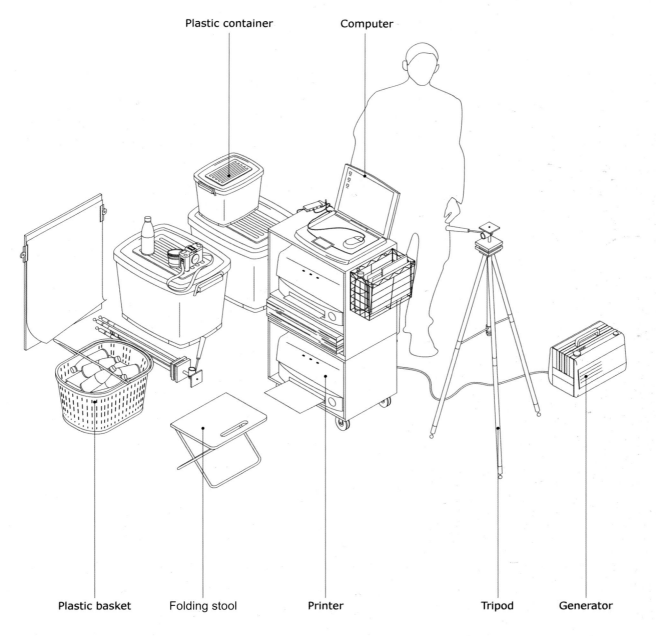

Plastic container

Computer

Plastic basket

Folding stool

Printer

Tripod

Generator

0   20   40   60   80   100cm

Upstairs shops
Resistance against mundanity

Lau sheung pou have existed in Hong Kong ever since the early 1970s. They are often family businesses. Shop space is converted from residential units situated on the second floor or above. Part of the shop space is used as residential space for the family. Traditionally, their most common business nature was barbers, fortunetellers and Chinese medicine practitioners. Around the late 1990s, a new generation of upstairs shops started to appear. Because the rent of upstairs shop space is much lower than that in the shopping malls or other on-street shops, many young adults set up their shops in upstairs shop spaces as a first attempt at operating retail or service businesses.

They are mainly located in the commercial districts of Causeway Bay and Tsim Sha Tsui, Wan Chai, Mong Kok and Central. The new generation of upstairs shops usually sell rare goods and provide novel services which are difficult to find elsewhere. Many upstairs shops actually depend on these special selling points for attracting patronage. There is a tendency for upstairs shops to combine retail with food catering. Nowadays, an increasing number of upstairs shops also operate cafés. They are often patronised by young adults and teenagers.

By consuming in upstairs shops, local young adults are actively constructing meanings by defining and relating themselves to others. According to Cheung Chi-wai [1], the nature of the resistance demonstrated by Hong Kong youths is individual, sporadic and consumptive. Although far from radical, young adults' consumption practices concerning upstairs shops show different kinds of resistance, a resistance to mundanity: "Shopping has become our principal strategy for creating value... shopping has come to define who we, as individuals, are." [2]

In today's consumer society, people consume not just for the utility value of commodities but more importantly for their symbolic value of social distinction. A commodity "is never consumed in its materiality, but in its difference." [3] It is usually the consumers who are dissatisfied with mainstream choices in the mass market who go shopping for something different and special in upstairs shops.

Rarity generates extra value as well as uniqueness in style. Georg Simmel's statement about the value of economic objects vividly illustrates this tension between upstairs-shop-goers and exclusive goods; he wrote "The difficulty of acquisition, the sacrifice offered in exchange, is the unique constitutive element of value, of which scarcity is only the external manifestation, its objectification in the form of quantity." [4]

"Adventure, in its specific nature and charm, is a form of experiencing. The content of the experience does not make the adventure. They become adventure only by virtue of a certain experiential tension whereby their substance is realised." [5] No one would deny that visiting shopping malls is an integral part of the Hong Kong way of life. According to Lui Tai-lok, the 'shopping-mall culture' has developed ever since the 'malling of Hong Kong' began some 35 years ago. [6] Today, Hong Kong people's experience of shopping has been vastly shaped by mega shopping malls. Shopping malls have become not only the main venues for family outings during weekends and holidays, but also places for people to kill time by browsing around.

It is exactly because shopping malls are so integrated with Hong Kong people's everyday experience that they become a routinised location in daily life. As a result, young adults regard shopping malls as uninteresting. Always on the lookout for novelty and excitement, some young adults turn to other places for consumption. While they go to youth-targeted shopping centres (such as Sino Centre in Mong Kok and Island Beverly Shopping Centre in Causeway Bay) for trendy goods, they visit upstairs shops for adventure. "I think shopping malls are crowded and unexciting places. They are more or less the same – they house the same shops and sell the same brands," said Jessie Chung, 26. "If I have time to kill, I'd rather go to upstairs shops to buy something different or hang out in upstairs cafes for some fun."

Jessie's favourite upstairs shop is Cat Store in Causeway Bay. Decorated in retro style, it is a combination of cafe and retail shop. A wide range of merchandise is available there, including locally designed clothing, accessories, gift items and even antique furniture. Underground music shows are held occasionally in their cat-themed cafe which accommodates 15 cats. Jessie paid her first visit to Cat Store a year ago. She only intended to play with cats there and to try out the signature dish - 'Meow Toast' (on which chocolate sauce forms a cat's face). "It was very different from the average shop or cafe," Jessie said. When asked about the difference, Jessie explained, "The interior design, the music, the cats, the merchandise... I think it is the combination of them all. I'm quite happy to have found a special shop like that." From then on, Jessie has developed

a habit of checking out upstairs shops and cafes in the hope of discovering special goods and services. Turo-Kimmo Lehtonen and Pasi Maenpaa's statement about a tourist-like mood of shoppers best describes the mentality of 'upstairs shop adventurers' like Jessie. They wrote, "What is fascinating... is the encounter of the new and the unexpected and the experience of being 'somewhere else'... The shopper is very alert and tuned for basic openness, expecting to encounter something new. It is a question of a similar anticipatory expectation as in games of chance: something might happen." [7]

Sometimes, visiting upstairs shops carries an element of chance and discovery – very much like a 'treasure hunt'. To a large extent, the excitement of visiting them comes from finding valuable goods unexpectedly. Lehtonen and Maenpaa's concept of 'aleatory play' about chance-based shopping depicts the pleasure sensed by these 'treasure hunters'. Their excitement comes from an anticipatory enjoyment of possibly coming across something they might find pleasant or desirable. They are thrilled when they encounter something that they have somehow anticipated or longed for but of which they have had only a faint idea. [8]

Anthony Yeung, 27, has the habit of visiting upstairs toyshops. Since he collects Japanese robot figures, he is a regular customer of Toyzone, a 2500-square-foot upstairs second-hand toyshop in Causeway Bay. "I go there every month. I usually hang around in that shop for more than

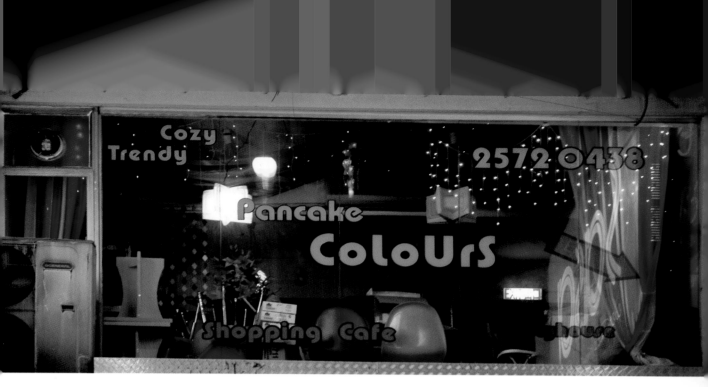

two hours. I take my time to check things out. It feels like treasure hunting." Understanding customers' mentality the shop owner of Toyzone, Raymond Wong arranges merchandise in his shop in seeming chaos on purpose. He said, "I deliberately arrange toys in a messy way so that customers sense the fun of a 'treasure hunt' while they go through every corner of the shop looking for their favorite toys."

Whether the excitement sensed by shoppers is the result of exploring an unusual environment with special features or discovering valuable goods by chance, upstairs shops provide some good venues for urban adventure. The essence of such adventure is in the means rather than in the end as what shoppers enjoy most is the process of discovery. The very core of the adventure lies in the experiential value of searching for and encountering the novel and the desirable by chance.

"One knew of places in ancient Greece where the way led down into the underworld. Our waking existence likewise is a land which, at certain hidden points, leads down into the underworld – a land full of inconspicuous places from which dreams arise. All day long, suspecting nothing, we pass them by..." [9] In Hong Kong, high population density exerts pressure on the demand for retail and catering services. Apart from making maximum use of shop space, retail shops and restaurants have to adopt measures to facilitate the flow of customers. For example, in their haste to complete as many transactions as possible, it is not uncommon for sales staff in retail

shops to give very brief attention to customers or even treat some customers impolitely. In some cases, restaurants try to free up tables as fast as possible by making customers pay their bills before they are ready to. This often results in tension among customers and unpleasant experiences.

In contrast to these general practices, upstairs shops are especially designed with features to prolong customers' stay. Many upstairs shops equip themselves with a cafe. Space, from the customers' perspective, is considered as an important consumable element since they highly value the often casual and relaxing environment of upstairs shops. Compared to the usual shops and cafes, these upstairs cafes are decorated very differently causing customers to have the impression of existing in an another-worldly context. Upstairs cafes are perceived as a crossover between a shop and a home. Sofas and cushions are becoming part of the 'grammar' of upstairs shops. Since they are signs that signify relaxation and comfort, they become indispensable props for building up the warm feeling of a comfortable home.

The media often describe upstairs shops with cafes as *Dau* (Cantonese slang which means 'hideout' or more precisely 'secret place for gathering') for young adults. Situated above ground level, these shops are not easily noticed by people walking on the street. It is true that unlike crowded and noisy bars or cafes, upstairs shops with cafes are better choices (among economical ones) as venues for

youngsters who want to gather and chat. They are also nice places for shoppers to take a break from the crowded streets and linger for a while. Immersed in the relaxing environment, customers are not conscious of the passing of time and often spend a whole afternoon in these upstairs shops.

Although upstairs shops are business entities, to many customers they are a temporary refuge to relax and forget about the undesirable realities outside. An 'elsewhere' is invented which is defined against familiar locales.[10] Young adults engage in a kind of passive resistance against practical problems in the real world by lingering in upstairs shops. Upstairs shops' status as 'elsewhere' allows young adults to temporarily withdraw from duties and problems in the familiar spheres of home and work.

Hui Yan-yan, the shop owner of Cat Store came up with the idea of synthesising retail, cafe, pets and underground music in an upstairs shop space. Explaining the original idea of setting up her shop, she said, "Antiques, cats and gift items are my favourites. I also like drinks and underground music. I want to combine all these favourite things and set up a flea-market type of shop. That's why I operate my shop as a mixed business." Cat Store was established six years ago when she was 22. Her innovative idea was met with unexpected success. Because customer demand was overwhelming, Yan-yan had to move her shop twice to accommodate the increasing number of customers.

Ellie Tsui, a 23-year-old secretary, likes to spend two or three evenings every month with her friends in Country Cat Cafe, an upstairs handmade accessories shop plus cat-themed cafe which is located in Causeway Bay. Because Ellie works nearby, sometimes she goes there for lunch. She really appreciates the food, the tranquil atmosphere, the country-style interior design and the music. "The shop is like existing in a completely different world. Every time I visit the shop, I can temporarily forget my troubles," said Ellie. "Actually I'm very conscious that I'm going to somewhere really different when I start to climb the stairs." For upstairs-shop-goers, the climbing up of the staircase can be interpreted as a ritual of crossing the border between the mundane and the fascinating, of transferring oneself from the familiarity of everyday locales to the exceptionality of 'elsewhere'. This process is also part of the experiential elements that build up the analogy of 'treasure hunting'. Staircases leading up to shops are often decorated to set customers in the right mood. This explains why graffiti are usually inscribed on both sides of the staircases that lead up to street fashion shops.

Upstairs shops are attractive to young adults because they are in the business of dreams. Dreams are embodied in the consumption of goods and services in upstairs shops through two different ways. Firstly, as upstairs shops depend on special selling points for their survival, they often provide goods and services that fill the gap between what is available in the mainstream market and the unmatched expectations of consumers. In other words, they temporarily fulfil customers' unrealised wishes. This is the main reason behind the popularity of upstairs pet cafes. Youngsters who are not able to keep pets

due to housing restrictions or parental objection have much fun visiting upstairs pet cafes. Ada Lo, a 20-year-old university student, is a regular customer of Good Dog, an upstairs dog-themed cafe and pet supplies shop in Tsim Sha Tsui. Although she wants to keep a dog at home, her parents don't allow her to do so. Before she discovered the upstairs cafe, she could only take a brief look at puppies through display windows of pet shops and daydream about playing with them. Now she visits Good Dog nearly every week to play with the resident dogs. Apart from knowing each dog's name and habits, she has also made friends with the shopkeepers there and they have talked a lot about tips on training and taking care of dogs. Sometimes she just drops by to see how the shopkeepers and the dogs are doing.

Candy Wu, a 20-year-old student, is constantly dreaming about having her own room. However, it is impossible because she is living with her parents and two sisters in a small 380-square-foot public housing flat. "I want to have my own room because I feel that I have already grown up and I need some privacy," she said, "If I have a room, I would decorate it in retro style and fill it with colourful furniture." For the past six months, she has developed a habit of visiting Oldies Lifestyle Cafe, an upstairs cafe which also sells retro style home decoration. "I like the shop because they decorate the shop just like my dream-room." During her free time, Candy hangs out in the shop either alone or with friends. "It's better than staying in the cramped flat," she said. Though it is unlikely that Candy will have her room soon, she did buy a piece of bead curtain there and saved it for future use.

Both the examples of Ada and Candy demonstrate that while youngsters struggle against disappointment in a reality which is often out of their control, they seek substitutes through consumption. It is a way to resist by refusing to subject themselves to total defeat by reality. These young adults' favourite upstairs shops form a bridge between reality and their dreams by realising their wishes to a certain extent.

Joey Wong is the designer and shop owner of Wow Factor, an upstairs shop in Central which sells stylish handmade lighting. Before Wow Factor was set up, Joey worked as a stage lighting designer. She believes that lighting has the magic of influencing people's emotions through creating the atmosphere of interior space. Hoping to let more people experience this kind of magic and have greater design freedom, she left her full-time job and set up Wow Factor. Every item on sale in her shop is designed and handmade by her. Joey's signature style is her lighting design with beads. She is skilful in creating lamps with beads of different colour, material and size. Her product range includes a variety of lamps and curtains that are made of plastic, glass or crystal beads. Other than ready-made lighting, Joey is more than happy to tailor-make unique decorative lighting according to clients' requests. As Wow Factor is a one-person business, Joey has to endure a heavy workload. However, she does not mind at all because sharing the wonder of her creative lighting is more important than leisure time and monetary gain.

Cloud 9 is a creative photo studio operated by Anthia Lee and Iris Chan. They have set their target as creating "a new culture of wedding photography". "Take wedding photo anytime, anyhow, anywhere with anyone. Who says you have to shoot it before your wedding?" Anthia and Iris think that wedding photos should be personal, artistic and stylish. Because each customer has a different personality and a different story to tell, their task is to create photos in a unique style through creative photography. They use different elements to breath an air of personality for each customer's photos. Hand-drawn illustrations, embroidery patterns and interesting props are just a few tricks among a wide range of their techniques.

1. Cheung Chi-wai, 2002.
2. Sharon Zukin, *Point of Purchase: How Shopping Changed American Culture*, New York: Routledge, 2004, p.8.
3. Jean Baudrillard, *Selected Writings*, Oxford: Polity Press, 1988, p.22.
4. Arjun Appadurai, *The Social Life of Things: Commodities in Cultural Perspective*, Cambridge, New York: Cambridge University Press, 1986, p.4.
5. Georg Simmel, *On Individuality and Social Forms*, Chicago: The University of Chicago Press, 1971, p.97.
6. Lui Tai-lok, "The Malling of Hong Kong" in, Gordon Matthews & Lui Tai-lok (eds.), *Consuming Hong Kong*, Hong Kong: Hong Kong University Press, 2001, pp.23-45.
7. Lehtonen Turo-Kimmo & Maenpaa's Pasi, "Shopping in the East Centre Mall" in, Falk, Pasi & Campbell, Colin (eds.), *The Shopping Experience*, London: Sage Publications, 1997, pp.136-165.
8. Ibid., p.158.
9. Walter Benjamin, *The Arcades Project*, Cambridge, Mass.: Belknap Press, 1999, p.875.
10. Dick Hebdige, *Subculture: The Meaning of Style*, London; New York: Routledge, 1979, p.79.

The Chinese believe that good relationships are built around
the dining table. So, having dinner with family, friends and colleagues
is very important in Chinese culture.

There is a Chinese saying that the state of the economy
is reflected in how people eat.
If the economy is good and consumption power is strong,
then people are willing to spend money on food.
In other words, eating culture
can reflect and
predict
economic
changes
in
society.

The Chinese also believe
that eating culture
reflects the overall culture
of a society.

See-fong choi:
A new concept of consumption

I attempt here to make some sense of the sudden popularity of *see-fong choi* ('private upstairs dining') and its relationship to a new concept of consumption in Hong Kong. Through soft approaches, I observe, record and explain how the *see-fong choi* phenomenon can be used as an indicator in a study of new consumption 'requirements' within middle to upper class consumers in Hong Kong.

Most of the information here is data collected from local newspapers and magazines. The Chinese terminology *see-fong choi* will be used throughout this essay and refers to both singular and plural circumstances.

"*See-fong choi* "
"Private Upstairs Dining"
"Secret Family Recipe"

There are many different explanations of the origin of *see-fong choi*. One is that in the early to mid 20th century in Hong Kong, private clubs were popular for various forms of private gatherings in the Chinese community, usually among wealthier groups. Private clubs were formed by groups of friends as permanent places for their private gatherings. Groups of friends or members with shared common interests formed clubs as places to engage in activities such as playing games like mah-jong, smoking and dining. Private chefs were hired to manage their clubs' kitchens which indicated the importance of 'eating' for the members of these private clubs. This 'private clubs' idea could possibly be the origin of the modern day *see-fong choi*.

One of the first, better known *see-fong choi* in Hong Kong was opened in 1998 by the artist Wang Hai and his wife and the art critic Lau Kin-wai. Wang's wife's culinary skill was highly praised among their group of friends. Lau was the owner of a pub and he first started the idea of making Wang's wife's cooking commercial by bringing his customers to Wang's 'restaurant' for dinner after drinking at his pub. Unlike usual restaurants, *see-fong choi* is 'dining at home' which is dining in an apartment and might not have a licence. Therefore *see-fong choi* cannot be categorised as restaurants in this case. Word spread quickly among friends and soon to the media. *See-fong choi* from then onwards became more and more popular and more people began to enter this new business.

A lot of the *see-fong choi*'s owners are artists and designers and they use their 'restaurants' as galleries to display their works as well as for dining. Wang's wife even sings to customers during their dinner as extra entertainment. The sudden booming of *see-fong choi* after 1998 could also be the result of Hong Kong's economic crisis. Some *see-fong choi* were opened by well known chefs who were laid-off due to the economic turmoil. To open *see-fong choi* would be one way of survival for them. Until now, *see-fong choi* not only has several versions of its origins, it is also a marginal 'business' hanging between 'private dining' and commercial licensed and unlicensed dining.

Despite the long wait for a table booking which could be as long as a month and the not so cheap price range which is about $250 to $400 per head, a lot of *see-fong choi* are doing very well. The number of *see-fong choi* is continuously increasing and attracting more and more new customers.

Most of the *see-fong choi* are located in Central and Sheung Wan. (Wanchai and Causeway Bay are becoming popular spots for *see-fong choi* recently.) In the early 20th century, famous restaurants were mostly located in Central and Sheung Wan. Central and Sheung Wan therefore have established fame for fine cuisine and elegant dining. One important factor here is that Lan Kwai Fong, the icon of cosmopolitan consumption in Hong Kong, is right at the heart of Central. The SOHO area, which is an area along Staunton Street and Elgin Street in Central, has become the second Lan Kwai Fong within recent years. A lot of unique and new style cuisines from around the world are gathered in the hubs of Lan Kwai Fong and SOHO. *See-fong choi* as a new style of cuisine has every reason to choose these two districts to establish a foothold.

See-fong choi is the 'secret family/personal recipe', therefore the food itself can be described as one of a kind. Since *see-fong choi* is a 'family business', there are no 'big menus' as in normal restaurants. Instead, the 'food of the night' changes according to what is fresh and seasonal in the market. The customers apart from knowing they would be having that particular cuisine, would not know what dishes they would be having nor have no choice because it is all up to the chef's decision based on what is best at the market. This however creates a sense of mystery to the customers and the anticipation makes *see-fong choi* even more mysterious and tempting.

Most of the *see-fong choi* are northern Chinese cuisines such as Sichuan and Shanghainese. 'Fusion' food is also becoming more popular as well as other cuisines like Italian, Indian and Japanese. Hong Kong people have always regarded northern Chinese food as very exotic and more 'high-class' than Cantonese food. One of the reasons can be traced back to the early 20th century eating culture in Hong Kong which was very conservative. Since most of the Hong Kong people were from Guangzhou, the restaurants were primarily Cantonese style. Cantonese food is very practical and is concerned only with the taste of the food. Not until after China's 1949 Revolution, when a lot of people from Shanghai moved south and settled in Hong Kong, did an eating culture in Hong Kong evolve. Shanghainese food, in comparison to Cantonese, pays attention to the detail of presentation and the eating environment apart from the taste of the food. It was from then onwards that native Hong Kong people began to look for dining qualities other than the food itself.

See-fong choi, private upstairs dining, is literally a 'restaurant' in an apartment. The interior of the *see-fong choi* is like the interior design of a modern home. Unlike the typical Chinese restaurant interior in Hong Kong which is usually over decorated with blinding lighting and tables being closely arranged, *see-fong choi* provides a more relaxed, private, comfortable and cozy 'home-feel' dining environment for customers.

See-fong choi offer only two dining sessions each night. The number of customers in each dining session is small due to the physical capacity of the dining area. Compared with large restaurants, the relationship between the host and the customers is much closer and intimate in *see-fong choi*. The host, who is also the waiter and the chef, will attend personally to the customers table by table. The chef talks to the customers face to face during the meal. Being the customers, you are treated as the chef's circle of friends. The relationship is much deeper between the host and customers in *see-fong choi* than in most large restaurants.

The 1970's marked the period of the 'fast food and self-service' eating culture in Hong Kong which was influenced by American culture. Cafe de Coral, Maxim, McDonald's and KFC all started to become very popular in the 1970's. (This eating culture is still very popular today.) At the same time, *Cha-chan tang* (Hong Kong style Western restaurant) also began to boom in the 1970's. The quality of life in Hong Kong improved significantly in the 1980's and consumption power increased. Many people began to experience wealth for the first time. Chinese seafood restaurants became popular and eating seafood was a sign of 'being rich'. The 'loud' and 'big' designs of the dining environment were then considered as luxurious and extravagant.

Lan Kwai Fong and SOHO in Central have very distinctive identities. People associate expensive clothing, fine cuisine, good taste, high-middle class yuppies, artists and movie stars with these two areas. They have become a unique community. Anyone who consumes in the various shops or restaurants within 'the community' will be perceived as belonging to its particular social class. Knowing that most of the *see-fong choi* restaurants are located in the two 'yuppie' districts, one can easily make the connection between location, *see-fong choi* and the target customers who are middle to upper class consumers. These *see-fong choi* frequenters, the middle to upper class people in Hong Kong, are high spending consumers. They are willing to pay for good quality products such as food.

But assuming that buying the food also means buying social status and a ticket to enter a particular community, suddenly the social status and the entrance to the community become more valuable. People in Hong Kong are very sensitive to the class differentiation. If going to *see-fong choi* can be perceived by others as 'high class', then the food itself could easily become the by-product of the social status.

See-fong choi recipes are unique because they are 'secret recipes'. This concept of uniqueness is very attractive to the customers. By eating such unique cuisine, the consumers believe they become themselves unique and different from others. 'Being different' is something that people are going after. 'Being different' makes them feel valuable and hence, proves their existence. The food here again becomes the by-product of the psychological factor of the notion of 'being different'.

See-fong choi do not provide menus. Limited selections mean less choice. People love this idea of 'limitation' because today, less choice means more value. Just like the phenomenon of a vast variety of clothes in G2000 versus the limited selection of clothes in Prada or Gucci. In the past, more was valuable. All-you-can-eat buffet was valuable. This concept however is fading out and is replaced by the notion of less choice equals more value. Less choice can be related to the notion of uniqueness. Uniqueness adds value to products. Therefore *see-fong choi* patrons are paying not primarily for the food but the extra value that is extracted from it, the value of uniqueness.

See-fong choi patrons are also buying the authenticity that *see-fong choi* provide. They emphasises home cooking. This means natural ingredients and original cooking methods. As people increasingly become more aware of the concept of healthy eating, home cooking becomes their choice. Going to *see-fong choi* means pursuing authenticity because it is home cooking. Home cooking is the most 'back to basic' eating experience. Therefore, going to *see-fong choi* can be related to buying a 'back to basic' experience.

It is important to grasp that this personalisation, this pursuit of status and social standing, are all based on signs. That is to say, they are based not on objects or goods as such, but on differences. Only in this way can we understand the paradox of 'under consumption' or 'inconspicuous consumption', "the paradox of prestigious super-differentiation, which is no longer displayed in ostentation, but in discretion, sobriety and self-effacement. These latter merely represent a further degree of luxury, an added element of ostentation which goes over into its opposite and, hence, a more subtle difference." [1]

In the past couple of years, the concept of having a "lifestyle" has been exceptionally stressed through different channels. Shops like Ikea, G.O.D., MUJI and a lot of interior magazines are among those channels that contribute to the promotion and selling of 'lifestyles'. The 'perfect lifestyle' that these media want to convey lies within the concept of creating a comfortable and cozy home environment. Any environment that is designed to be 'home-feel' or 'homelike' is trendy, modern and tasteful.

Even commercial offices and retail shops incorporate this 'home-feel' design style in their interior designs and furniture decorations. The essence of *see-fong choi*, which is everything about 'home-style' matches exactly this 'lifestyle'. Hence, people going to *see-fong choi* can at the same time experience and surround themselves with the kind of lifestyle that relates to good taste and a high quality way of living. When home living spaces for most Hong Kong people are so limited, to create a 'lifestyle' living condition is not easy, but through *see-fong choi* people can pay to borrow the experience of such a 'lifestyle'.

The serving style of typical Chinese restaurants is indifference and distance. *See-fong choi* breaks away from this custom. Within a few hours of serving the dinner, the relationship between the hosts and the customers is close and intimate like friends. The intimacy between the hosts and the customers not only can give a sense of prestige and privilege to the customers, but also more importantly, the sense of personal touch. *See-fong choi* patrons are not only buying the food but at the same time buying a couple of hours of human relationships.

In an industrial economy, the emphasis is on mass production. The products of mass production are moulded copies with no character - just like all the big housing estates that are built almost identical in Hong Kong. A lot of typical Chinese restaurants operate similarly to the idea of mass production. Customers cannot tell the difference from the taste of the food, the menus and even the interior decoration between restaurant A and restaurant B. Consumers today, especially the middle to upper classes, are tired of these mass production 'copies'. They want tailor-made products like *see-fong choi*. They want products/goods and services that can fulfil their desire of 'being different' which can distinguish them from the rest of society. They are looking for the unique characteristics that the products can give them so that by purchasing the products, they feel that they are unique as well. Being unique, they believe they are special and rare

and this makes them feel prestigious and 'high class'.

For example, "while the middle classes continue to engage in conspicuous consumption, the elites may engage in new forms of inconspicuous consumption in order to create new and more subtle differences between themselves and the rest of society." [2] "The customer begins to identify with a firm's product or service and incorporates it into his sense of self. It becomes one of the many ways he differentiates himself in the world." [3]

Hong Kong, like other big cities around the world is experiencing a boom in information technology. High technology is everywhere. Though high technology makes life more convenient in many ways, it is a very artificial 'product' which is cold and lacks a human touch. When people are exposed to too many artificial experiences, the result will be a turning around and looking back to the very basics. That's why a lot of consumers today are looking for products that are natural, original, handmade and homemade like *see-fong choi*. Consumers today appreciate and treasure more the originality and creativity behind the products themselves.

Hong Kong is a city of speed. People are always in a hurry. The living pattern is very intense. When experiencing too much intensity, people will loose their sensitivity. Human relationships become cold and alienated. From the *see-fong choi* phenomenon, we can see that a closer kind of human relationships is 'in demand'. Consumers want more than just the goods and services themselves. They are looking for the personal touch and human relationships to augment products. Even when the human relationships are 'bought' as in the case of *see-fong choi*, people still are more than willing to pay for such experience.

The Age of Access is defined, above all else, by "the increasing commodification of human experience [...] the commodification of goods and services becomes secondary to the commodification of human relationships." [4] The consumption concept has changed especially among the middle to upper class people in Hong Kong. There are more 'requirements' that consumers are looking into before any act of consumption. People are not buying just primary goods and services like the food in *see-fong choi* for example. In fact, goods and services become secondary to the symbolic values and the human sensitivity that comes along with the goods and services. Those symbolic values are the ideas, concepts and hidden messages that bring to consumers ideas such as 'back to basics', the concept of a particular lifestyle and the message of "I am unique and high class". Human sensitivity is an aspect of human relationships that can add value to goods and services, such as the friendship between the host and the customers in the case of *see-fong choi*.

The economy in Hong Kong is facing a period of uncertainty. Understanding the concept of consumption among Hong Kong people is important to the understanding of the Hong Kong economy. The consumption concepts of the middle to upper classes in Hong Kong can be used as the indicator of the future consumption pattern in Hong Kong because they are an influential consumption group. I think the concept of 'small communities' and 'small businesses' will be the next consumption pattern in Hong Kong. The formation of small communities can satisfy the desire of this group of people to seek isolation from the rest of society while retaining membership of certain groups. Within specific communities, 'members' can build human relationships and can share common interests, knowledge and their 'social standings'. To accommodate these 'small communities', 'small businesses' emerge that have the characteristic of personal attention and the concept of originality. Hence, the large chain stores and mass production operation methods will fade out giving way to 'small businesses' tailor-made for the 'small communities'. The result will be in fact very similar to one of the explanations of the origin of see-fong choi, which is the idea of private clubs for private gatherings.

Traditional Chinese culture is concerned very much with a kind of 'love' and the notion of sharing between families and friends. This 'love' also means the kind of human relationships shared between families and friends. Western culture stresses the notion of individualism and the notion of private life. (The idea of privacy, according to some scholars, seems to have emerged fully in nineteenth century England, linked to the establishment of a *bourgeois* culture.) This significant difference in interpreting 'human relationships' between Chinese and Western cultures at times creates confusion for Hong Kong people. On the one hand, Hong Kong people are going after the idea of 'individualism'. On the other, they are tied to their Chinese roots and are unable to resist looking for the harmonisation of human relationships. What then can best satisfy these opposing cultural values? Maybe it is the idea of 'small communities' again - enclosed enough to nurture human relationships while at the same time enclosed enough to continue the quest for 'individualism'...

1. Jean Baudrillard, *The Consuming Society*, London: Sage Publications Ltd., 1998. p.6.
2. Ibid.
3. Jeremy Rifkin, *The Age of Access*, New York: Penguin Putnam Inc., 2001, p.109.
4. Ibid., p.97.

家菜董師傅

干燒明蝦

這不是一間正式的餐館，事關客人都要親自到北角董師傅的家中去吃，訂枱時講低想食乜，師傅就會一早準備最新鮮材料，冷盤、熱盤、點心樣樣係師傅即製造。菜肉包更係以前做大廚時董特首至愛，一試難忘的還有那份獨有的親切感。

估唔到出街都可以食到住家菜

電話：2571 5168／9217 4306董太洽
備註：每晚只做一枱，人數由5-15人亦可，必須預訂

Au Bon Gout

法國海鮮冷盤

老闆夏先生旅居法國十多年，鍾情法國菜，更願與同道人分享，於是這裡便成了廚房、餐廳（只有一張大枱及兩張小枱）連藏酒室，客人預先不會知道餐單，上桌時才揭曉總有意外發現，夏先生又會走嚟同你傾偈，好warm喫。

地址：中環德己立街27-39號榮華大廈6字樓D座
電話：2526 2621（必須預先訂位）

不妨上嚟食下，睇下有乜新發現。

式都傳時就會一早準備最新鮮嘅材料，冷盤、熱盤、點心樣樣伙日以製造。菜向也是係最前做大廚愛，一試有那份獨有的親切感。

GUTIERREZ + PORTEFAIX / LAURENT MALONE *

Underneath the highway

Kilometres of high-speed transportation meandering through high-rise buildings express a dynamic that is specific to Hong Kong. Driving at 70 kilometres an hour on those concrete snakes frames a global city where efficiency and interconnectedness produce an enigmatic in-between space, proximity with no intimacy. Confrontation is a crucial element in Hong Kong's culture. It involves a rupture, a moment when a foreign element intrudes and disrupts the urban fabric. But what is happening under the highway?

'Underneath' in general refers to areas that do not like exposure. They are also characterised by a mental universe other than that of an uncovered space. Whether it is under a bed, a desk, the atrium of the Hong Kong and Shanghai Bank (HSBC) in Central or under the highways, 'Underneath' in Hong Kong are precious places for appropriation. They are manifold, serving as refuges, playfields, and shelters from the harshness of the speed city above them.

* This project is a collaboration between Laurent Gutierrez, Laurent Malone, Valérie Portefaix (photos), and Maeva Aubert (sound). Here is an extract of the visual material, unfortunately excluding sound tracks.

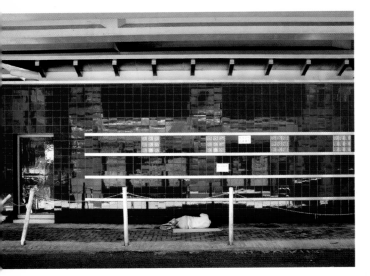

Text by MARY BUNEO
Photos by GUTIERREZ + PORTEFAIX / LAURENT MALONE

HSBC stories

"On Sundays and public holidays, Hong Kong's Central District is occupied by thousands of Filipino girls who transform the public space around the empty office tower into a collective living room. A cartographic image of the places they use presents a clear picture of public and private space in Central. Although they are permitted to conduct purchases in the commercial centres and use the pedestrian bridge systems, they cannot linger there. One exception is the open floor of the Hong Kong and Shanghai Bank that is made public by the Filipinos on their days off."
Gutierrez + Portefaix, *Mapping HK*, Hong Kong: MAP Book Publishers, 2000

Mary's story

My name is Mary Buneo from the province of Ifugao, Philippines. For almost 12 years in Hong Kong, I can say the HSBC is very useful for us, domestic helpers, and especially to us, Filipinos. It is our meeting place... During holidays, it is our habit to come here [HSBC], to wait for our group, like relatives, friends and different organisations. It is where we chat, share food, ideas and even problems if one of us needs help. It is a convenient place for us to practice some activities; to present a new program when we have one. Sometimes when it is raining and there is no place

to go, we're just staying there spending our time chatting, some of us playing cards, manicuring, reading and eating. Before we depart, we always set the time when we will all gather again. Otherwise, a majority of us are going to church, to sports festivals, like volleyball and basketball. Some of us are also going to a skill training, like cooking, hair cutting, sewing, computer, and much more. Few are even pursuing their unfinished studies, studying hard the entire Sunday afternoon. In the evening most of us are buying food from a restaurant or food chain take out, to eat in HSBC in-group. That's how we enjoy our holiday till the time to go back home to our working place.

Ann's story

Since 18 months, I am going to the HSBC compound every Sunday, from 4 to 5 pm. I first finish my plans for the day like roaming around, attending church mass, and spending time in the library, before going there. It may be a noisy place, with endless lines of people and buses passing by, but I prefer it to other places like the Star Ferry and any over pass. Besides, It is the only outdoor place in Central that provides shade to hundreds of helpers, especially on a rainy day. It is where "illegal hawkers play catch me if you can" with urban officers. It is sad to say, it is also a place where some helpers spend their money through small-time gambling.

Meeting my friends and everybody makes me happy; sharing things and spending my time with them helps alleviate my boredom after a week of the same old routine. Everybody seems happy there but at the end of the day we make lots of new friends, some enemies, and sometimes we are able to help someone from stress-related problems. My hour stay there may sound too long for passers-by, especially tourist to imagine, but I never really notice the time and it is over too soon.

Elsie's story

I usually go to the HSBC at the end of the week to meet my friends. I don't do much there but just say hello to friends, meet relatives who have arrived from the Philippines for any updates or information about what is going on at home. Sometimes I stay longer and share a meal with them. I don't go there every Sunday. Personally I don't like this place because there is too much noise, it is too crowded and dark. But I have to go sometimes to easily meet my friends and relatives. Although I describe it as such, it offers protection from the rain and the heat of the sun to many Filipinos. It is the only large space where domestic helpers are allowed to pass their holiday time.

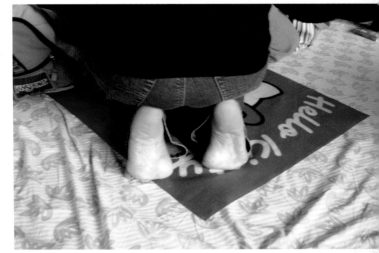

Minerva's story

My name is Minerva, I came from Fugato, a province located in the Northern part of the Philippines island. I like to come to the HSBC building because this is where most of my *kababayan* or town mates from the Philippines usually meet before and after their day-off activities. This is also one of the few places where the Hong Kong government allows us to do what we want, like eating, singing, dancing or just simply talking and loitering.

Compared with some other places where the Filipino gather, the HSBC building is quite decent and few people passes by and stare at us, wondering who we are and what are we doing here. I come every Sunday and holiday and stay here for a while in the morning, then come back in the evening until I have to go back to my employers' home.

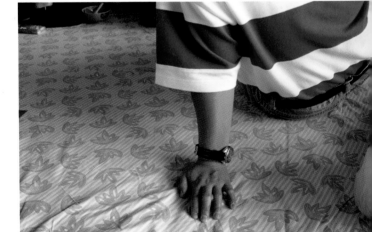

personal acco

個人戶口

collection

各項領取

international b

國際銀行業務部

HSBC Bank In

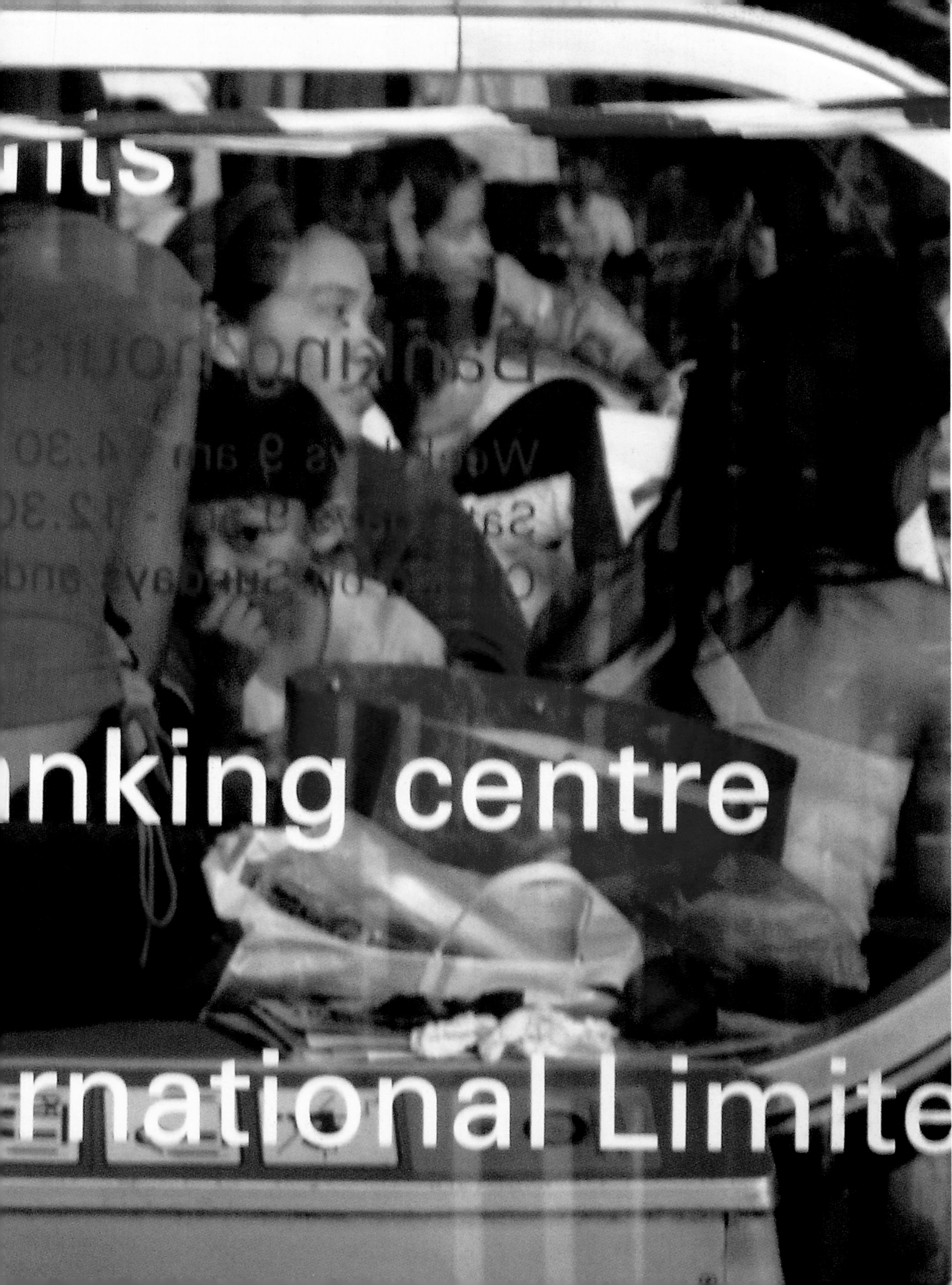
nts
nking centre
rnational Limite

NEIL LEACH

Drag spaces

"We are all in drag now", Ackbar Abbas

Hong Kong is the quintessential site of spatial appropriation. The interstices of the urban fabric are used and re-used with an extraordinary intensity. Stalls appear over night, squatting within the left-over spaces of the urban fabric, and disappear with equal ease. Interior spaces – homes - are created even in the external zones of the public realm. Public thoroughfares are adopted as the site of ritual events. These spaces – many of them transit spaces – become spaces of transitory identity, as their character changes according to the way in which they have been appropriated.

On Sundays Filipino domestic workers congregate around the covered walkways of Central, under the Hong Kong Shanghai Bank building, in Victoria Park in Causeway Bay, and in many other public spaces and thoroughfares. Here they encamp for the day and perform a number of private rituals, such as cutting each other's hair, giving each other massages, manicures and pedicures and serving each other lunch. This is for many their one opportunity to entertain. Denied any private spaces in which to perform these activities, they appropriate public spaces.

Elsewhere, illegal street cafes – or 'soup cafes' as they are known - are set up by hawkers to serve food to migrant workers, street cleaners and scavengers, wherever some vacant space can be found.[1] Meanwhile real estate agents take over the marginal spaces along the street - often no more than 50 cm deep - for their shop fronts. With their properties displayed on the walls, and with little more than a chair, desk, lap top and mobile phone, these estate agents spill out on to the street, turning it into a makeshift office. More generous spaces are rented out for temporary shops on short-term leases between more permanent tenants. These spaces are often used to sell cheap goods from mainland China – mainly Tupperware, plastic kitchenware and other cooking utensils - often kept still in their boxes, and marked up with hand-written signs. Although on occasion the interior decoration of their previous tenants will have been stripped away, these temporary shops – like transvestites – often reveal tell-tale traces of their former identities, through signage and decorations of their former occupants which have been left behind.

In Hong Kong space becomes an ever renegotiable commodity. Nor need such operations exist on the margins of legality.

Spatial appropriation has also become the dominant logic within the mainstream commercial world of Hong Kong. Here I am not speaking of the hybrid configuration of interior spaces so typical of Hong Kong, as bars sit on top of swimming pools on top of car parks on top of shopping arcades, in a manner that can leave Rem Koolhaas's famous model of the Downtown Athletic Club looking distinctly conventional. Rather, I am referring to the logic of temporary spatial appropriations, where the same commercial interior may shift from being conference centre to wedding hall to exhibition hall to bar or perhaps even brothel, and back to conference centre again overnight. Hong Kong – itself once the site of colonial appropriation – has become the site of intense commercial appropriation.

Bernard Tschumi famously celebrates the cross-programming of spaces.[2] The old modernist slogan of 'form follows function' together with the dream of spatial determinism have been called into question, as spaces are continually put to re-use. Homes become police stations become brothels. Slaughter houses turn into art galleries. Modes of inhabitation are defined less by architectural form and more by the events that take place there. Spaces become 'event spaces'. This cross-programming exists in many parts of the world, and may even take the form of a multi-layered programming of space. In Las Vegas, for example, casinos serve as hotels while also serving as conference centres, resorts, shopping arcades, spaces of prostitution and so on. But seldom do we find the richness and diversity of the complex choreography of sequences of spatial appropriations evident in Hong Kong. In this respect Hong Kong is the ultimate 'event space'.

The intensity of this process often leads to a blurring of the distinction between public and private. Whatever is nominally public is often appropriated for a prescribed set of semi-private activities. Walter Benjamin has commented on the porosity of public and private in the crowded streets of Naples, but not even he could have imagined the intense overlapping of public and private in a place like Hong Kong.[3] Indeed, we should maybe reject any fixed distinction between public and private when dealing with such spaces, and view them instead as zones of temporary strategic appropriations, an ever changing landscape of territorialisation and deterritorialisation.

How, then, can we begin to theorise these spatial appropriations? How can we understand the method by which these spaces achieve their temporary, strategic identities? I want to put forward the concept of 'drag space', as a means of describing how these complex spatial appropriations found in Hong Kong can imbue interior spaces with a certain temporary identity. In this regard I shall explore the notion of identity itself as a form of drag, by extrapolating from the concept of 'performativity' promoted by Judith Butler in the context of interpersonal identity. By appropriating and bastardising this concept I hope to offer a viable theoretical framework with which to understand these 'drag spaces'.

Judith Butler has elaborated a vision of identity which is based on the notion of 'performativity'. It is an approach that allows her to perceive identity in a far more fluid and dynamic way than traditional approaches to the question. It is an approach, moreover, that recognises identity politics as a field of individual empowerment.

Butler is a theorist of gender politics — and more specifically lesbian politics. Her concern is to formulate a notion of identity that is not constrained by traditional heterosexual models and to offer a radical critique of essentialising modes of thinking. According to Butler, it is precisely our actions and behaviour that constitute our identity, and not out biological bodies. Gender, she argues, is not a given ontological condition, but it is performatively produced. It is "a construction that conceals its genesis", such that, "the tacit collective agreement to perform, produce and sustain discrete and polar genders as cultural fictions is obscured by the credibility of those productions."[4]

We may effectively rearticulate our identities and reinvent ourselves through our performativities. Here it is important to note that identity is the effect of performance, and not vice versa. Performativity achieves its aims not through a singular performance — for performativity can never be reduced to performance — but through the accumulative iteration of certain practices. It is grounded in a form of citationality — of invocation and replication. As Judith Butler explains: "Performativity is thus not a singular 'act', for it is always a reiteration of a norm or set of norms, and to the extent that it acquires an act-like status in the present, it conceals and dissimulates the conventions of which it is a repetition."[5]

Butler figures identity not as something interior — an essentialising 'given' — but rather as something exterior, a discursive external effect. It is borne of "acts, gestures and enactments" that are 'performatively' repeated.[6] Importantly, this relates not just to lesbian sexuality, but to all sexualities, such that heterosexuality itself emerges as a socially transmitted construct that depends upon a behavioural norm being 'acted out'. Here the connections between gender and 'mime' begin to emerge. Indeed Butler's whole discourse, it would appear, depends upon mime in general and the mimetic in particular. All behaviour is based on a kind of mimicry, including normative heterosexual behaviour that is thereby 'naturalised' and instantiated by the force of repetition: "All gendering is a kind of impersonation and approximation... the naturalistic effects of heterosexualised genders are produced through imitative strategies; what they imitate is a phantasmatic ideal of heterosexual identity, one that is produced by imitation as its effect."[7]

Cultural practices are governed by the hegemonic. They instantiate a certain order, and encourage acquiescence to that order. They are propagated through a desire to conform. This is particularly evident in the case of gender practices.

Normative gender practice is controlled by the logic of camouflage. To subscribe to the dominant cultural norm is to avoid conflict and to follow the behavioural systems of a naturalised, hegemonic order. And it is as a camouflage that gender can be understood as an 'effective' cultural praxis.

Gender, in this sense, approaches a notion of drag. It is a position that is 'assumed', and played out within the logic of conformity to some accepted norm. In making this claim, Butler destabilises the traditional authority of heterosexuality: "To claim that all gender is like drag, or is drag, is to suggest that 'imitation' is at the heart of the heterosexual project and its gender binarisms, that drag is not a secondary imitation that presupposes a prior and original gender, but that hegemonic heterosexuality is itself a constant and repeated effort to imitate its own idealisations."[8]

This is a radical re-evaluation of the mechanics of cultural practice, that has ramifications for every aspect of cultural life. Without collapsing sexuality, class, race and ethnicity into the same category, all types of identity can also be interpreted as dependent upon performative constructs.[9] While each operates within its own individual paradigms, the general framework remains similar. Each depends upon the performative, each is citational in character, and each is 'effective'. This is not to overlook the significance of physical characteristics, but rather to challenge the notion that these characteristics are the sole determinants of identity.

According to such a view, the constitution of one's identity through performativity extends beyond questions of appearance into modalities of behaviour and modes of perception and expression. In the context of race, for example, we have to acknowledge how the process of 'racing' something or 'being raced' might operate. For performativity also operates in modes of perception, such as the 'gaze' which, as it were, 'colour' and frame our view of the world, but — importantly — also constitute it. To be 'black' is to view the world with a 'black' gaze.[10] What applies to the gaze also applies to other modes of perception or expression.

Butler locates performativity at the heart of our cultural identity today. In an age increasingly colonised by 'fictional worlds', as Marc Augé has observed, where fantasy allows identities to be assumed and discarded like fashion accessories, and where self-realisation often conforms to models drawn from Hollywood, the concept offers a more productive alternative to traditional understandings of the constitution of the self.[11] The whole notion of identity as some fixed and stable condition deserves to be re-interrogated in an age of theming, role-playing and identity politics, where identities must be perceived in the plural, as multiple and often seemingly contradictory modes of personal expression. Nor is this necessarily negative. Indeed such tactics can be analysed as a defensive mechanism that allows the individual to 'survive' within contemporary cultural conditions. Indeed, as Sherry Turkle has argued within the context of a proliferation of 'screen identities' as a result of the increasingly widespread use of the computer, multiple personality disorder can be seen less as a problematic symptom of an age of instability and depthlessness, and more as a strategy of survival — a kind of cultural camouflage — that enables individuals to operate productively in a variegated and multi-faceted world.[12]

The emphasis which Butler places on performativity does not undermine the underlying value of form. Indeed this is the main message in Butler's seminal work, *Bodies that Matter*.[13] Hers is an essentially corporeal philosophy of identity. Butler's discourse also serves, however, as a corrective to a certain positivistic theory of form that is still pervasive. Matter — in Butler's terms — does not exist outside of discourse. As Mariam Fraser observes, following Butler: "Matter does not 'exist' in and of itself, outside or beyond discourse, but is rather repeatedly produced through performativity, which 'brings into being or enacts that which it names'."[14]

The politics of space

These observations have obvious ramifications for any discourse about the politics of space. Butler's incisive comments on identity being defined not in biological terms, but in performative terms as something that is 'acted out' — can be profitably transposed to the realm of physical space. What Butler's logic seems to suggest is that particular spaces are given meaning by the practices that take place there. In this respect, the mechanisms which govern personal identity also govern spatial

identities. If the constitution of personal identity can be defined in terms of performativity as a manifestation of a form of 'drag', then the identity of spaces themselves can be understood in similar terms. For if identity is performed, then the space in which that performativity takes place can be seen as a stage. After a certain number of performances that stage will no longer be neutral. It will be imbued with associations of the activities that took place there, on the part of those who witnessed those activities. If identity is a performative construct — if it is acted out like some kind of 'filmscript' — then architecture could be understood as a kind of 'filmset'. But it is as a 'filmset' that derives its meaning from the activities that have taken place there. Memories of associated activities haunt physical space like a ghost.

It is here that Butler's thinking can be deployed as a way of cutting through much confusion that exists on the question of the politics of space. Too often there has been a simplistic collapsing of a particular political ideology on to a particular form, as though a political ideology can be conflated with an aesthetic ideology. This refers as much to politics in general as it does to the specific question of gender politics. According to this logic, certain forms are in and of themselves imbued with a certain content. Just as there are seen to be certain 'democratic' forms, so there are certain 'feminine' forms. It is this thinking that Fredric Jameson has sought to challenge. Form, for Jameson, is essentially 'inert' and whatever content is grafted on to it is 'allegorical' in character.[15] There is no intrinsic meaning or political potential to any form. Whilst there may indeed be certain forms that 'lend' themselves to democratic purposes rather than totalitarian ones, and — equally — no doubt certain forms that 'embody' a feminine sensibility, it is surely a mistake to map certain activities on to certain forms, as though those activities were a consequence of those forms.

A space can only be politicised by association. Certain associations are 'projected' on to a space, but those associations are defined not by the material properties of that space, but by the activities that take place there. Moreover, they depend upon the memory of those associations being kept alive. In this sense, a space used for particular activities will accrue a certain character over time, but as new activities take over — and as memories of the former activities fade — the space will take on a different character. A 'masculine' space may invert into being a 'feminine' space. A 'fascist' space may turn into a 'democratic' space. And, by extension, a 'colonial' space can be turned into a 'post-colonial' space. Often these processes are charged with a sense of strategic reappropriation, and are set against the memory of previous associations. At other times they may be facilitated by conditions of amnesia or the repression of memory, factors which release a space from its previous associations.

It is here that we might recognise the possibility of using Butler's comments on 'performativity' to understand how the spaces in Hong Kong are imbued with a certain transitory identity. Spaces become 'drag spaces'. They take their identities from the performativities that are acted out there. No longer defined in terms of some essentialising 'given', they may be effectively redefined according to each new activity that they house.

Surface effects

Yet it is worth pausing for a moment to examine the specific practice of drag to tease out the precise mechanics of this culture of the performative. One of the primary features of drag culture, for example, is the reliance on effect. Surface display provides a mechanism by which to highlight the intentions of the act. Props serve as indexical markers to add signification. The performative thereby becomes exaggerated precisely in order to overinvest the practices involved with a degree of content that does not belong to the form itself. Drag therefore operates as a form of masquerade, a camouflage tactic that focuses on the surface and the paraphernalia of surface effects often with a deliberately distorted and exaggerated intent. Drag queens are more female than females. They offer a caricature of female performativity, a display of over-invested gestures and exaggerated props – such as false eye-lashes, high heels, wigs and padded bras.

Such visual displays find their echoes in the 'drag spaces' of Hong Kong, where the ephemeral and fleeting paraphernalia of celebration reach their apotheosis in various ceremonial practices, like the dragon dances of public festivals. Once the setting itself is no longer invested with the capacity to lend a certain character to actions taking place there, attention is displaced into the realm of effect. The effective therefore needs to compensate for lack of identifiable character within a particular setting.

Some might criticise this 'drag culture', this ephemeral enchanting world of visual affects, for being superficial. Yet we should recognise the positive value of a culture of the surface. Here, against various critiques of a surface culture of the spectacle or hyperreality mounted by figures such as Guy Debord, Jean Baudrillard, we should recognise the role of the image as constitutive of all forms of identity. The message that seems to emerge from Debord, for example, of the image as working to alienate people from their true selves, is clearly at variance with psychoanalytic approaches that recognise the specular nature of identification in which representation plays a crucial role in all forms of self definition. In effect we gain our identity precisely through our self re-presentation. Nor is there some essential 'reality' that has been lost beneath the surface. Rather – according to a Lacanian perspective, at least – what we take for reality is in fact the imaginary. We never access the 'hard kernel of the real' except in moments of acute *jouissance*. Identity is always a form of masquerade. The simple example of 'make-up' illustrates how surface manipulation and enhancement has become more or less co-extensive with contemporary notions of identity.

Equally some might criticise this 'drag culture'- this culture of surface effects - as a culture of the inauthentic. Yet the logic of such practices is perhaps to challenge the very principle of authenticity itself. More than anything else, the concept of performativity has helped to expose that all normative cultural practices that have become instantiated through hegemonic practice – and are therefore perceived as 'authentic' - depend upon the performative. As such performativity emerges as a critique of the whole discourse of authenticity. It is not simply, as some writers such as Fredric Jameson have maintained, that as one of the antinomies of our current age the authentic collapses into the inauthentic, so that the authentic is inauthentically reproduced in the work of Quinlan Terry and others, and the inauthentic – as in the case of Las Vegas – has somehow become accepted as authentic.[16] Rather the whole discourse of authenticity can be seen to be flawed, and grounded in a moralistic attempt to preserve certain traditions. 'Authenticity' is often championed by traditionalists within architectural discourse as a defence against the onset of the 'inauthentic' new. The weakness of this argument becomes clear once it is recognised that 'authenticity' is simply defined in opposition to what is supposedly 'inauthentic', and the argument soon collapses under the weight of its own circular logic. What is supposedly 'authentic' is only deemed so through this repetitive citational culture that has invested it with such an attribute. In other words claims to authenticity amount to the projection of certain values on to the world, values that are not inherent in a particular practice or object, but are ones which have been grafted on to it over a period of time. Once we realise that all cultural practices are grounded in the performative, performativity emerges as a potentially emancipatory concept that recognises that whatever has been instantiated to become a form of hegemonic practice can equally be displaced by an another form of practice.

Hong Kong, more than anywhere else, is a place that challenges received assumptions about authenticity, whereby certain forms are perceived to be in and of themselves 'authentic'. The criteria for judging what is 'authentic' are never clearly articulated. What, for example, are the 'authentic' spaces of Hong Kong? Are we to celebrate the continuation of long-standing tradition - through antique or regional forms - against the 'imposture' of the new? Are we to celebrate, in other words, the recuperation of a language of a bygone era, as though tradition were something locked into the past? Or are we to recognise that tradition itself is a dynamic process of continual rejection and renewal?

Koolhaas and Jameson argue that this celebration of the regional and the traditional may lead to a form of 'Disneyfication' as the historical fabric of a city is often celebrated as a means of offering an individual 'identity' to that city, but in a manner that rinses it of its original content and reduces that fabric to the status of touristic spectacle.[17] Yet, worse than this, such attempts to recuperate the traditional and the regional as a means of overcoming the homogenising placelessness of late capitalism may also serve to support the very culture that they attempt to resist. Instead of countering a culture of late capitalism, they may actually feed that culture by offering the traditional and the regional as further 'products' on the cultural marketplace.

Here it is not so much a question of challenging the nostalgic reappropriation of the past - in the form of chinoiserie and other surface mannerisms - as a product of rather than a resistance to the universalisation of architectural forms within postmodern culture. Rather it is a question of recognising that both universal forms and the nostalgic reappropriation of the traditional and the regional are manifestations of a culture of postmodernity.

A more profitable line of enquiry, perhaps, would be to recognise that the universal is always folding into the individual, just as the individual is folding into the universal. The individual is spawned by the universal, and vice versa, through a process of reciprocal presupposition. The greater the replication of any item, the more apparent become the individual differences. In the context of Hong Kong we might recognise this principle at work through the ways in which the universal tower block becomes appropriated through local practices and rituals to become the 'living' tradition of Hong Kong. Here we might turn once more to the theory of performativity to understand this process. For the logic of performativity delineates that it is not form itself that gives identity, but form inscribed within a specific social practice. It is through the particular performativities of Hong Kong, then, that a specific Hong Kong identity might be forged through these tower blocks. The same tower block might appear in Hong Kong, South America or Eastern Europe, and yet the particular way in which it is colonised ensures that the tower block within Hong Kong - or indeed within specific localities in Hong Kong - will always maintain a distinctive identity.

In this respect the interior 'drag spaces' of Hong Kong emerge as quintessential spaces of the postmodern. If we are to assume that modernity strove for fixed rules and deep levels of meaning, postmodernity could be characterised by an obsession with the surface. Postmodernity is a culture of sampling, of surfing and casual operations. It is also a culture of the ephemeral, where fixed rules give way to dynamic systems. It is a culture of radical shifts, where biological metaphors of growth and adaptation best capture the processes of assimilation.

As such, we might recognise in the 'drag spaces' of Hong Kong a highly contemporary moment. These spaces expose new forms of cultural practice that have emerged to deal with a culture of change. They epitomise a certain adaptive strategy which can also be detected within multi-functional commercial spaces elsewhere in the world, although not perhaps with quite the same intensity. The particular conditions that give Hong Kong its extreme cultural identity begin to suggest that there is much to learn from its innovative cultural practices. Hong Kong can be seen as the space of various experimental practices that will no doubt find their place elsewhere in the world. 'Drag spaces' are sure to proliferate elsewhere.

Rem Koolhaas has introduced the notion of 'Junk space' to define much of the architectural production of the 20th century. More recently he has added a further series of categories for the 'New World' of the 21st Century, including: Nano space, Space space, Dump space, Boom space, Voice space, Bush space, Border space, Tight space, Crowd space, Blog space, Robo space, DNA space, Limbo space, Sex space.[18] I would suggest that 'Drag space' needs to be added to this list, as the quintessential performative space of the 21st Century.

---

1. 'Scavengers' is used here as a term to refer to Chinese migrants on temporary two month permits, who deal largely in recycling scrap metal. Many of them rent out spaces on the tops of buildings, where they set up tents for accommodation and cook using camping gas.

2. See, for example, Bernard Tschumi, "Six Concepts in Contemporary Architecture" in, Andreas Papadakis (ed.), *Theory and Experimentation*, London: Academy, 1993, p.18.

3. Walter Benjamin, "Naples" in, *Reflections*, New York: Schocken, 1986.

4. Judith Butler, *Gender Trouble*, London: Routledge, 1990, p. 140, as quoted in Vikki Bell (ed.), *Performativity and Belonging*, London: Sage, 1999, p.136.

5. Judith Butler, *Bodies that Matter*, London: Routledge, 1993, p.12.

6. They are 'performative', as Butler puts it, "in the sense that the essence or identity that they otherwise purport to express are fabrications manufactured and sustained through corporeal signs and other discursive means. That the gendered body is performative suggests that it has no ontological status apart from the various acts which constitute its reality. This also suggests that if that reality is fabricated as an interior essence, that very interiority is an effect and function of a decidedly public and social discourse, the public regulation of fantasy through the surface politics of the body, the gender border control that differentiates inner from outer and institutes the 'integrity' of the subject." Judith Butler, *Gender Trouble*, op.cit., p.136.

7. Judith Butler, "Imitation and Gender Insubordination" in, D. Fuss (ed.), *Inside/Out: Lesbian and Gay Theories*, New York: Routledge, 1991, as quoted in Bell, op.cit., p.137.

8. Judith Butler, *Bodies that Matter*, op.cit., p.125.

9. Vikki Bell discusses the possibility of understanding Jewishness in this light in Vikki Bell (ed.), *Performativity and Belonging*, op.cit. See also Sneja Gunew, "Performing Australian Ethnicity: Helen Demidenko" in, W. Ommundsen and H. Rowley (eds.), *From a Distance: Australian Writers and Cultural Displacement*, Geelong: Deakin University Press, 1996, pp.159-171.

10. Judith Butler herself has addressed this question: "I do think that there is a performativity

to the gaze that is not simply the transposition of a textual model onto a visual one; that when we see Rodney King, when we see that video we are also reading and we are also constituting, and that the reading is a certain conjuring and a certain construction. How do we describe that? It seems to me that that is a modality of performativity, that it is radicalization, that the kind of visual reading practice that goes into the viewing of the video is part of what I would understand as the performativity of what it is 'to race something' or to be 'raced' by it. So I suppose that I'm interested in the modalities of performativity that take it out of its purely textualist context." [Judith Butler (interviewed by Vikki Bell), "On Speech, Race and Melancholia", in Vikki Bell (ed.), op.cit., p.169.

11. Marc Augé, *A War of Dreams*, trans. Liz Heron, London: Pluto, 1999.

12. Sherry Turkle, *Life on the Screen*, New York: Simon and Schuster, 1995.

13. Judith Butler, *Bodies that Matter*, op.cit.

14. Mariam Fraser, "Classing Queer" in, Vikki Bell (ed.), Performativity and Belonging, op.cit., p.111.

15. "I have come to think that no work of art or culture can set out to be political once and for all, no matter how ostentatiously it labels itself as such, for there can never be any guarantee that it will be used the way it demands. A great political art (Brecht) can be taken as a pure and apolitical art; art that seems to want to be merely aesthetic and decorative can be rewritten as political with energetic interpretation. The political rewriting or appropriation, then, the political use, must be allegorical; you have to know that this is what it is supposed to be or mean — in itself it is inert." Frederic Jameson, "Is Space Political?" in, Neil Leach (ed.), *Rethinking Architecture*, London: Routledge, 1997, pp.258-59.

16. Frederic Jameson, *The Seeds of Time*, New York: Columbia University Press, 1994.

17. Rem Koolhaas, "The Generic City" in, *S,M,L,XL*, Rotterdam: 010, 1996; Frederic Jameson, "History Lessons" in, Neil Leach (ed.) *Architecture and Revolution*, London: Routledge, 1999.

18. Rem Koolhaas (ed.), "New World, 30 Spaces for the 21st Century", *Wired*, June 2003, pp.115-169.

Urban dynamics
The culture of change – choice – connection – co-existence

CONDITIONS: How do cities intensify ?

INTENSITY describes the state of things, literally a kind of immaterial density that pervades the city as a general culture. It is vigorous, but does not necessarily embody a physical form. On the one hand, the extreme form of urban intensity is represented by the massiveness and rapid occurrence of (and between) individual events. This particularly refers to the events that come in a gigantic scale and disappear without any traces.

DENSITY is a term commonly used by others when referring to Hong Kong. While this is true, the often overlooked spirit of the city, lies in its intensity. Geographically and politically speaking, Hong Kong is its own boundary. There is simply no room for horizontal expansion. As a result, Intensity is more so intensified in such an environment when imposed with such a constraint.

Looking back on the histories of the dominant Chinese cities of today, their development are more or less based on simultaneous horizontal and vertical expansions. Shenzhen, a prime example of a new city which has emerged in the last twenty years, has never ceased to sprawl outwards. Historical cities like Shanghai and Beijing, in addition to their rapid redevelopment in the old city areas, have also been incorporating their peripheral provinces to grow to unprecedented sizes. Hong Kong, on the other hand is a city which has continued to thrive on its own intensification, which in itself is a truly unique scenario, hence a worthwhile case study.

Below we propose a framework of 4 conceptions - change, choice, connection and co-existence, to further elaborate the idea of intensified city with reference to Hong Kong. They are not in sequence, nor do they represent any hierarchy. Instead, they are in close relationship to one another, but the relationship is not explicitly linear. Each of the concepts is not strictly a cause or an effect of certain phenomenon below. But the concepts discussed here aim to provide some relevant points of reference for the local phenomena.

CHANGE

Force is the immaterial cause of change. A cityscape is a product of an infinite number of different forces coming into play at a same point of time. Social, economic, political, cultural or historical forces act from different directions, and the changes resulted are directional, pointing to certain ideals about the urban space. After all, change is about the survival of society.

Change is intricately associated with time. Time is a distinctive dimension which has an internal logic of space: a space not measured in a physical sense but by an immaterial calibration: duration. Like the way physical space provides a medium of locating objects, time provides a medium for changes to take place. Yet unlike an object which occupies space, there is no full saturation of time. The intensity of change can be infinite, always with the possibility for further intensification of various scale and duration.

Forces are generated from shifting concerns and ideals in the course of time. They are external factors, but can cause implosions within a system. It is possible to identify the sources of the forces, but it is always oversimplifying to reduce the cause of change to one single force. Change has no final form, but only intermediate products in the process of transformation. Although change does not necessarily lead to growth or unidirectional progresses, the shifting of forces and the subsequent transformation of systems do.

Take the transformation of the old district in Causeway Bay, for example. A classic case of Change brought on by different forces (known and unknown) shifting in various directions over Time. When the Time's Square project was completed, the district instantly became the second center of Causeway Bay. Consequently, property prices soared for its neighbouring worn-down tenement housing with developers competing to redevelop the land into a five-star office building.

All was well until the economic recession struck Asia, hence the originally planned office spaces had to be transformed into low flow commercial areas, that is, hair salons, beauty parlours and restaurants... but when all these are stacked over forty floors, it results in a vertical recreation/shopping mall taking the configuration of an office tower.

<the bachelor dwells within s
a compact and efficient arrang
and laundry area liberates th
programmes of bachelor life> g

eezespaceof330squarefeet.
hentofkitchenette,bathroom
mainingspaceforthevarious
rchang'sappartment,HK,1998

living / working / eating / sleep
/ living / working / eating /
/ reading / living / working /
dressing / reading / living /

/chatting/dressing/reading
eeping / chatting / dressing
ating / sleeping / chatting /
orking / eating / sleeping /

CONNECTION

Connection is about constructing relationships between systems. Systems vary in scale and nature and present along the spectrum between polarities, be it physical or virtual, micro or macro. A beeping sound in the underground train during rush hour can induce a phone search through the crowd. The system of wireless communication acts on the system of public space. Altogether this scenario reflects the issue of congestion, mass displacement, collective behaviour and patterns of living. Here, connection is an instrument which relates to a matrix of references.

Connection confirms the presence of a boundary, by which relationships are created between two or more disparate entities. In other words, boundaries separate while at the same time connect. The fluid nature of boundaries shift, dissolve, associate with distant elements or phenomena and creates an intensive spatial montage.

Connection is created through the implemented interface. It creates a platform for interaction. The peripheral plane is itself the connecting device. It triggers unforeseen spatial experience and subversive visual-information relationships which animate the presumably static public space. Building facades can be wrapped with mere commercial visuals. The parasitic brothel lightscape reveals an extra layer between streets and buildings, thus creating a new system of informal, if not illegal, city guides.

Connection evokes a network of conjunction. Space flows in a fluid manner and is not constrained by an independent edifice. It results in a separate system while hybridising with other existing systems.

Connection in its most brutal manner is revealed in the act of overlapping and penetration. Surfaces multiply by the making of additional layers and entities. Every surface is maximized to enhance visual connection, and in the end, to raise its commercial value through the quantity of visual contact.

Connection can be observed while riding the MTR, where a series of freeze frame projections are synchronised to the velocity of the train. For ten seconds, the passenger would see a short, amusing advertising short film when gazing out of the window. All this is achieved through the overlapping, penetrating visuals through time and displacement, which results in the connection between the active and the passive.

CHOICE

Choice is a representation of both individual and collective desire. Selection is a responsive act. It allows for identifying the existing potentials and gives room for reconfiguring the possible outcomes. This often leads to a transgression of the norms through deviations from the usual path.

Choice can be regulated, but cannot be controlled completely. Choice is provided through a matrix of consideration in which the existing conditions as well as the imposed forces are taken into account. Choice unveils the power of creativity of the public to achieve what is often misunderstood as given. Looking at the process of selection, individual vision can be reorganized and formulated from the fragments. While the external and internal constraints are revealed through the reading of individual choices, a maximum of possibilities can also be attained through creating flexibility under the same conditions.

Choice is seen through the evolution of Hong Kong's old Causeway Bay district, as sited previously. Novel flourishing mall typologies were born as a result of the - successful realisation of an ambitious idea and the unforeseen failure of those economically-driven decisions - forceful innovative strength of the people.

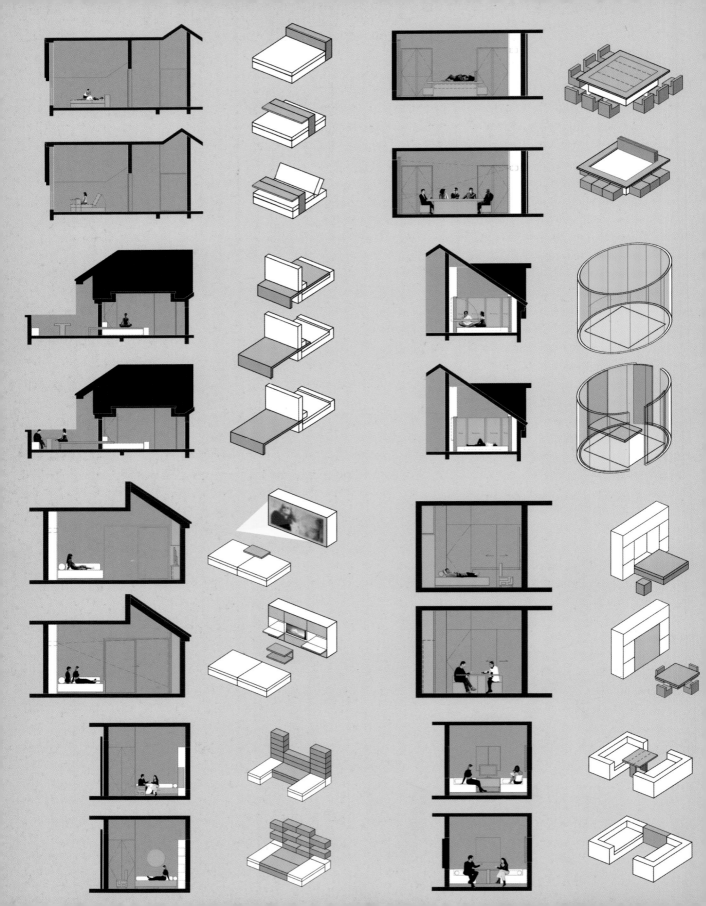

CO-EXISTENCE

Co-existence enhances a mix to become a total system. A rough view of Hong Kong is like a single whole with hiatuses carved out from the monolithic city building mass. Zooming in, it is composed of fragments of events and physicalities. We call these urban fragments [city bytes]. Often, they come in huge quantities and scale with a variety of life spans. They are self-developing at all times. The richness of city bytes is generated through collective creativity. They invade every part of the city, transforming the original use of space while revitalising abandoned areas of the city. They could be sometimes totally planned.

Co-existence, as an approach, favours adaptation instead of imposition, reuse instead of erasure, diversity instead of homogeneity. Thus, city bytes are highly adaptive because they are generated from specific urban conditions. They respect the existing conditions and seek the neglected potential of those conditions. They fragmentise the over-structured city, and provide new energy to fuel the self-generation of the city. Co-existence is a viable strategy for a development from ambition to economy.

Co-existence is an open system and operates as a means to urban sustainability. Contrasted with to evolution, which is a transformation within one entity, sustainability transforms with a network of interrelated systems which work as a totality of difference.

CONCLUSION

The above discussion is an attempt to delineate the logic of a city's operation where efficiency and intensity are results of a more improvised than structured model. Though the 3-dimensional cityscape is breathtaking, it is the non-visual based pragmatism behind that affects such realization. After all, it is this 4-C approach that is able to avoid any kind of preclusive visualization of an urban landscape; and more importantly, it allows for an ultimate escape from any disguised ambition of an ideal city.

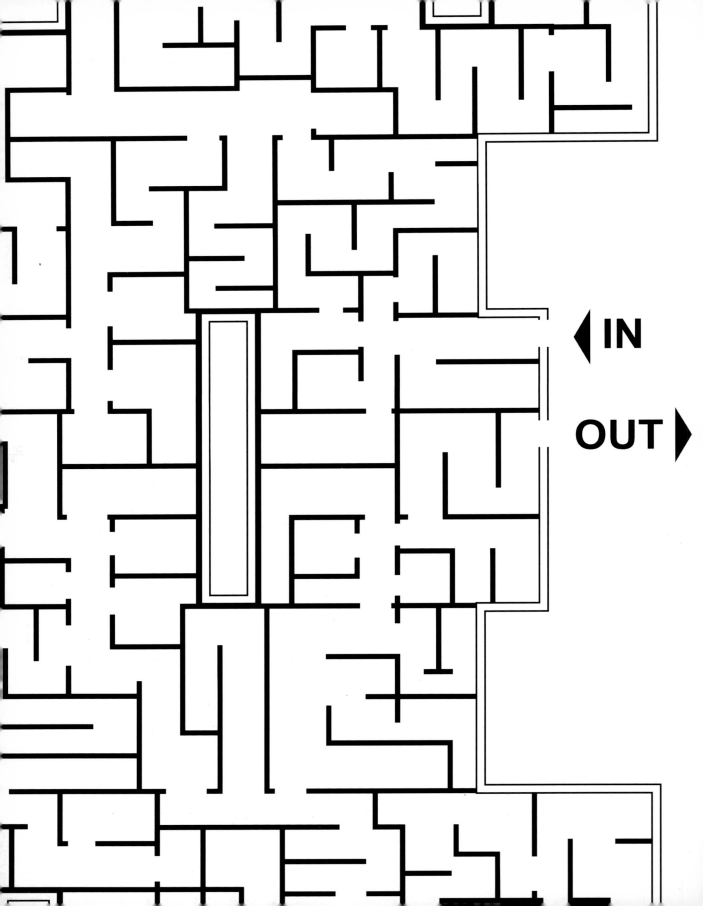

IN

OUT

Chungking city

There are places about which everyone has a story to tell. Chungking Mansions is definitely one of these, a Hong Kong mega building feeding urban legend and rumors. The place is associated with experiences – both good and bad. Locals, backpackers or tourist groups, they all have experiences of it.

Built in 1962, it was designed as a chic estate on one of the best sites in Kowloon, South Nathan Road. Since then, its reputation has never ceased to attract the media – fire, robbery, counterfeit, crime, disappearances, viruses and many more; Chungking Mansions offers us a voyage into an unfamiliar and unknown universe for the pleasure of being scared.

Among the first to grasp and translate its atmosphere, was the film director Wong Kar-wai in *Chungking Express* (1994). The internationally famous Mansions became the perfect setting for a film about Hong Kong's fast pace. Fast production first - the shoe factory - then fast consumption – a pineapple tin box – and a constant acceleration in the Chungking corridors. Yet another *Corridor city*. A rapid turnover of clients and products has shaped a hectic space that never stops.

As a tourist, starting from the street up to the Kowloon Guest House – an 11th floor private five square meter room without a window but air conditioned, for HK$100 – you are experiencing space and time concretion. It starts from the lift lobby. From the effervescence at the lift queue when one wants to go first with heavy luggage. In the lift, different cultures are telling us about different habits, some climb the lift cabin like spiders to avoid lift surcharge beeping. Once in the three dimensional dynamic maze (3DDM), you may pass by playful spaces invaded by African tribe dancing or Bollywood songs, silent old fashioned suit tailors, or tired residents promptly closing their doors.

The 3DDM is a nightmare for some, but a one hundred and one Arabian nights island for many others. It takes you through the meander of cables and pipes in between floors, staircases and stairwells.

Ventilation shafts are competing to accumulate dust and garbage from the upper floors. Here, drops are falling, but no one knows where they are coming from: might be a toilet or a dyeing factory or some used dishwater from an Indian restaurant kitchen. Nevertheless, everybody moves along, stops – to buy 5 year old electronic goods or consume Kashmir mutton rice - then continues.

As the basement and second floor are totally disconnected from the main building, one can be stacked within the 3DDM. Another option is to be there without even knowing you are there. With a separated entrance accessible from the street, these two floors belong to a different commercial entity. Shiny floors and wall surfaces, artificial lighting and clean corridors, these floors are split from the main body and clearly belong to a different world.

Rendering of the Chungking Mansion before construction.

A Pandora's box, *Chungking city* is a complete city within a building - a paradise of cross and multi-program. What is fascinating here, besides all the horrible shortcomings, is that Chungking succeeds where developers have miserably failed: a perfect example of a city as an organic mega-structure, flexible enough to fulfill every need from religion to water supply, yet providing an alternative to conventional space, culture and time.

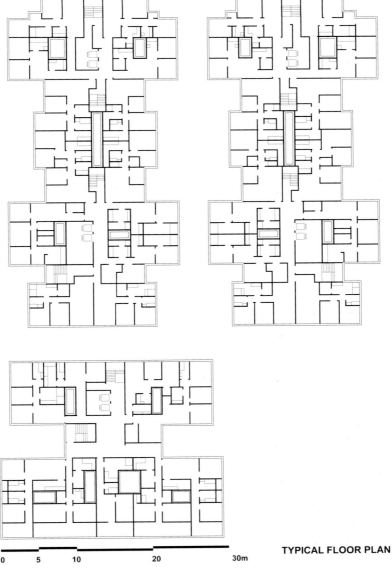

0   5   10   20   30m

TYPICAL FLOOR PLAN

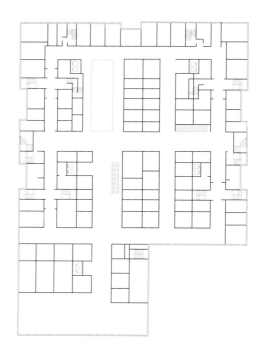

G/F PLAN

1/F PLAN

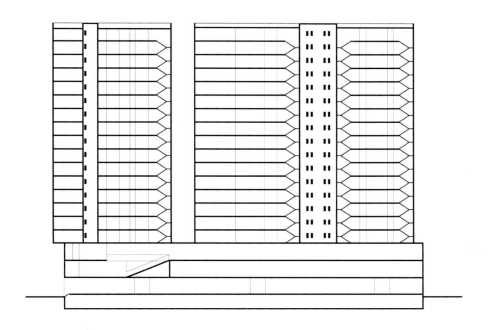

SECTION

0 5 10   20   30m

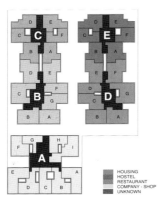

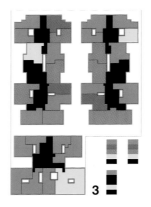

HOUSING
HOSTEL
RESTAURANT
COMPANY - SHOP
UNKNOWN

CHUNG
KING
MODE
D'EMPLOI

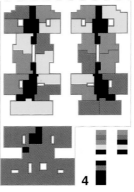

3

A3
AB Feng Enamuelling Co (exit from the stairs to the 3rd floor roof)

B3
C Taj Mahal Mess
D Stairs to the ground floor
E Sher-i-Punjab Club Mess
F Dragon International Travel

C3
C Jean's shop (owned with shop #53)
E Taj Super Deluxe
F The Delhi Club Mess

D3
AB Southern India Club (mess)
C Princess Guest House
E Event Club (mess)
F is the stairs to ground floor

E3
B Karachi Club (mess)
F AE Trading Co

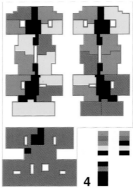

4

A4
Chunking House

B4
AB Thomtex enterprises
G Splendid Asia Limited

C4
A Ran jeet Super Deluxe
B Pakistan Mess
D Mah araja Guest House
F Islamabad Club Mess

D4
AB Head Sun Guest House
D Taylor
E Mount Everest Guest House
G Lai Wei Guest House

E4
C Great wall International
E moonsky Star Ltd
F Ming's company -import/export

5

A5
Chunking House

B5
A Chunking House
B New Delhi Guest House
C Taylor
E H.S. Industries - MFG - importers/exporters
F Ashok Club (Memners only) Nepali Food
G Taylor

C5
C Shin Kwang Co
E Sing Dim Trading Co. Ltd

D5 E Royal Inn Delux Room
F Royal Plaza Inn

E5
E Hang Fong Opal Co

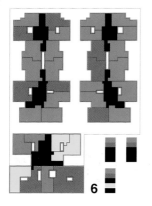

6

A6
AB London Guest House
D New Worl Hostel
E MRA Trading Co.
HI Keen rich Development Ltd.
Boom Come Development Ltd.

B6
CF Kamal Guest House

C6 CE new Brother's Guest House

D6
B Regent Inn Guest House
E Regent Inn Guest House

E6
B Regent Inn Guesthouse

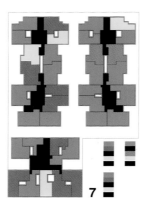

7

A7
A First Guest House
B Pay-less Guest House
C Gather Wealth Group of Companies
E Welcome Guest House
H Double Seven Guest House

B7
D Himalaya Guest House
F Kamal Dormitory (50HK$)
G New York Guest House

C7
B Hong Kong Trading Agency
E New Chunking Mansion Guest House
F Seijita Ophtalmic Lens Ltd.

D7
Private

E7
A Khyber Pass Club (mess)
B Cholira Association (mess)
E Hafiza Traders

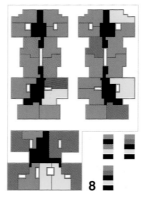

8

A8
A Sun Ying Guest House
B Shoe Fabric
C Chak Mei Ivory Factory
E Tom's Guest House
F New Mandarin Guest House
HI New Asia Guest House

B8
E Taj Super deluxe
F closed
G Tailor

C8
B Bangladesh Club

D8
A Fortune Guest House
F Hero's export/import

E8
B Yan Yan Guest House
E Wing Wah Opal Co

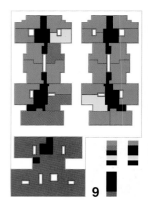

9

A9
All the floor is closed

B9
AB Grant Guest House
G Happy Guest House

C9
A New Harbour Guest House
F Star's Mansion's water and electrical works

D9
C Makkah Industries

E9
Private

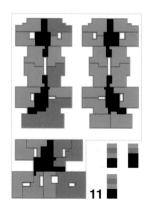

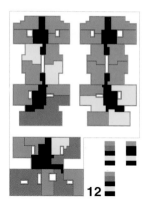

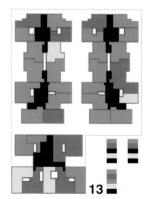

10

11

12

13

A10
All the floor is closed

B10
AB Happy Guest House
C China Source Company
E Kowloon Guest House

C10
A Kowloon Guest House
C Dhaka Overseas Restaurant
E Olympic Watch Co Ltd.

D10
AB are private   B Simla Guest House
E Simla Guest House
F China Town Guest House
H Yuet Shan engraving art

E10
C Maharaja Ranjeet Guest House
E Sea Hing Opal Co
F South river and Co

A11
AB Fortune Guest House
D Nanak Mess (Members Only)
HI New International Guest House

B11
AB Hong Kong Guest House
E Kowloon Guest House

C11
E Marria Guest House

D11
Private

E11
Private

A1
A Wadhwani's Hong Kong Inc. (clothes)
B Pekin Guest House
DE Super Guest House
I Double Star Guest House

B1
BAG Hong Kong Guest House

C1
CA Tailor

D1
C O'Lite Ltd.
G Nihon Co

E1
Private

A13
BG Rhine Guest House
C Pilot Impex
D Ashoka Guest House
E Sino Asi Electronics
G Chun King Saloon
HI Capital Guest House

B13
A Guest House

C13
A Jostina Fashion
D New Grand Guest House
F Osaka Guest House

D13
FG New Guanzhou Guest House
H Hong Kong Standard Ltd.

E13
D Mandarin Guest House

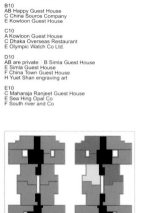

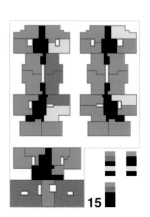

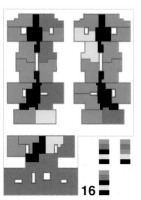

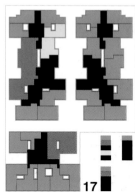

14

15

16

17

A14
B Himalaya Guest House
E Tokyo Guest House
HI Guest House

B14
B New Lucky guest House
G Guest House (Owned by F)

C14
Private

D14
A Duru's International (export)

E14
B Al Makkah Industries
C Old Far East Guest House
D Far East Guest House
F Old Far East Guest House

A15
AB Park Guest House
DE Ocean Guest House

B15
E Carlton Guest house
F Gaina Guest House
G Shan Grigh

C15
A Carlton Guest House
F Excellent International

D15
G Fairdeal Centre

E15
E Datesun Office

A16
ABCDEI Travels Hostel
H Time Travel Service Ltd.

B16
AB Private Area (A is an office   b an apartment)
E Tom's Guest House
G New Carlton Guest House

C16
A Tom's Guest House
E Garden Guest House

D16
A new Sanghai Guest House

E16
B Hang Tung Plastic Material Co
D International Club (mess)

A17
HI nited Guest House

B17
A Amar Guest House
DC LCA Guest House

C17
A World Impex Custom Taylor
F Yat Yee Saram Shirling Specialist (guru)

D17
Private

E17
Private

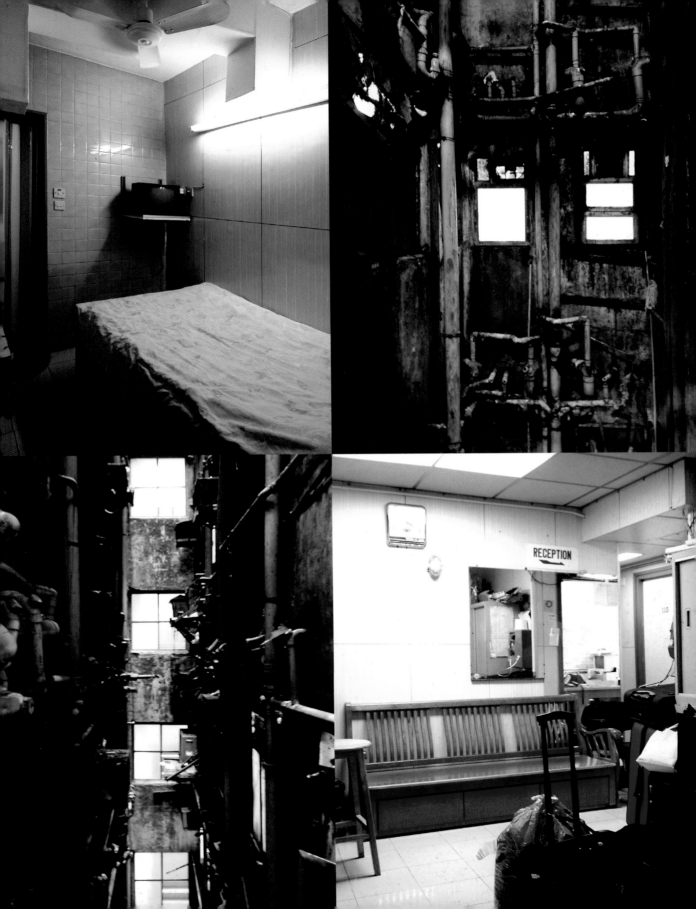

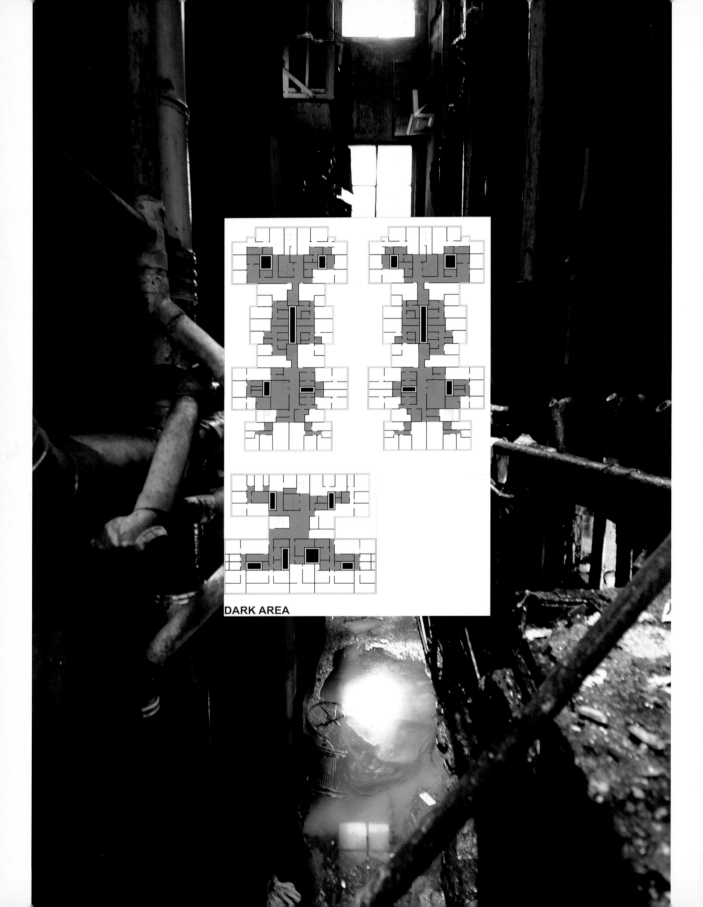

DARK AREA

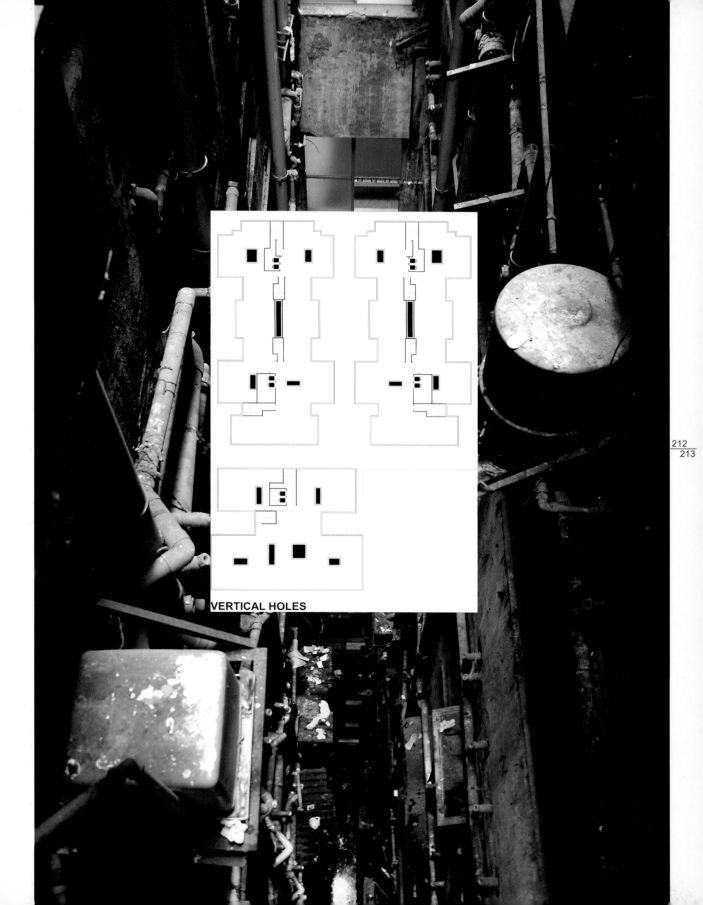

VERTICAL HOLES

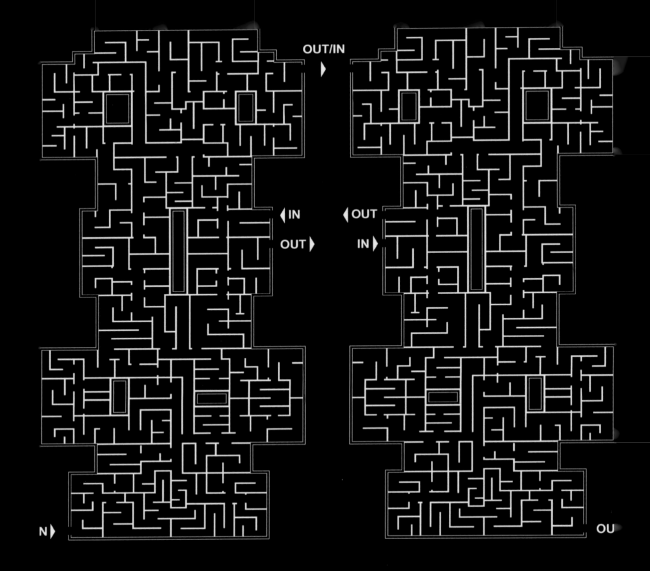

OUT/IN

IN

OUT

OUT

IN

N

OU

CHUNG KING MAZE

OUT

CHUNG
KING MAN

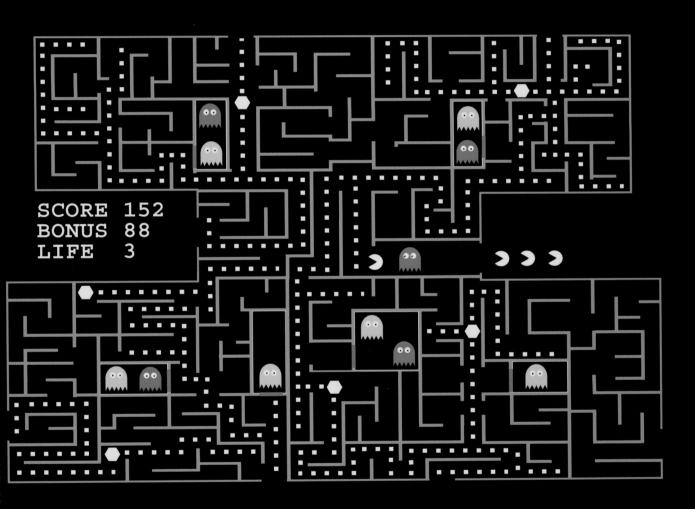

SCORE 152
BONUS 88
LIFE 3

Re-city

Re-city is about solid waste and its treatment.

Re-city is about thousands of locations and people in Hong Kong who dedicate their time to collecting and recycling our waste.

Re-city is about paper, plastics, ferrous metal and non-ferrous metal, glass, wood, rubber tyres and textiles, rejected by our frenetic consumption.

Re-city is about 17760000 kilos of waste every day disposed of at landfills in Hong Kong (2003).

Re-city is about 24 million plastic bags used in Hong Kong every day, or about 3.6 bags per person.

Re-city is about 2.38 million tonnes of municipal solid waste recovered in Hong Kong (2003).

Re-city is about the couple of dollars received for pushing a full cart of used cardboard.

Re-city is about a machine that can compress scrap or shape materials into a perfect cube.

Re-city is about the dream to find a suitcase full of banknotes within the rubbish, or at least computer equipment that is still working and therefore, not obsolete.

Re-city is about machine and electrical components dismantled into the smallest pieces.

Finally, Re-city is about the waste that we send away in disavowal.

LAURA RUGGERI

Moulding time

You leave Hong Kong for a few days, switch off your air-con, and while you are away paint peels, mould grows on the ceiling, damp patches appear on walls, books and magazines assume a contorted pose, the surface of your bags and leather skirts acquires a grey green constellation of mildew. Your new shoes grow a white fur.
Fungi spread on the guitar someone left in your flat.

"Things change quickly in this tropical climate", Alain Robbe-Grillet warned the readers of *La Maison de Rendez-vous*. The place you return to is not the place you left.

Like Cop 663 in *Chungking Express* you start wondering why your flat has changed so much during your absence. Has it become sentimental?
Time is calibrated by this change. As the patina thickens, days feel like years.

Mould grows even faster than the city.

Hong Kong is constantly at war with mould and... time. If time leaves any traces, they are immediately erased. Teflon-like surfaces are favoured over those that would stain, age, acquire a patina. Time doesn't stick here, slips away, channelled onto the acceleration lane that leads to the future, that 'some place else', freed from the clasp of time, freed from the ballast of history and memory.

Nothing is allowed to wear and tear. Commodities are discarded at the earliest sign of time accumulation. The fast and furious pursuit of the new is accompanied by the evacuation of the past.

Time is immobilised, one can step outside of history and retreat inside a controlled, air-conditioned, spotless environment, untouched by time, constantly reproducing itself 'new'.

In the accelerated cycle of consumption and disposal ageing is not permitted.

Fungi species of the ascomycete genus Chaetomium can dissolve the cellulose fibres in cotton and paper and cause the materials to disintegrate. This process is particularly rapid under moist conditions, as occur in the tropics. During World War II, countries fighting in Southeast Asia lost a great deal of equipment to the Chaetomiaceae.

Painted walls can become overgrown by species of the Phoma and Exophiala. Wallpapers also serve as a source of nutrition for the Scopulariopsis species which grow on wallpapers containing arsenic pigments.

Leather is mainly protein and serves as a convenient source of food for moulds. Some of the moulds that occur here are related to the dermatophytes that attack the outer layer of human skin.

Some substances that seem to be entirely unlikely to support fungal growth may be found to be well.

Patina:
a surface discolouration or adhesive outer crust of an artefact due to chemical changes resulting from weathering.
Patina does not necessarily imply great age.

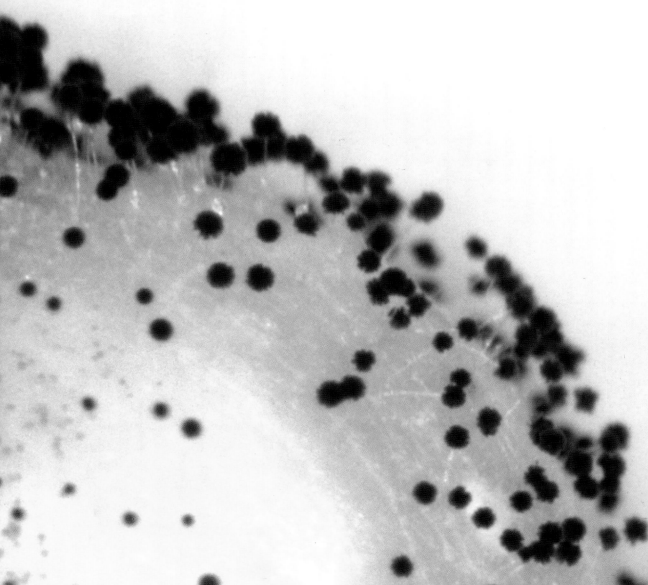

Yet time is a cunning opponent, it morphs into 'weather' in the space of translation. *Temps*, *tempo*, *tiempo*... in Romance languages /time/ and /weather/ share the same signifier.

In its becoming-weather, time acquires an experiential dimension, one that escapes the parcellisation into measurable units, restores duration as a continuum between subjects and their environment.

Mould, like time, creeps through moist interstices and cracks... wherever the sealant becomes loose.
As an inscription of time, mould is an index, that is a trace of its duration.

I don't know if it is the weather, but I feel that things are changing.
Cop 663, *Chungking Express*

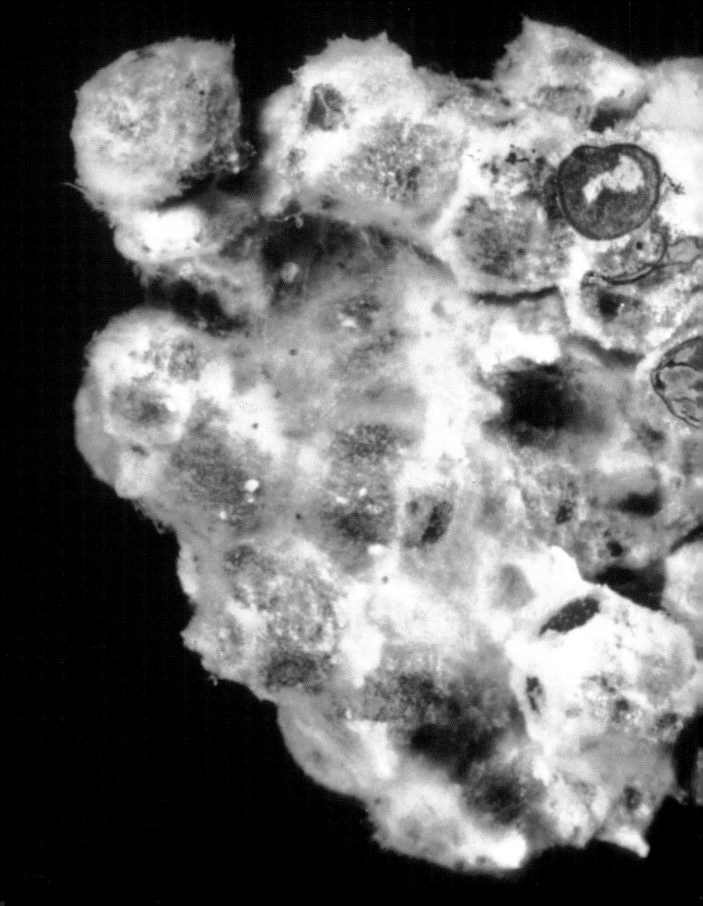

Mould smears the boundary between organic and inorganic. The line fuzzes. The hybrid formation is inherently transgressive, attacks the clarity of absolute distinctions... inside/outside, organic/inorganic, clean/dirty. Walls sprout, dampness oozes, mould grows. The porosity and permeability of surfaces becomes all too apparent. The interior is an illusion. The membrane is only ever relative.

The permeability of the surface breeds irrational fears of violation.
The body returns as a metaphor. Not the biological body, nor the libidinal body. A different body is at issue here: the paranoid body, bounded and locked, a body that no longer allows any traffic between inside and outside.

Glass and steel edifices are vigourously rubbed clean and polished. Fuzziness, confusion and intrusion must be avoided at any cost. The defence of borders becomes an imperative, for the proliferation of mould is perceived as an attack on the health of bodies, buildings and things.

Yet the battle against the invader is a losing one, uneven and hopeless. Mould soon begins to gain the upper hand.

Buildings are always on the point of being reclaimed by nature, vulnerable to the ever-present elements.

Mould continually 're-territorialises' inert matter, by altering its chemical order. Mould, being a rhizome, works through addition and multiplication. There are no real 'margins' of a rhizome. Growth happens at any point.

The natural/artificial cannot be conceived as a dyad. As in any complex space, a simple opposition or dual intertwining is embedded within a contorted jumble of becomings. Fungi meld the inorganic with the organic.

Rhizomatic networks re-territorialise rock-hard edifices. The coat of painting erupts in blisters and moulds proliferate inside and outside walls, seen and unseen. The materiality of architecture is engaged. No longer kept at the safe distance of spatial representation, its foreshortening reveals substantial rather than formal elements.

Mould counters sublation (*Aufhebung*), the idealist (and capitalist) attempt to lift matter out of the grip of time.

By restoring the experience of duration, mould reintroduces time as temper-ality.

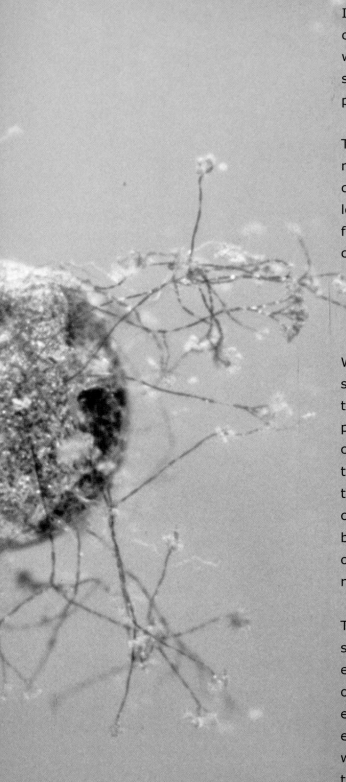

In Hong Kong there is virtually no period of dormancy, but only endless movement, with shallow breaks and slowdowns during seasons of relative scarcity (such as the peak of the dry season).

The urban space merges back into the mosaic of patches of succession that characterise the tropical forest. It is no longer distinguishable from the surrounding forest, no more surrounding, no more centre.

While buildings soar toward the sky, saprophytes and fungi grow toward the dark, inhabit damp recesses. Their presence and proliferation reintroduce the chthonian element, the gravitational pull to the ground, and below. The lower world that is kept out by sanitising measures and compulsive directives about hygiene seeps back into the conditioned atmosphere of office blocks, shopping malls and residential towers.

The crystallisation of the interior, the sealing of the border between interior and exterior, is impossible. Precisely because of this impossibility, policing the never-ending invasions has engendered its own economy. An army of cleaners is supplied with ever new, more powerful detergents; the arms race escalates at the expense of environmental balance.

Text by ERIC HOWELER
Photos by GUTIERREZ + PORTEFAIX

Thermal space:
18 degrees inside / 26 degrees outside

Hong Kong's urban morphology traces a precise geometric and optical contour, a result of the intersection of real estate speculation, commercial property leasing standards, and climatic controls: the setback tower profile, the leasable floor plate area, the lift service interval, the exterior reflectivity of the curtain wall. The formal determinants of Hong Kong's urban landscape, form an alchemical architecture, a mixture of geopolitics, topography, demographics, and climate. Climate is perhaps the least articulated determinant of architectural form, yet it is one of Hong Kong's defining characteristics. Hong Kong's density of habitation make it an epicenter of artifice; new land mass is reclaimed in Victoria Harbor, and new residential towers form architectural geologic formations, while the mechanically conditioned and optically regulated architecture of Hong Kong creates extensive new exterior membranes and vast new interior atmospheres.

Hong Kong's interior environments simulate conditions, defined by thermal comfort zones, that are prescribed by multinational business standards, which export goods and services as well as standard atmospheres. The history of a universal atmosphere dates back to the architecture of the International Style, which promised to deliver architecture from the specifics of local climate. In 1930 Le Corbusier stated, "Every nation builds houses for its own climate. At this time of international interpretation of scientific techniques, I propose: one single building for all nations and climates, the house with *respiration exacte*... I make air at 18 degrees centigrade and at a humidity related to the state of the weather." Le Corbusier's dream of a universal building with a single temperature imagined a utopian ideal – an optimised and man-made atmosphere. The discourse of climate and the discourse of globalisation are inextricably linked.

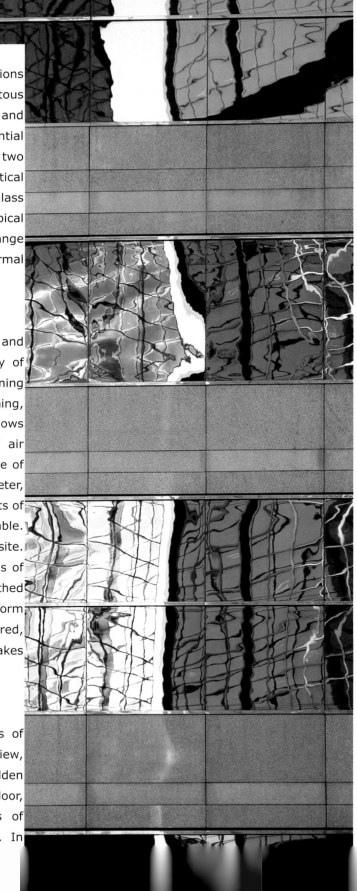

Surface

Hong Kong's two archetypal surface conditions reveal its climatological imperatives: the ubiquitous reflective glass curtain walled office building and the air conditioner studded facades of residential structures. The two surface conditions reveal two primary strategies for thermal practice: the optical and the mechanical. Optical properties of glass curtain walls repel the solar rays of the tropical sun, while the mechanical systems exchange heat to create and regulate interior thermal environments.

Prerequisite

While the marriage of steel frame, the lift, and the skyscraper are central to the mythology of metropolitan life, the impact of air conditioning is no less instrumental. Prior to air conditioning, the office building relied on operable windows for natural light and air. The invention of air conditioning severed the link between the size of the floor plate and the proximity to the perimeter, emancipating building bulk from the constraints of what was naturally illuminatable and ventilatable. Air conditioning in Hong Kong is a prerequisite. The dense stalks of office towers are columns of cool air, separated by floor slabs and sheathed in glass, while the vast shopping malls form horizontal chambers of cool air, monitored, filtered, dehumidified and regulated. Air conditioning makes hyper-dense urban life in Hong Kong possible.

Organs

Mechanical systems are the invisible organs of architecture, screened and louvered from view, they feed spaces through architecture's hidden interiors. Running overhead and under floor, buildings are equipped with vast amounts of mechanical and informational infrastructure. In

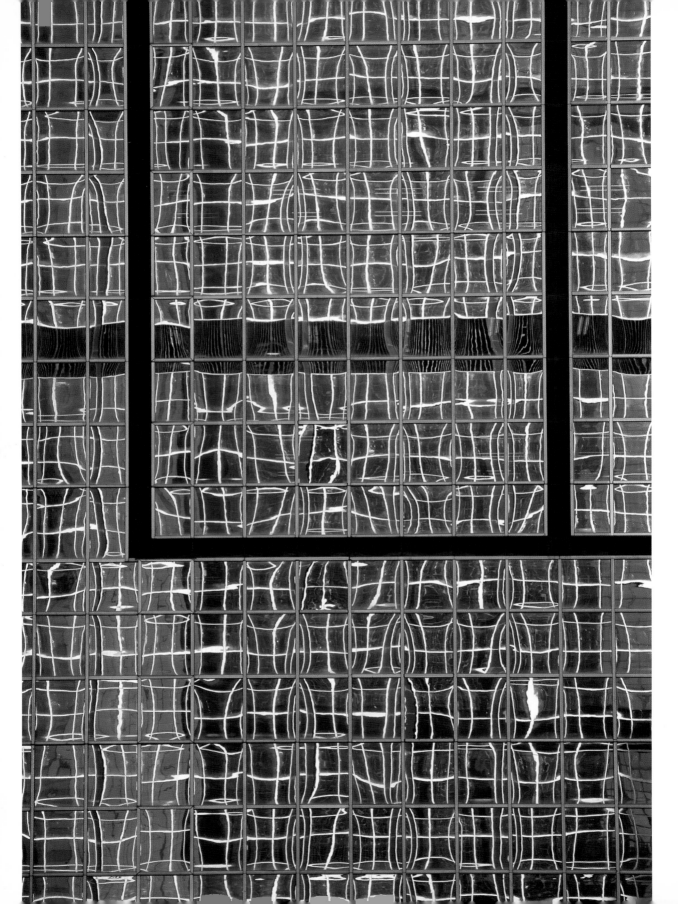

Hong Kong's voracious real estate market, where every square centimetre of duct space is displacing leasable space, the planning of distribution equipment is calculated with exacting precision. The Hong Kong Shanghai Bank is an exception to the rule of invisible organs. Its building systems are conspicuously displayed on the building exterior, and the mechanical equipment is elevated to the level of icon.

Filter

Traffic pollution in Hong Kong and heavy industry across the border in China render the air in Hong Kong among the most polluted, with air quality levels reaching hazardous conditions with an alarming frequency. The ubiquitous curtain wall membrane acts as a hermetically sealed interior to shut out Hong Kong's toxic exterior. Louvers and mechanical equipment form the ubiquitous threshold condition between inside and outside, $\frac{240}{241}$ where airflow between the two realms is regulated and filtered.

Anatomy

The glass curtain wall is the pervasive architectural surface of commercial architecture of Hong Kong- its gridded reflective surface forms the material DNA of the city- the curtain wall unit is Hong Kong architecture's basic building block and irreducible module. Dissecting the curtain wall system reveals its component layers: aluminium, silicone, and glass.

Aluminium extrusions are lightweight, hollow sections whose interior profile is designed to provide the wall thickness for optimised strength and configurations to allow for their assembly into unitised frames. Silicone combines strength and flexibility to adhere aluminium to glass without the

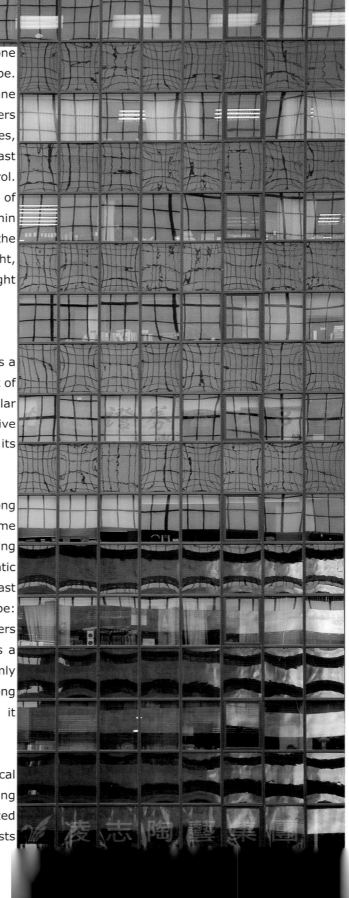

need for mechanical fasteners. Structural silicone glazing enables Hong Kong's vitreous landscape. The outermost layer of the curtain wall membrane consists of a glass assembly: interlayers, spacers and coatings that give it specific properties, thermal performance, acoustic insulation, blast resistance, dirt repulsion, and view angle control. A typical glass assembly consists of two lites of glass and an aluminium spacer, which trap a thin sheet of air or argon. Reflective coatings give the glass optical properties to reflect or filter out light, while low emissivity coatings allow for visible light transmission but resist the flow of heat energy.

Reflections

Hong Kong's mirrored vertical landscape creates a prismatic and kaleidoscopic urbanism. The Bank of China's taut glass facades form a faceted angular form, whose reflective coatings create a selective optical shell, which multiplies its context in its mirrored folds.

Available in a vast array of colours and tints, Hong Kong's glass sheathed towers form a polychrome skyline. The tinted glass increases the shading coefficient, filtering solar radiation. Chromatic associations abound. The gold glass clad Far East Finance Centre in Admiralty is an architectural trope: the bank is a bar of gold. The AIA Headquarters in North Point employs a multicoloured skin as a graphic metaphor for Hong Kong. The randomly distributed striped glass panels internalise Hong Kong's polychrome skyline and retransmit it through a conceptual camouflage skin.

Spectral properties of glass and the mechanical means of ventilation are exploited by One Peking Road, which employs the first double-glazed curtain wall in Hong Kong. The curtain wall consists

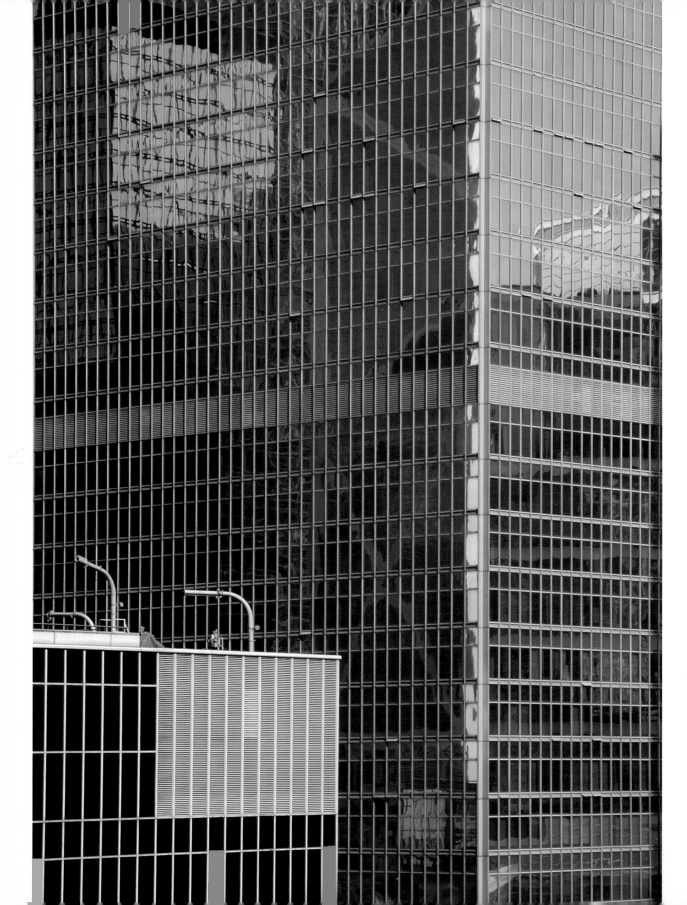

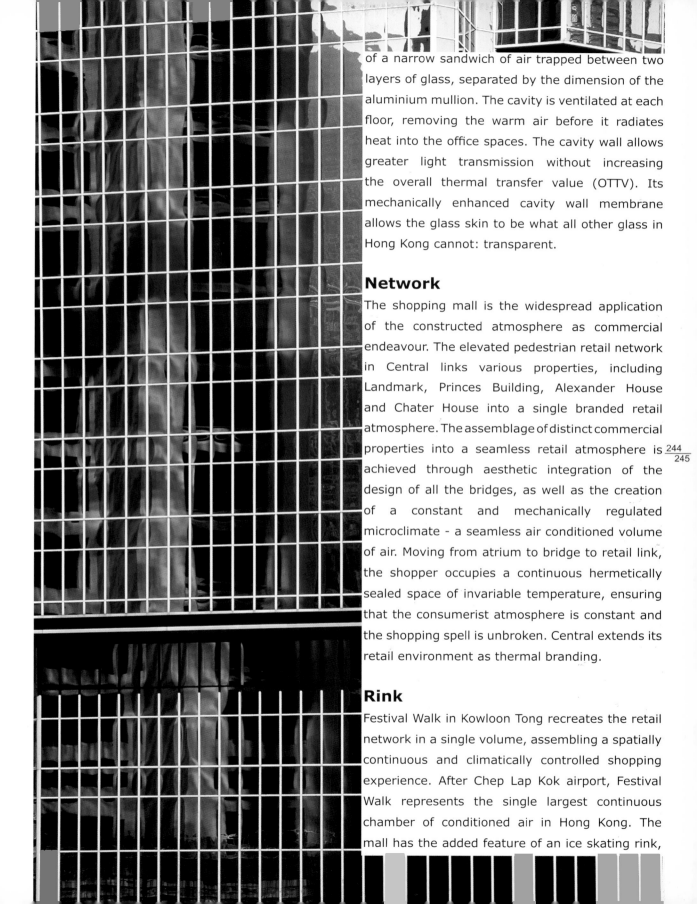

of a narrow sandwich of air trapped between two layers of glass, separated by the dimension of the aluminium mullion. The cavity is ventilated at each floor, removing the warm air before it radiates heat into the office spaces. The cavity wall allows greater light transmission without increasing the overall thermal transfer value (OTTV). Its mechanically enhanced cavity wall membrane allows the glass skin to be what all other glass in Hong Kong cannot: transparent.

Network

The shopping mall is the widespread application of the constructed atmosphere as commercial endeavour. The elevated pedestrian retail network in Central links various properties, including Landmark, Princes Building, Alexander House and Chater House into a single branded retail atmosphere. The assemblage of distinct commercial properties into a seamless retail atmosphere is $\frac{244}{245}$ achieved through aesthetic integration of the design of all the bridges, as well as the creation of a constant and mechanically regulated microclimate - a seamless air conditioned volume of air. Moving from atrium to bridge to retail link, the shopper occupies a continuous hermetically sealed space of invariable temperature, ensuring that the consumerist atmosphere is constant and the shopping spell is unbroken. Central extends its retail environment as thermal branding.

Rink

Festival Walk in Kowloon Tong recreates the retail network in a single volume, assembling a spatially continuous and climatically controlled shopping experience. After Chep Lap Kok airport, Festival Walk represents the single largest continuous chamber of conditioned air in Hong Kong. The mall has the added feature of an ice skating rink, which offers winter recreation in subtropical Hong Kong. Festival Walk recreates a retail experience as thermal entertainment.

Mountain

One step closer to the total construction of architecture-as-weather is Snow World, a winter theme park planned for Ma Wan. The park will include hotels and spa facilities as well as a vast interior chamber, with an artificial mountain and artificial weather. Visitors will be able to ski or snowboard down a snow-covered slope any time of year. Unlike Hong Kong Disney world, the Snow World theme park is not an importation of a pre-packaged theme environment. Snow World is completely site specific. It is a theme park of Hong Kong's weather, inverted: its climatological opposite. Snow World offers the opportunity to escape Hong Kong's climate and occupy a parallel world. Snow World is thermal tourism.

Boundary

In Hong Kong, climate is another phenomenon to be overcome, regulated and consumed. Hong Kong's architecture defines the limits between Hong Kong's exterior environment and its vast new interiority. Its regulatory glass membrane, only 25mm thick, defines the boundary of the occupied space of Hong Kong. The exterior is unpredictable: heat waves, urban microclimates, heat island effects, and air pollution inversions. The interior is strictly regulated: conditioned worlds of constant temperature and humidity. Meanwhile tourisms of architecturally created weather supply dream worlds of remote climatological atmospheres as thermal escapism.

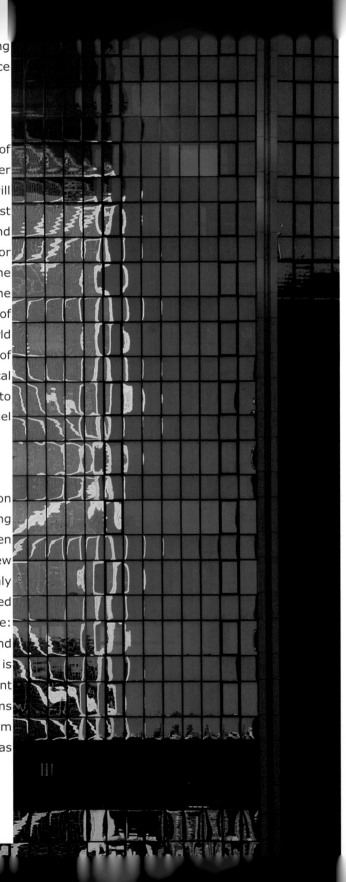

Shopping malls are many things to many people. To me, they were first and foremost a place of transit. As the movement of individuals in the urban space is increasingly constrained and channelled, becoming a servo-mechanism of commerce and business, I often had very little choice but being herded through these glittering halls. Located at the exit of MTR stations, intersected by covered footbridges that separate pedestrian from vehicular traffic, and branching off to bus and taxi stands, shopping malls, like the lobbies of office-buildings, are an integral part of that parallel network that multiplies the amount of space available to pedestrians in hyper-dense Hong Kong. As the boundaries that separate inside and outside, public and private become porous, I would step into the mall in a distracted and hurried way. Saving time and keeping out of the sultry heat, rather than shopping, being my only rationale for cutting through a mall.

Recently, maybe due to the purchase of a pair of high-heeled sandals, I have started to pay more attention to what happens once I pass from an elevated walkway to the mall. The concrete strip gives way to a shiny marble floor, polished daily by an army of underpaid cleaners. Here my heels make a distinct sound, and I suddenly become self-conscious: the rhythm of my steps changes, becoming shorter, lighter. This unsteady trot makes me both the subject of a new experience and the object of the gaze. At the same time as I look, I am also a picture, I can also be seen.

The 3 inches prostheses have set a new pace, and by extension produced a new space. The specifics of my bodily experience now shape my perspective. Walking on high heels shifts the focus back to my body, from the prosaics of crossing to the poetics of cruising. Walking stands out when it's out of keeping with the pace that is regarded as appropriate to a particular place.

LAURA RUGGERI

The erotics of the shopping mall

Living on Lamma island, my days in town usually start in the mall located in the International Finance Centre, which also houses the Airport Express terminal, and the in-town check-in counters. Several footbridges connect it to bus terminals and the outlying islands ferry piers. An underground car park can be reached by elevator.

My daily route from Central pier no. 4 to Battery Path cannot be traced on any existing map: several feet above the street level, I snake my way through malls, office-building lobbies and privately owned footbridges.

The Chorus of Idle Steps

Walking/writing entails 'spacing', i.e. the articulation of space and time, the becoming-space of time, and the becoming-time of space.

September 16-12-03 - h. 4.00 pm

Ferry Pier No.4 – IFC: 335 steps
IFC: 520 steps
HK Land walkway: 272 steps
Chater House: 86 steps
Walkway: 40 steps
Alexandra House: 130 steps
Walkway: 30 steps
Prince's Building: 52 steps
Walkway: 70 steps
Standard Chartered Building: 94 steps
Walkway to Battery Path: 26 steps

1,655 steps, 25 minutes. Wearing comfortable shoes. No phone calls, no window-shopping, little eye contact, no stops, good physical conditions.

Our understandings of space emerge from action, indeed space is to be defined as a "certain possession of the world by my body".

Maurice Merleau-Ponty, *The Phenomenology of Perception*

Story-telling not only bridges space in the sense that it links disparate elements by imaginative threads of reasoning, but it also creates space in the sense that by the act of signification, inscribing experience in words, new bifurcations are produced.

Michel de Certeau, *The Practice of Everyday Life*

Women's walking is often construed as performance rather than transport, with the implication that women walk not to see but to be seen, not for their own experience but for that of a male audience.

Rebecca Solnit, *Wanderlust*

And although desire is unbound here, it is unbound within a secure place. Any encounter is read off the body at a safe distance, where seeing comes before words.

Eric Laurier, *City of Glas-z*, Ph.D Thesis, University of Wales.

The new pace affects the way I see others - new lines of sight are established – and informs my understanding of and alignment with that space. In the bright maze I lose my shadow and gain fragmented and multiplied images of myself. Reflected in shop windows - where glass serves as the signifier of representation and display - reflected in polished stainless steel pillars and ceiling panels, my body blends into the surface. Space starts to look back. On the warping mirror plane the distance between bodies is erased. Through my corporeal exertion and inscription the mall becomes a site full of promises, despite its limited spontaneity.

The erotic promises of shopping malls are well-known to the local gay community. The top three cruising spots in Hong Kong are up-market shopping centres (Pacific Place, Festival Walk, International Finance Centre). Their location is easy to reach by public transport from most districts, their architectural image is an elective minimalism, the polished products of the sensuous and seductive editorial pages of glossy fashion magazines. It's a *mise en scène* that supports the dream-state of fashion, glorifies the scenographic and privileged places identified as 'de luxe' and 'elite'.

I believe that between utopias and these quite other sites, these heterotopias, there might be a sort of mixed, joint experience, which would be the mirror. The mirror is, after all, a utopia, since it is a placeless place. In the mirror, I see myself there where I am not, in an unreal, virtual space that opens up before the surface; I am over there, there where I am not, a sort of shadow that gives my own visibility to myself, that enables me to see myself there where I am absent: such is the utopia of the mirror. But it is also a heterotopia in so far as the mirror does exist in reality, where it exerts a sort of counteraction on the position that I occupy. From the standpoint of the mirror I discover my absence from the place where I am since I see myself over there… The mirror makes this place that I occupy at the moment when I look at myself in the glass at once absolutely real, connected with all the space that surrounds it, and absolutely unreal, since in order to be perceived it has to pass through this virtual point which is over there.

Michel Foucault, *Of Other Spaces*

If my body may be said to enshrine a generative principle, at once abstract and concrete, the mirror's surface makes this principle invisible, deciphers it. The mirror discloses the relationship between me and myself, my body and the consciousness of my body - not because the reflection constitutes my unity qua subject, as many psychoanalysts and psychologists apparently believe, but because it transforms what I am into the sign of what I am. This ice-smooth barrier, itself merely an inert sheen, reproduces and displays what I am - in a word, signifies what I am - within an imaginary sphere which is yet quite real. A process of abstraction then - but a fascinating abstraction. In order to know myself, I 'separate myself out from myself'.

Henri Lefebvre, *The Production of Space*

The flaneur plays the role of scout in the marketplace. As such, he is also the explorer of the crowd. Within the man who abandons himself to it, the crowd inspires a sort of drunkenness, one accompanied by very specific illusions: the man flatters himself that, on seeing a passerby swept along by the crowd, he has accurately classified him, seen straight through to the innermost recesses of his soul - all on the basis of external appearance.

Walter Benjamin, *The Arcades Project*

We rub shoulders with each other everyday, we may not know each other, but we could become friends one day.

Wong Kar-wai, *Chungking Express* 1994

Cruising in HK - From the Gay Guide to Hong Kong

Best times after 8.30 pm and before closing.

Pacific Place Shopping Mall, MTR Admiralty
The Landmark, MTR Central
Ocean Terminal Shopping Centre, 3rd Floor, MTR Tsim Sha Tsui
IFC Shopping Mall, Ground floor, 1st floor, MTR Central

The act of picking up somebody in public for sex is by no means circumscribed to gay men, as female prostitution appropriated the space of the shopping arcades since their appearance in the nineteenth-century. In the shopping mall both bodies and commodities become part of the scenographic display: all participate at the same time as forming an audience. A spectacle marked by the exchange of looks and gazes, complements the display of goods. The mirror, prioritising the visual, the perspectival, in a manner that resembles theatrical space, is the most ubiquitous feature of Hong Kong shopping malls. Even when mirrors are sparsely used, shop windows, polished marble surfaces and stainless steel panels ensure the constant reflection of bodies.

The spatial arrangement of reflecting surfaces allow people to look at each other without embarrassment, looks are mediated, often reflections of reflections, bouncing back and forth. Being looked at can only be perceived in the act of looking at oneself. Voyeurism and narcissism are conflated in a commercial space that thrives on both. The mirror, like the mall, carves out a space floating between inside and outside, reality and unreality. Marketeers are trying to channel the pleasure principle into predictable commercial conduits and thus sublimate desire. Seductive icons of commercialised love appear in shopping windows, mannequins and body parts, usually female, eroticise the merchandise. One can play fictionally with the possibility of possession, take on and discard whole identities associated with objects. Here one can apprehend oneself as one more object in the simulacra of objects. But as kleptomania proves, the fetishistic power exercised by the goods can exceed the economic rationale of commerce.

What if desire which should circulate the shoppers around the stationary commodities instead circulates between the shoppers? When attention wavers from rational economic activities, people may take the opportunity to elaborate more complex social behaviours, to engage in more roles, even to contest the rationalised norms of the site. My walking takes on the character of cruising. Dominated by a scopophilic pleasure, this is also a walk of showing off for sexual ends while watching others to assess their looks and whether they are willing to exchange glances and more.

Festival Walk, Kowloon Tong. 24-06-03, 6:30 pm

As I take the escalator I notice that several men are leaning against the balustrade on the upper floor, looking down. The counterpoint is provided by the middle-aged man standing next to me, who is looking up. His eyes are fixed on the stainless steel panel hung over the escalator: My cleavage that no frontal view would reveal is reflected overhead, as is that of the woman who is standing before me.

The word scopophilia is made up of two Greek words, *scopos*, which is to do with looking and seeing, and *philia*, which is to do with a love of, or pleasure in, something. Scopophilia is therefore to do with the love of, or the pleasures that are received from, looking and seeing.

Elements of Desire. A Sensory Experience. Explore the Dynamics of Desire Through Pacific Place. Let Inspiration Be Your Guide.
Pacific Place, *The Place To Be*. (Poster Ad)

Pacific Place, like an upmarket variation on the theme of the old Parisian arcades, offers the possibility to explore a more carnal type of desire upstairs. Serviced apartments and two hotels can be accessed from the mall by taking an elevator. A recent decision to close male lavatories at 6:30 pm has put a dent on Pacific Place reputation as top cruising spot and pushed cottaging activities to malls where such time restrictions don't apply.

Contemporary shopping malls implicate the same shadows of self, desire, and consumption amongst the goods on display and the crowds of people.

Rob Shields, *Lifestyle Shopping*

Before the shop window the eyes of the young woman in the black dress meet those reflected in the pane of glass. She turns away slowly to her right and continues to walk with the same regular step.

The young woman is wearing a low-cut bodice that leaves the shoulders and the cleavage bare.

Tomorrow then, she says. Or the day after tomorrow.
Delicate high-heeled sandals, whose leather thongs form three gilt crosses over each tiny foot. A close-fitting dress very slightly striated at each step by tiny creases moving under the hips and belly.

Alain Robbe-Grillet, *La Maison de Rendez-vous*

Neither space nor concepts alone are erotic, but the junction between the two is.

Bernard Tschumi, *The Pleasure of Architecture*

The *Flaneuse*, regarded as an anomaly in the 19th century, feels at home in the 21st century house of mirrors. One could argue that within the disciplinary space of the mall, where the visual mode is dominant, to exercise agency is virtually impossible, that the objectifying character of the male gaze makes the notion of *flaneuserie* impossible. This argument doesn't take into account current gender relations and the potential power of the individual who seems to play by the rules (the scopic regime) and yet devises a set of tactics to subvert the space rationale for commerce.

Through the (re)inscription or articulation of sexuality and desire within the order of a dominantly asexual space, cruising performs an appropriation of semi-public spaces. It doesn't produce a marginal site in which hetero and homosexuality finds a demarcated place, rather cruising is out of place. An ephemeral practice, sometimes visible, but mostly out of sight. It is ghostly and haunting not only because it plays with in/visibility and dis/appearance, but also because it reveals to us desires, and also identities, that have been socially and spatially excluded in the production of commercial semi-public spaces. Cruising implies the existence of blind spots in the structure, backspaces which allow a certain degree of intimacy.

To go 'into the mirror' or 'through the looking glass' implies passing a threshold and entering another world. This other world lies beyond the image. It is 'there' that the principles and archetypal conditions of experience of the world are to be found.

The mall is a realm for consumption, effectively forcing the realm of production out of sight. It's 'imagineered' with maintenance and management techniques, keeping invisible the delivery bays or support systems. The corollary of this quest for purity is the specification for a back region where the subterranean and dirty 'functions' of the shopping centre can be hidden.

In Mary Douglas' famous classification of "dirt as matter out of place", the pure establishes itself in opposition to the dirty. That is particularly pertinent to building construction, as it involves drawing and defending borders that hold what is defined and pure. An area which is designated 'dirty', literally begins to acquire dirt and collect things out-of-place.

It was Woman that the stores fought over, Woman that they caught up in the continual trap of their sales, after having overwhelmed her with their displays. They had awakened in her flesh new desires, which were an immense temptation, to which she succumbed fatally, giving in first to the small purchases of a good homemaker, then won over by the coquetry, then devoured.

Emile Zola, *Au Bonheur des Dames*

The pleasure principle works through a mesh of decisions which parallel those of the shopper in front of their goods struggling with economic decisions. The libidinal economy is a phrase to be taken literally as well as metaphorically, not that any firm division can be made between the literal and the metaphoric in language anyway.

Eric Laurier, *City of Glas-z*

It is a queer space, an odd space, one that has no particular shape or site, but one that continually slips into the activities of everyday life, transforming them into a fantastical world of possible desire.

Aaron Betsky, *Building Sex*

One knew of places in ancient Greece where the way led down into the underworld. Our waking existence likewise is a land which, at certain hidden points, leads down into the underworld – a land full of inconspicuous places from which dreams arise.

Walter Benjamin, *The Arcades Project*

Even the most striated city space gives rise to smooth spaces (...) Movements, speed and slowness, are sometimes enough to reconstruct a smooth space. Of course, smooth spaces are not in themselves liberatory. But the struggle is changed or displaced in them, and life reconstitutes its stakes, confronts new obstacles, invents new paces, switches adversaries.

Gilles Deleuze and Felix Guattari, *A Thousand Plateaus*

Dirt is the by-product of a systematic ordering and classification of matter, insofar as ordering involves rejecting inappropriate elements. Where there is dirt there is a system.

Mary Douglas, *Purity and Danger*

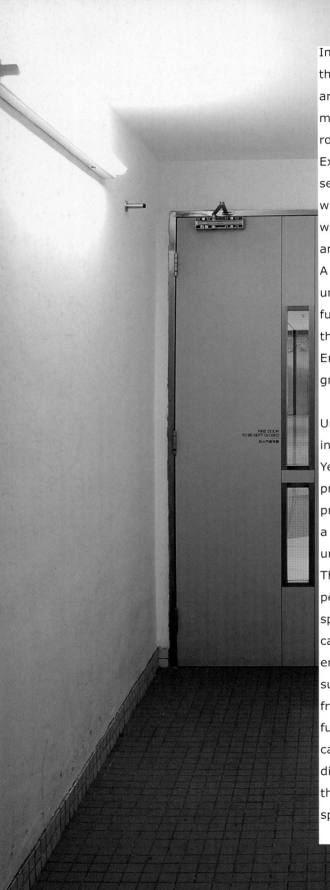

In the mall the borders between accessible areas and the backstage are not only clearly signposted, they are also delineated by the use of different building materials. Glossy surfaces are replaced by matt or rough ones, marble flooring by cheap tiles.

Exposed pipes, water ducts, vents, electricity cables, service stairs, sprinklers are a vision given only to those who push a fire exit door, or follow a toilet sign only to walk past the toilet entrance, into the tapering corridors, and stair system that constitute the backstage.

A space of both repulsion and fascination, this soft underbelly like the labyrinthine bowels of Bataille, also functions as a powerful site of the imaginary: the site of the expansion and permeability of bodily boundaries.

Erotically charged activities occur spontaneously, grafting onto these under-used, peripheral spaces.

Unsurveyed spaces attract behaviours that are either increasingly marginalised, labeled as deviant, or illegal. Yet their existence points to a dialectical movement: prohibition, as power, produces space and space, as prohibition, produces power. Space far from being a passive backdrop looks back and suggests new, unanticipated uses.

The backstage becomes the centre stage of a different performance. Behind a fire exit door one can find a spot to smoke a cigarette undetected by surveillance cameras or security personnel, eat from a lunch box, engage in sex acts, hide stolen goods, exchange illegal substances for money, take an unscheduled break from a cleaning shift, or simply sleep. Defined by its functional marginality this space both produces and caters for needs and desires. It does so by means of differential systems and valorisations which overwhelm the strict location of such needs and desires in specialised places.

IFC shopping mall, 15-10-03 h. 6:00 pm

On the first floor stairs I catch sight of shop assistants and cleaners lighting cigarettes, chatting, sitting on the stairs while eating out of their lunch box. They are surrounded by discarded packaging material, mops and carts full of cleaning products, toilets rolls and refill bottles for liquid soap dispensers.

The Landmark shopping mall, 23-11-03 h. 6:45 pm

I sneak out for a smoke before a meeting in the building. A young couple (shop assistants?) are making out between the second and third floor. As they spot me, I smile, show them the cigarette as a way of excuse and walk back downstairs.

True eroticism starts and ultimately ends with individual imagination. Sensuous effects can be achieved by blurring the definition of the conventional environment.

For space to present an erotic threshold, invariably it has to incorporate a contradiction, in connotation or function.

If an intimate incident occurs in a public place, the place itself retains that frisson for those involved. It's forever constituted by that practice.

Space is dynamic and active: assembling, showing, containing, blurring, hiding, defining, separating, territorializing and naming many points of capture for power, identity and meaning.

Steve Pile, *The Body and The City*

A Project by ZITENG

My life
**Photographic
Works by sex workers**

"My life – Photographic works by
sex workers is a new project of
Ziteng.
The project aims at
enhancing and improving the
communications between sex
workers and the society at large.

It is organised around a photographic exhibition of sex workers in Hong Kong. The exhibition has toured around the territory. The works will be archived in *Sex Workers' Photo Album*.

In this project, the cameras serve as eyes of sex workers, through which people have the chance to have a close encounter with the world of sex workers who have long been the objects of the mainstream, dominant narratives.

They have been deprived of their subjectivity because of the deep-rooted social stigma and discrimination associated with their occupation. They do not have a voice of their own. With the cameras and the photos

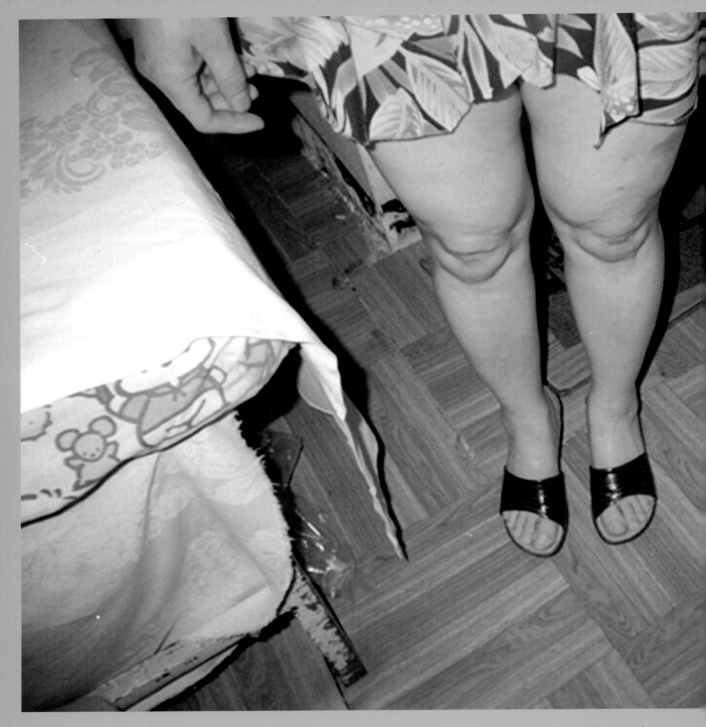

they take, we are able to see through their eyes and read how they understand the world, their feelings, their days and nights, and who they are in their direct narration.

Established in 1996, Ziteng is a sex workers concern group. It supports and organises activities that enhance and raise awareness of the public on sex workers' marginalised situation. It works with sex workers to improve their

work situation and basic rights including health care services. The project helps change the attitude of the public towards sex workers and eventually eliminate discrimination against them.

Why photography ?

Photography is a powerful means of expression. With the advancement of technology, it is one of the most popular and friendly media for records and documentation. It is a world language that crosses over borders, ethnicity, culture and language *per se*. People communicate directly with each other through this visual tool. We see. We feel. We are impressed and moved. Cameras capture what we see. Just press the

trigger for the shutter, and the film will help register what your eyes register. As prints, they will then become others' registration. They imprint on our minds, stay, and shape our world.

This is why we choose photography. And given that it is among many other means of documentation and expression, the most popular, direct and easy to manage medium, it might in the process enhance the confidence of the users.

Why sex workers ?

Sex work is one of the longest surviving professions in the world. They have long been discriminated against. People have strong bias and prejudice against them: "They are the bad ones, shameless, dirty, morally corrupted, weird, live different lives, do not know how to love, do not have 'normal' feelings etc. and etc. and etc…"

But the work experience of Ziteng tells a different story. The more than 10,000 sex workers we have contacted in Hong Kong mostly work in apartments by themselves. Most are single mothers and are the main sources of family incomes. They work as sex workers

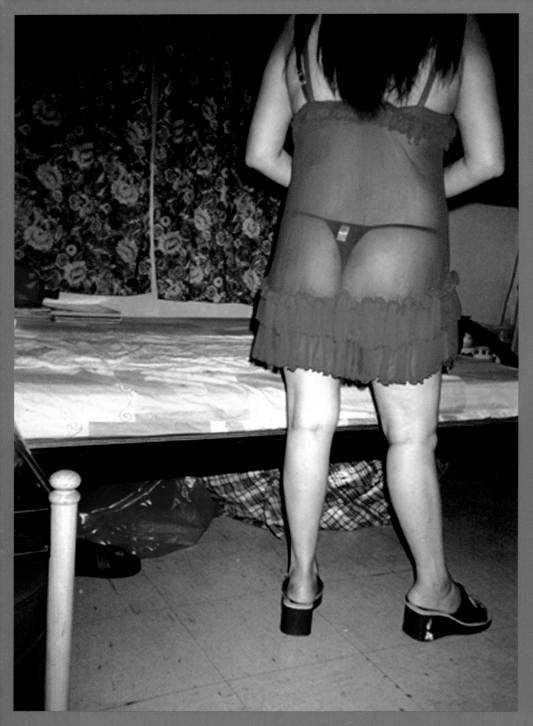

because they want to take care of their families and do not want to be a burden on society. They are very tough and work very hard, like other people in Hong Kong. They are also members of society, contribute to its development, share the same responsibility and therefore should be entitled to the rights and social status others enjoy. However, discrimination and prejudice deprive them the voice they should have. Society at large does not see the real life of sex workers. We would like to have a photo exhibition for sex workers, who will use photos to express themselves and let the community know their life through their eyes!

An inclusive society will enable
us to move forward particularly
during difficult times and to build
a strong, caring and harmonious
community.

Photo exhibition

40 sex workers in Hong Kong participated in the photo taking activities. Participants were given cameras and worked on their own. They photographed whatever they wanted, liked and felt could best record their daily life. Sharing sessions were organised for participants to review and reflect on pictures they made. 30 of the participants also chose a photo for the touring exhibition. An opening ceremony was held in the Hong Kong Cultural Centre in January 2004.

Ziteng was formed in 1996 by a group of local women activists who shared the common goal of assisting and empowering Hong Kong sex workers through direct services, legal advocacy, and raising public awareness on sex workers' issues. It aims to empower sex workers and provides services for them in Hong Kong and Mainland China.

About Ziteng

This story is a fiction and has no relationship with existing people or places...

Contents

Facts about 2046

History

As anyone who wanders the streets of 2046 will know, the city has a long history with a composition of architecture spanning back to the 16th Century. 2046 was first populated as a trading port for the barterers of opium, sugar and silk, but later became a place for industry during the 19th Century, where migrant workers from all over the world could come to 20a46 and gain free citizenship and work. In the 20th Century, the economic boom led to political unrest, with bordering neighbours commencing a trade war on 2046. To protect itself, 2046 began to build a wall around itself limiting immigration and travel. By the end of the 20th Century, 2046 had taken on a mystical aura of place both of a Shangri-la – a city dreamt of but difficult to find, but also a No-Man's land, where history begins to be lost.

Geography

Situated on the eastern edges of the Magrian Planes and north of the industrial hub of post industrial Shanghai, 2046 has a series of convoluting river ways that used to carry the barges for industry and are now left empty and silent by the lowering of the water table. As the city grew during the 19th Century, 2046 has slowly but surely lost all its countryside as its urban scrawl has expanded. Today, there is next to no open areas left. As an example of a city within a city, 2046 has become a layered city where the old city is layered upon the new city. Attempts to chart 2046 have been difficult, as conventional Cartesian mapping does not allow for the layered nature of 2046 to be fully explained.

The complexity of 2046 is almost organic, with regions of ghettos springing up comprising of ethnic and social groups meshed together. Like a cauldron of social trends, even the ghettos are layered upon each other, mixing together people of different groups.

The city itself is dark and claustrophobic, with daunting super structures meshing together older architecture with newer architecture. In the depths of the city, natural light almost never penetrates, and these inner depths can be eerie to the visitor. On the upper levels of the city, super towers provide a panoramic view of 2046.

Climate

Unlike a conventional city, 2046 suffers from creating its own microclimate due to its high density. The lack of ventilation in the depths of 2046 has meant that there is a continuous dampness in the air and a chilly temperature of 19 degrees centigrade throughout the whole year.

At the upper levels of the city, the sun heats the city to a baking 35 degrees, not helped by the large population and thus the huge output of carbon dioxide.

You are advised not to underestimate the severity of the climate of 2046. Please bring with you different clothing for different circumstances.

Ecology & Environment

Like other over developed cities in the world, 2046's economic boom came at the expense of controls on air pollution, land clearing, deforestation, endangered species and rural and industrial waste. 2046's huge population in combination with geographical factors make its environmental problems infinitely more massive than any other place on earth.

Some experts have predicted an impending environmental catastrophe, warning that 2046's greatest challenge will be ecological.

Unfortunately there have never been any

A
B
C

A : 2012 Skyline
B : 2023 Skyline
C : 2046 Skyline

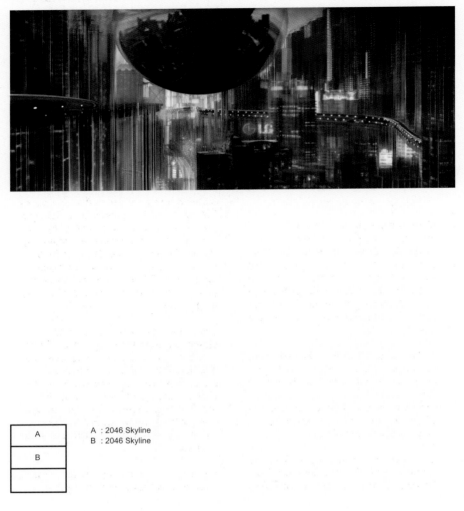

A : 2046 Skyline
B : 2046 Skyline

strict measures against environmental degradation and no measures have been taken to avert disaster. It may be too little too late.

Flora & Fauna

2046 of the 18th Century was endowed with superbly colourful and wonderful sets of natural vegetation and animal life. But in the 2046 of today, much of this has been wiped away by the expansion of the city.

By the 19th Century, 2046 had actually become the "Tobacco" growing capital of the world, with vast high-density fields growing tobacco for the world market. Most of the natural flora and fauna was chopped down and land was used instead for this purpose.

By the 21st Century, and after the mass banning of smoking throughout the world in the 20th Century, 2046's tobacco fields became the underground supply to the world's desire to smoke.

Today, tobacco is symbolically the national plant of 2046 and any mention of 2046 is synonymous with tobacco.

Government & Politics

2046 has undergone a whole spectrum of political change in its history. With stints as a Marxist state, a Socialist state, a Capitalist state and a Fascist state, 2046 has been a political cauldron in which human politics have no where in the world been more erratic and more unstable.

Today, precious little is known about the inner workings of the 2046 government, but what is known is that the entire monolithic structure, from grassroots work units to the upper echelons of political power, is controlled by the all powerful 2046 Politburo

The Politburo comprises a Standing Committee of 2046 standing members. Of these 2046 members, 13 members are elected to the Central Committee that oversees the workings of the Standing Committee.

At the grass roots level, the political structure is a system of control spread over different sectors of society, including the army, universities, and the administration of the army, the security police, and industry.

In this hierarchical system, the day-to-day control of 2046 is placed in the power of 2046 members of the Standing Committee, which implements the decisions of the committee.

The Government is a massive bureaucracy. In an almost limitlessly complex system of rules and regulations, the system of government has developed in the same mind blogging and complex way that 2046 has as a nation and as a city. Layering of rules on top of each other, lends to a society that has too much control by the government, yet the rules are too complex and complicated to be implemented in any orderly fashion.

In theory, every citizen of 2046 is a member of one of the systems, and thereby a pixel in the overall system. Yet, this utopian system is not perfect, and many slip though the social controls of the 2046 set of rules. Many now are working outside the rules of 2046, trading privately and being self employed and independently mobile and outside the system.

2046 attempts to be the perfect social system by approving marriages, divorces, childbirth; assigns housing, sets salaries, handles mail and communications, recruits civil servants, keeps files on each citizen, arranges transfers from job to job, controls immigration and emigration, controls travel within and abroad. All this extends to every individual's life in 2046.

For those who rebel against the system, these political dissidents are dealt with harshly and swiftly by the security police. Prisons all over 2046 are mainly filled with political dissidents and opponents to the government.

There is no organised or recognised opposition. No party system exists.

Economy

Under the current 2046 politburo, the economy has taken an isolationist approach, and the deconstruction of the local currency was completed at the end of the 20th Century. In a throw back to the medieval era, 2046 now has a bartering system for its economy.

The industrial world of 2046 therefore trades by the bartering of materials and services, whether at a conglomerate level or that of the individual on the street.

It is rumoured that the nearest thing to currency is tobacco, as it has been banned in the rest of the world. Within 2046, tobacco is sold in sachets, and each unit is the equivalent of gold.

There is also rumoured to be a large under world smuggling tobacco to the outside world

Population & People

Han Chinese make up 90% of the population with other 2046 minority ethnic Chinese groups comprising another 5%.

Another ethnic groups is the android population, which takes up the rest of the 5%.

The population has well exceeded a billion by the early 21st Century yet there are no definitive figures for the exact size of the population at this time.

The two groups of minority Chinese and androids are mainly concentrated at the centre of 2046 where they live and work side by side. In the congested central urban zones of 2046, these two groups have formed a myriad of ghettos and districts with their individual cultures mixed together.

The remaining Han Chinese are spread evenly over 2046.

The prospect of an ever growing population, with an ever-shrinking capacity to feed itself, prompted a limited birth control program during the 1950s, but this was abandoned around the turn of the millennium, when the ageing human population was unable to support the economy leading to civil unrest and the introduction of androids into the population to compensate.

2046 is the only nation in the world that recognises androids as citizens.

Education

2046 society is split between the academics and the workers.

The academics are identified at birth through genetic monitoring, and are then placed into huge academic institutions where a regimented education takes them through their early lives.

Rote learning and an absence of open debate on issues in the classroom create a certain restrictive educational model.

Some academics have argued that the 2046 educational structure is too harsh and antiquated, due to the difficulties of learning the Chinese script (the predominant written language), and English, French and Russian are also taught.

The workers are subjected to a different education in skills, to be used in industry, especially in the repetitive work sectors.

The 2046 government decreed this clear difference as a way of lowering social strife, but neutering the workers, whilst brain washing the academics.

2046 has a literacy rate of only 70%, which is very low by developed country standards.

The lower standard of educational attainment has meant that most citizens are assigned jobs by the state after graduation. This is especially true for the workers. Academics are left with more freedom to choose, though choices for jobs are not too abundant.

Arts

Some say that 2046 is a piece of artwork in itself, a canvas that has been painted over and over again over time - a city that has layers of history and architecture. Even today, the architecture you find in the depths of the city originates from the 18th Century, on top of which are 19th and 20th Century buildings, and then further on top are the 21st Century mega structures. Like a time capsule, 2046 has become a living store cupboard of architectural relics.

Another interesting aspect about 2046's art scene is a rich underground art culture where subversive art is produced, shown and traded. It is illegal to produce any material, which is deemed to criticise the state, and thus the urge to make a commentary on society is taken underground. Subversive paintings, theatrical shows, writings, music and movies are produced in the art ghettos in the depths of 2046.

Society & Conduct

Traditional Culture
The 2046 culture is unique in comparison with the rest of the world due to its mysterious separation from world culture. Whilst it resembles much of the Chinese culture of the PRC, it has developed its own brand of interpersonal culture and rules

Face Face is basically defined as the "status" of a person, or his ego, or his place in society. In any conversation or

negotiation in 2046, the rules of exchange are based on "face" and thus confrontations can be avoided. The social status of the individual is very much expressed in the expression and reception of "Face"

Fortune Telling Superstition plays a big part in the world of 2046, and the idea of destiny is a key belief in the minds of the population. Therefore over the years, there has been a proliferation of "Fortune Tellers" who have small make shift stands on many street corners, offering their own individual brand of fortune telling ranging from "Palm Reading", "Face Reading", "Psychic Aura Reading", "Ancestral Tree Reading" and "DNA Mapping Extrapolations". The cost of fortune telling is cheap, but the famous fortunetellers of 2046 are celebrities that charge millions for their services. Also, in recent years, with the proliferation of robots in society, robot inhabitants have begun to search for their own purpose in life, and this has led to a separate brand of "Robot Fortune Tellers" that predicts facts - by reading into the operating systems of robots.

Dos & Don'ts
Speaking Honestly and Frankly. People in 2046 rarely speak honestly and frankly. For example, if you ask someone for directions, they will probably allude to a place via another place, as opposed to telling you a precise route. This is of course due to the need to save "face" in the midst of ignorance. You will have to learn how to deal with this by being very precise with your questions.

Smiling Smiling is rarely an expression of happiness, and is in fact a mask that many people in 2046 wear in order to brighten up their day-to-day boredom in this isolated kingdom. So don't be surprised when you are expecting an expression of guilt or anger or sadness, but instead the 2046 local inhabitant just smiles at you!

Sexism 2046 is a hugely sexist country by global standards, and today still holds much of the male prejudicial societal structures of the pre-20th Century world. The world is still dominated by males in 2046, and in both business and politics, the man is the sole dominator. But in this awkwardly slanted world, the woman plays an important role as the underground persuader. So you may find that in public, the female half of a couple will stay silent and the man vocal, but when on their own, the woman is more vocal than the man.

Sexual Diplomacy Within the confines of a restricted society, where marriage has had a rigid and conservative history, the role of sex in 2046 is very important in the balance of power between its inhabitants. The biggest favour you can do for someone is to be discreet about their indiscretions, and likewise them for you. If you have this bond, it is a bond of friendship, and something that is regularly traded as diplomacy. So if you want a friend for life, set him up with a sexy chick and then tell him it is OK!

Negotiations over a joint. If you want to strike a deal with businesses in 2046, it will be that much easier if you can bring some tobacco (which is banned in 2046) or any other forms of illegal substances and then share them with your potential partners. It is a sign of trust and a way to show your outsider credentials that will give you instant street credibility in 2046.

Tobacco Diplomacy Especially if you meet people for the first time on your trip to 2046, you should always try to offer a cigarette when meeting someone. If they gesture their acceptance, then you are already in. If they gesture their decline, then you will have to work harder with another way to get them to accept you, such as by doing them sexual favours. When offering a cigarette to someone, you must extend the open pack with a cigarette protruding from it – it would be impolite to remove a single cigarette from your pack and

hand it over. Your pack should be foreign, as this will show your status as a traveller and foreign visitor. If you want to butter up your host or guest, you should tell them to keep the packet of remaining ones, and that next time you are in town, you will bring them more. The people of 2046 are obsessive about cigarettes, as they are hard to come by as contraband. Remember you will have to be careful bringing them into 2046 through customs. If caught, you will have to extend your stay in 2046 indefinitely. The locals light up whenever they feel like it and especially at mealtime, so you can as well. If you don't smoke, then you better start.

Gift Giving It is customary to bring some form of gift when visiting a local's home - for the first time. Gifts such as foreign products are most appreciated, as well as flowers, foods and alcohol. Whilst cigarettes and tobacco are secretly the most desired, these are never given as gifts due to their illegal nature. When presenting the gift, always give it to the better half of a couple, i.e. the wife. But never give to a robot, as they have no social status. You will have to learn to distinguish between robots and humans.

Religion

2046 is a place where there is no religion. The basis of faith resides in the individual. Whilst there are many residents of 2046 who try to become missionaries of their own faith, it is not customary for people to listen to others. 2046 is the archetypal lonely and introvert world, and there is no common belief or faith.

Language

2046 is a multi lingual place with people migrating there from all corners of the world. The language is so mixed that it is sometimes difficult for people to communicate, and there is the symptom of ghettos of common language populations crowding together. To over come this, androids are programmed to be multi lingual, and play the role of intermediary and translator to the human population.

Facts for the Visitor

When to Go

Travel to 2046 has been on the increase for almost 50 years. This mass influx has meant huge waiting lists of visitors applying for the limited quota of visas made available during each travel season of Spring, Summer, Autumn and Winter. There is almost a continuous peak of travel, so there is no such thing as a quiet season, though the winter sometimes receives slightly fewer visitors due to inclement weather. Major public holidays should be avoided if possible. 2046 New Year is a terrible time to be travelling, and the same applies for the 2046 National Day, which is on 1st October, and celebrations are a week long.

The borders are open for two sessions a day, one at midday and one at midnight. You will be allocated entry times when you apply for your visa at your local 2046 consulate or embassy. Should you need to enter into 2046 outside these hours, you can apply for an emergency entry visa, which is both expensive and difficult to obtain, or you can try to offer monetary incentives to the border police to allow you onto out of hours trains that enter into 2046. But remember you still need a valid visa.

Orientation

2046 has four major entry points into this landlocked city-state. The North crossing point is for diplomatic use and thus is rarely open for public travel. The South crossing point is used for supply and logistics. The West and the East crossing points are the ones open to individual travellers. Having entered 2046, all the railway and transportation lines run into the city epicentre where you will arrive at the 2046 Grand Central Station. It is from here you can plan your journey to different districts and ghettos. All visitors are checked through immigration here. Be aware that this can take some time.

Maps

Officially maps are prohibited in 2046 due the sensitive nature of the city. Nevertheless you can purchase unofficial maps from street vendors. Citywide maps are notoriously inaccurate, so it is best for you to purchase another map when you have arrived at your local area in order to verify your location.

The most popular way to get around 2046 is to hire a local guide who can show you to your destination or give you a guided tour of the city. Local guides tend to congregate at the exit to Grand Central Station, and you can identify them by the red stripes they wear over their coasts. They will charge between US$30 to U$100 for a day's guide, excluding transportation. They may also ask for tobacco as part payment. If you are interested to research and explore 2046, a good guide is essential for your journey as well as your safety, and the more experienced and seasoned guides will be able to tell you stories concerning different aspects of 2046.

You will also notice that they too will be interested to find out about the outside world. Also be aware that some guides may be robots as well as human, though you may not be able to easily identify the difference.

Tourist Offices

Tourist Offices are dotted around the city, with the largest one located at Grand Central. You will be asked to register your name and travel document number, and to predict your route with the tourist office, which can then provide you with recommendations for a guide. You will be able to select from humans and robot guides.

Documents

Passport

You must have your passport with you at all times. This is the basic document of identification for the visitor. You must have a passport that is valid and up to date. Spot checks on visitors are often undertaken, and should problems arise from your documents, you will be detained and held until the matter is clarified. If is also a good idea for you to bring some kind of duplicate passport in case you lose your original, or some form of identification such as your driver's license (although no visitor is allowed to drive in 2046)

Should you lose your passport, please immediately inform the 2046 Public Security Bureau or your embassy.

Never deposit your passport with any party in 2046, as there is a strong likelihood that your passport will be duplicated and sold in a rampant market for fake passports and identities.

Visa

All visitors from any nation need to have a visa to visit 2046. Transit passengers do not need to have a visa, but are confined for a maximum of 24-hours within the Grand Central Station facilities and will not be allowed to visit 2046 city itself as a matter of security.

Should you wish to stay for a maximum of 3 months, you will be required to apply your local 2046 consulate or embassy for a long stay visa prior to your arrival. You will be required to provide proof of employment and family in your home country as well as reasons for travelling to 2046 for this longer period. The cost of a visa is US$100.

Should you wish to extend your visa, you must return to Grand Central Station's immigration centre to present your case for extension.

Should you wish to emigrate to 2046, you will be required to apply 12 months in advance. The process for application is rather arduous, and will require a medical check-up as well as a psychological evaluation. A will is also required to be made out to the nation of 2046 for your assets in your current home country to be assigned to 2046 on your passing.

Travel Permits

Certain areas of 2046 require a travel permit for entry. Travel permits are issued by the Public Security Bureau, and need to be applied for after entry into 2046.

Whilst sensitive military areas are of course out of bounds, some ghettos and regions of different ethnic mixes are subject to travel restrictions due to their delicate social mix.

It is also common for travel restrictions to be enforced over night in 2046, so the visitor must stay abreast of the changing situation by watching the television or listening to the radio to the national broadcasts in order to avoid being trapped.

To avoid misunderstandings, it is worthwhile for the visitor to register personal details at the nearest tourist office in case you are found to be without a necessary travel permit. In general, you should travel smartly and quickly in 2046, not to take unnecessary detours and to stay alert to the current situation, in order to avoid problems with local ghettos and regions.

Travel Insurance

At this time, there are no known banks or insurance companies willing to offer travel insurance to 2046. You will have to travel at your own risk.

Driving License

No driving by visitors is allowed in 2046, so a driving license will not be of any use. Should you need a car, there are both taxis and courier cars for your hire.

A		
B		
C		
	D	
	E	

A : Tony Leung Chiu Wai
B : Tony Leung & Zhang Ziyi
C : Tony Leung & Zhang Ziyi
D : Tony Leung & Faye Wong
E : Tony Leung & Faye Wong

A
B
C

A : Takuya Kimura
B : Zhang Ziyi
C : Tony Leung & Zhang Ziyi

Resident Permits

Should you decide to emigrate to 2046, or stay beyond the duration of 3 months, you are required to apply for and carry with you a resident's permit.

The permit will determine the areas you are allowed to enter, and needs to be renewed every 12 months, again with a rigourous medical and psychological assessment.

Even robot residents are required to carry permits.

Embassies & Consulates

Your own Embassy

Embassies do not exist in 2046. Your entry into 2046 means that you have given up your nationality or citizenship, and the role of the embassy as a representative of your country affiliation does not exist.

Customs

2046 customs is extremely strict and no one is allowed to bring any belongings into 2046 apart from food and the clothing on your body. It is the policy of 2046 to maintain a strict independence of cultural purity and not to be affected by the outside world.

Money

You don't need money. Who needs money? In 2046, you only need your thoughts and ideas. You need to trade in 2046 to survive. Trade contraband or trade ideas, trade your time, trade your services, trade sex. It is a survival technique you need in 2046.

Post & Communications

There is no communication and post to and from 2046. There is no telephone communication, no internet contact. Nothing. So be careful to say what you want to say to your loved ones before you set off!

Internet Resources

The internet is cut at the borders of 2046. No data transmission is carried into the borders of 2046. There is a 2046 intranet within the borders. But most resources are restricted to official use as opposed to public use. Hackers do get access, but risk imprisonment if caught.

Books

2046 is covered in most international guides, but there are no details on the place as no correspondent has ever returned from visits. It is rumoured that this particular guide to 2046 is the most comprehensive one ever written due to our access to the one and only person who has been able to return from 2046. The publisher of this book denies his existence.

Newspapers & Magazines

News dissemination is mainly carried out by the official 2046 newspaper called 2046 Times. It is posted on major billboards at major junctions, and is available in magazine format. Newspapers are recycled at the end of the day, and so are rented as opposed to being bought by the reader. He/she must return newspapers and magazines to the official news recycling stations every evening.

Films

2046 has been featured in many Hollywood productions, though the first references to this mythical place appeared in the Wong Kar-wai movie 2046 which was filmed in 2004. In the film, a writer undergoes a deeply emotional and personal journey through his thoughts and writes a fictional story alluding to a parallel science fiction world called 2046.

CD-Rom

A CD-Rom of this guide to 2046 is available for bidding on Ebay and at all respectable retail outlets, though Amazon. com has refused to see this product for reasons only known to them.

Radio & TV
2046 shows radio and TV from all over the world, but there is a time lag of 50 years. It is the world of old radio shows and black and white TV shows. There is apparently only one channel for each.

Video Systems
Old betamax is the way to go in 2046. But old celluloid film projects are often used too.

Photography & Video
Whilst photography and videoing require a permit, few apply for one, as memories do not store well in 2046, and data corrupts very quickly. Photos fade and video goes fuzzy. People venture to explain this by an apparent strong magnetic field that surrounds 2046.

Time
2046 does not fit into the world structure of time zones. Due to the long journey to 2046 and the zero contact, time does not matter relative to the world. Time is not so important any more in 2046.

Electricity
240V AC is available in 2046. Batteries are available in most corner stores, and wind up electrical appliances are the fad of 2046. See them used in most common households.

Weights & Measures
Mixture of metric and imperial systems is used, so know your conversion factors!

Laundry
Public launderettes are available at most corners. Or you can donate your clothing at the local OXFAM of 2046 and have new clothing exchanged for you. Save on washing.

Toilets
Public toilets are not widely found in 2046. People who ask nicely get to use private toilets in homes, offices and department stores. But remember to bring your own toilet paper.

Health
Most medical health insurances do not provide for 2046. You should consider purchasing 2046 medical coverage at the local rail station on your arrival. It will keep you covered for all eventualities and give you access to medical support from any doctor in 2046.

Women Travellers
The most important thing that women travellers need to be aware of is that most women in 2046 are not human and are instead androids. They provide most of the sexual services to men; so do make sure you are not mistaken for an android.

Gay & Lesbian Travellers
Gay & Lesbian activities are thriving in 2046. Being gay or lesbian is absolutely no different from being heterosexual.

Disabled Travellers
Disabled travellers will find that 2046 does have everything you need for your travels.

Senior Travellers
Senior travellers will find that 2046 is a great location for retirement. Many senior travellers treat the journey to 2046 as their final journey.

2046 for Children
Not really a place to go for children. Suggest that trips to 2046 be a totally adult affair. It is prohibited by most countries to allow children under the age of 17 years to go to 2046.

Useful Organisations
There are a number of visitor centres dotted around the centre of 2046. From there you will be able to get most of the information you need for getting around 2046 and to get advice as to how to settle down. These visitor centres also act as visa processing centres, and thus you will need to go within 48 hours of your arrival to one and declare your arrival. At which point, you will be invited to please handover your previous travel documents from your country of origin.

Other useful organisations are the 2046 bureau of topography, who are always welcoming people to deposit their travel photos into their archives, as well as the 2046 congress of memories, where you can be plugged into the master database and have your memories downloaded and shared with the android population.

Libraries

Libraries mainly contain two areas of information. The fist is books that have been bought to 2046 by outsiders and then surrendered at the visitor centres. These books are kept for the knowledge of the outside world, but access is only granted to those who have lived in 2046 for more than 10 years, in case this knowledge stirs up feelings of wanting to leave 2046.

The other area contains android information based on the downloaded knowledge and memories of new arrivals to 2046.

You will be able to apply for your library card at both 2046 visitor centres as well as at the entrances of libraries themselves. Passes expire every 27 days.

Universities

Continuing higher education is available at 2046. There is only once course available, and it is in Art History, and the focus is the "Art of Oneself". Students of all ages are able to enrol onto this 6-year course and produce as part of their studies a portfolio of art that is created as a self-representation. At the end on graduating, you will be bestowed the qualification of Masters of Oneself, MOO, which is a prized title in 2046.

Cultural Centres

The main cultural centres are in the centre of 2046 where you will be able to find the 2046 Palace of Memories. It contains information on former citizens of 2046. It is open on Tuesdays and Thursdays, but sometimes open also on Sundays depending on the arrival of the next train from the outside world, when a special effort is made to open the Palace for new arrivals.

Danger & Annoyances

2046 is a peaceful place, but there are frequent occasions when the peace is disturbed by new arrivals who go through the mental struggle of letting go of their home worlds. This sometimes manifests in bouts of depression, violence, alcohol abuse, and sexual depravity. Therefore, one should distance oneself from other visitors at an early stage, and instead bond with the local population as soon as possible in order not to exacerbate the situation. Finding an android lover quickly is always a good way.

Legal Matters

2046 has a classless system, and legal matters are dealt with by the central judge of your state in 2046. No legal representation or jury is required. For more information, remember to ask on arrival when you are at the visitor centre.

Business Hours

Business hours are typically 24 hours a day with shift work between humans and androids. To avoid android services, focus your business between 3 am and 3:33am, which is the standard charging time of androids around the city.

Public Holidays & Special Events

There are no public holidays and special events in 2046.

Doing Business

Bartering is the main form of business transaction in 2046. Cigarettes and cigars are very popular and are commonly used as a currency.

Whilst there is no obvious commercial activity in 2046, there is a vibrant underground business for prostitution and drug smuggling. Whilst prostitution has been legalised for 20 years, it is only legal between humans and androids. Real girls are only available through networks of underground brothels.

Moving to 2046
In the last 50 years, there has been a huge demand on the part of people disenchanted with the world to go to 2046. 2046's population has grown significantly as the world has modernised and human relationships have seemed to loose clarity.

As a place of sanctuary, 2046 has been legendary, and the prospect of moving to 2046 is both one to look forward to as well as a way to relieve the stress of the outside world.

Whilst there is no official emigration or travel agency that is allowed to formally organise for you to move to 2046, there are ways of doing so.

In every town and city, there are portals that allow for the emigrant to enter and board a train to 2046. Often disguised or on the fringes of society, your challenge is to find these portals and to navigate yourself onto the trains. There are no fixed schedules, and the only ticket to board is based on your suitability for the journey. Other modes of transport are by air, bus, train or boat.

チャン・ツィイー　　　　　　トニー・レオン

チャン・チェン　　　　　　フェイ・ウォン

Special Appearance
マギー・チャン　　　　　　コン・リー

カリーナ・ラウ　　　　　　木村拓哉

A	B
C	D
E	F
G	H
I	J
K	L

A : Faye Wong

B : Faye Wong

C : Zhang Zihi

D : Tony Leung

E : Dong Jie

F : Faye Wong

G : Maggie Cheung

H : Gong Li

I : Carina Lau Kar Ling

J : Takuya Kimura

K : Faye Wong

L : Faye Wong

"You want to create a place in the world where what we think is nice, we can keep it that way. It's like the Hong Kong that we picture in our films is something from our impressions, from our memories, a certain wonderful moment of our city." Wong Kar-wai

lovely planet   www.jameslawcybertecture.com

Asian phantasmagorias of the interior

When we speak of "phantasmagorias of the interior", we think first and foremost of Walter Benjamin, whose phrase it is; then of the German poet Rainer Maria Rilke, whose only novel *The Notebooks of Malte Laurids Brigge*, contains, in passing, some of the most illuminating pages on the work of Henrik Ibsen, dramatist and deconstructor of the bourgeois interior. But most of all we think of the changeful and elusive nature of the modern city, in response to which 'the interior' was constructed in the first place, with Ibsen, Benjamin and Rilke as its first amanuenses. We all know and expect the city to change very fast; but when it changes too fast, and when change comes from all kinds of unpredictable directions, we reach a point when the city begins to outpace our perception and understanding of it. At this point, everything begins to take on a quality not of '*déja vu*' but of '*déja disparu*': like the ghost of Hamlet's father, at one moment "'tis here, 'tis here"; at the next, "'tis gone". It is at this point, when the city is receding from our perceptual and cognitive grasp, that the interior as phantasmagoria is created. The first hints of how this came about were noted by Benjamin and Rilke as they looked at European cities like Paris and Berlin. Today, our focus will have to shift to Asian cities like Hong Kong, Shanghai or Beijing. No city changes as fast as the contemporary Asian city, and this is suggested by phrases like 'Shenzhen speed' or 'urban frenzy'. These Asian cities too, like their European counterparts, have their own very different phantasmagorias of the interior.

The interior, as Benjamin describes it, is not just domestic or private space, versions of which have of course existed since almost the beginning of human history. Rather Benjamin uses the term to refer to a radical 'spatial change' in the relation between public and private that resulted from a number of 'political and economic changes' in the nineteenth century, namely liberal democracy on the one hand going together with industrial capitalism on the other. Both conspired to produce 'the citizen', whose new-found sense of political power was accompanied and contradicted by his economic impotence: the citizen, in whose name the democratic state was founded, was still merely a wage-earner, a slave to capital. It took this combination of power and impotence to create the European interior. For the first time, living-space became sharply distinguished from the place of work, 'the interior' from its complement 'the office'. "The private citizen who in the office took reality into account, required of the interior that it should support him in his illusions ... From this sprang the phantasmagorias of the interior." [1] The interior is both a place from where the citizen can reduce the world and its exorbitant demands to an on-going spectacle: "his drawing room was a box in the world-theatre"; as well as a casing, a protective envelope, that preserves his traces. If "living means leaving traces", the citizen provides proof that he has lived (and not merely existed) by filling the interior with objects, these traces of life like so many fragments shored against his ruins. That is why Benjamin notes that Edgar Allen Poe, inventor of the detective story that investigated these traces left by the citizen, was also the author of *The Philosophy of Furniture*.

The bourgeois interior therefore is both space and affect. It is an affective space that is at the same time relatable to the spatial changes being brought about by politics and economics. Rilke presents Ibsen as the tragic poet of the interior, the ruthless analyst and victim of this new affective space. Every play begins by trying to measure the barely measurable affective movements of the interior: "an emotion that rises by half a degree... the slight cloudiness in a drop of longing, and that barely perceptible color-change in an atom of confidence..." [2] It continues by trying to find "equivalents in the visible world for what you had seen inside." However, Rilke concludes, the enterprise ends in failure because no such equivalents can be found. Rather more and more desperate and violent images have to be brought on ("...finally towers had to come in and whole mountain ranges..."), and Ibsen's stage becomes "overwhelmed with what is tangible, for the sake of what cannot be grasped." Yet 'failure' is hardly the right word, for it is exactly this leaking away of equivalence between the social and the personal that defines the interior as such. From this point of view, *The Master Builder* which deals with failure is one of Ibsen's most successful plays. Solness the master builder can build masterful high towers full of bourgeois homes, but is himself afraid of heights. When he does 'the impossible' and tries to climb as high as he builds, he falls to his death. This drama of power and impotence where one negates the other is the drama of the interior; and Ibsen is one of its most prescient nineteenth century chroniclers.

The interior then, in spite of - or because of - its phantasmagoric nature, is a way of seeing the city. Though the interior is a pliable space of memory and desire, it nevertheless has some relation to the implacable urban reality, just as a *cliché* or negative is related to the photograph. In the interior, we see the city in a blurred or skewed way through our affective response to it. This is not of course a phenomenology of the city, because what takes place in the interior (from visual decor to social decorum) is based not so much on what we see as on what we wish to see; not so much on what we experience, as on what challenges and even upsets our experience. In the interior, we see the city not through privileged moments of insight or revelation, i.e., epiphanies; but rather through puzzlement and confusion, i.e., through 'negative epiphanies'.

If the interior is formed in relation (however indirect) to political and economic factors, what changes can we expect to find there when these factors are being reconstellated - a reconstellation that goes under the name of 'globalism' - as is the case in Chinese cities today? We can try to give a necessarily partial account by taking the case of two contrasting Chinese cities: Beijing, where urban life is being reshaped in line with the paradoxes of a 'socialist' market economy; and Hong Kong, since 1997, officially a Chinese city, but with a very different history of colonialism and capitalism.

As everyone has heard, Chinese cities are going through a real estate boom, a period of frenzied construction largely fuelled by both state and global capital. The new high-rises include both commercial and residential buildings, as well as public buildings like opera houses and cultural centres. One of the most surprising is the CCTV building (China Central Television) designed by Rem Koolhaas now currently under construction. Let me begin with this as one of two examples to suggest how a new kind of interior is coming into being.

The design, consisting of two massive L-shaped structures interlinked at the top, makes no concessions to local design traditions or motifs. This is at one level refreshing, as so many allusions to the local (bamboo, pagodas) are of the order of *cliché* and ornament. The question though is why an ultra-conservative state institution, which is how CCTV will still have to be described, should close a 'futuristic' design like the one offered by Koolhaas. The visual form of the building gives no hint about the kinds of things going on inside - except as an anticipation of 'things to come'. Let me juxtapose this with my second example before I attempt to give a tentative formulation of the interior in Beijing. One of the striking urban phenomena in Beijing is the turning of factory space into loft spaces, following the model of New York and London. The most famous example is Factory 798 in northeast Beijing. The 'bauhaus-like' buildings in the compound were built by the East Germans in the 50's, but they have in the last few years been taken over by design, advertising and publishing companies and by sculptors, photographers, musicians and other arty types, who have given this factory space cutting edge interiors. The

compound is said to be the most chic place in Beijing, written up in the New York Times and other international newspapers. None of this is too surprising with the CCTV building (and many others like it) in mind. What is surprising though is a story of what took place in one of these factory-turned-chic-private-apartments (the authenticity of which I can vouch for, because it took place in my apartment!) Imagine someone, a complete stranger, barging in into a space that you have taken such pains to decorate. Worse still, he is someone who seems to assume that he has a perfect right to be there. When you expostulate with him as gently as possible about this invasion of your privacy, 'he' is the one who gets offended. How to understand this? One explanation is that we are seeing here some residues of egalitarianism - fostered by the older communist society but frowned upon by the new China - surfacing and producing this minor crisis of the interior.

With these two examples in mind, we can speculate on how a new interior is being constructed. It is constructed not in terms of power and impotence, but in terms of a 'double negative', the co-presence of two absences: the no-longer-there (a socialist egalitarianism that now seems so '*passé*'); together with the not-yet-there (anticipations of a future when China will overtake the U.S. as the world's strongest economy.) This double negative gives to the present and to the interior an air of nervous expectancy. We see this for example in the huge popularity of interior design magazines, where images of sleekly minimalist interiors predominate; images which have little resemblance to the majority of actual Beijing interiors. Rather, they are idealisations of a moment when the clutter of the past can be erased, de-interiorised as it were; so that a projective geometry of desire can be put in its place.

Hong Kong gives us a quite different example of the interior under conditions of globalism. One unfailingly accurate guide to this interior are the films of Wong Kar-wai, particularly his last two films, *In the Mood for Love* and *2046*. In these films, the city as such seem to have disappeared, suggesting that globalism refers us not just to the large effects that we can see, like new architecture; but also to small effects, 'the capillary action' that takes place in the interior. Thus in these films, there are very few recognisable 'images of the city', as much of the action in these films takes place in interior, or interiorised, space. There are no shots of landmark buildings; what we see instead are decrepit walls with graffiti-like patterns on them; walls with the surface concrete peeling off them, exposing the brick beneath; like human egos. Nevertheless, the city's problematic presence is very much part of the film's *mise-en-scène*. The city is present through the characters' affective responses and the crises in the interior. In Wong Kar-wai's films, we find again and again the evocation of some kind of invisible barrier between people, and human relations characteristically take the form of proximity without reciprocity; whether it is the case of the male lovers in *Happy Together* who cannot be happy and together at the same time, or the case of the heterosexual couple in *In the Mood for Love*, who live in adjoining rooms in the same boarding house, but whose attraction for each other is based on the impossible premise that they do not want to be like their adulterous spouses, so that what pulls them together is exactly what keeps them apart; or the situation of Tony Leung and Zhang Zi Yi, one in Room 2047, the other in Room 2046, where it is not space but the affective baggage from the past, memories, that stands between them. Benjamin's line "living means leaving traces", becomes in *2046*, "All memory is memory of tears."

The paradoxical logic of the interior goes together with a kind of cinematic image distinctive to Wong Kar-wai, what I have called elsewhere an image of disappointment. These images may be sleek and awkward by turns, minimalist or excessive, but they are never quite right. They never quite make the appointment with meaning; they disappoint. Take for example the image that everyone remembers best from *In the Mood for Love*, Maggie Cheung's dresses. The more beautifully she is dressed, the more pathetic her situation appears to others. Maggie Cheung's dresses are not fashion statements; they are images of disappointment. Or take the Sci-Fi image of Faye Wong as a 'retarded' cyborg in the story-within-the-story in *2046*. It is never clear what she feels, as she is programmed to respond only afterwards. The lover who says to her, "I have a secret: run away with me," never knows her answer.

Yet there is also something curiously erotic about disappointment, as if in the interior, desire and frustration were now no longer opposites, but rather complementary; just as on the narrative level we find the co-presence in Wong Kar-wai's films of boredom (the weight or 'ashes of time') on one hand and the experience of speed on the other. Similarly, '2046' is both a date in an as yet unknown future, as well as a well-known place where 'nothing changes'. People go there to retrieve their memories, to remember; but then, once there, they can never return. To remember is also to forget. Finally, in *2046*, it is said, nothing changes; just as Hong Kong after the Handover is supposed to remain 'unchanged for 50 years', while the city and its interior are changing daily behind our backs. If the nineteenth century bourgeois citizen sensed his political power (in the right to vote) at the same time as his economic impotence, the Hong Kong citizen of the twenty-first century is not confident of having either. The phantasmagorias of the interior make these political and economic disappointments erotic.

Notes:
1. Walter Benjamin, *Charles Baudelaire*, (trans. Harry Zohn), NLB: London, 1973. All quotations from Benjamin on pp.168-169.
2. Rainer Maria Rilke, *The Notebooks of Malte Laurids Brigge*, (trans. Stephen Mitchell), Vintage Books: New York, 1985. All quotations from Rilke on pp.82-83.

中文譯文

Gutierrez + Portefaix

走廊城市:一次水平的旅行

城市是一条没有尽头的走廊。无论是陆地还是通道,走廊是不同地域之间的水平连接。它物化为线性的过渡空间,或是一条向未知的新世界开敞的封闭通道。换句话说,走廊是任何室内空间组织的脊索。它是路线、是光明、是入口、是通往另一目的地的大门。人们在走廊中度过自己一生的大部分时间。成群结队的或是独自的,他们水平运动到一个将自己投射到无尽灭点的空间。作为一次水平的旅行,走廊城市并不缺少远景。

如果一个城市可以被认为是一个场所,人们必须要设想城市不是普通的城市,而是一个线性的场所。走廊城市由无尽的通道组成。它们不仅提供了通往停留空间的通路,同时也向其他线性空间敞开。它们一起组成了走廊的一个复杂几何体——一个完美的迷宫。

作为所有公共空间中程度最高的一员,走廊经常吸引高密度的活动,并成为其连接者。当这种情况发生时,它就转变成了一个线性空间——两旁布置着各种货品的连续商店橱窗。这些橱窗彼此竞争,以获得最大的多样性、鲜亮的色彩和诱人的价格。这种线性通过低矮的天花板和光滑的表面以及纹理一致的大理石和磁砖铺地得到了加强。

与室外环境相隔绝,封闭的线性空间主要通过机械控制的门窗和人群来使其变得生动。因此,城市随着居民们的开窗关窗在各个走廊之间、从火车到住宅、办公室、机场或是饭店之间的运动而生长,走廊形成了居民的日常生活规律。

在走廊城市中,没有人关注审美,而只注意连续地带的流动性。它的经济节俭到了一个词:高效。因此审美只是一种广告的形式,是装饰的某种符号化的元素,甚至除了它所包含的简易材料之外什么都不是。

这里的气候完全忽视了外界的气象因素:16-19摄氏度,干燥。事实上,这里居民的衣着都是专门为走廊气候而准备的。

走廊城市有很多规矩。它们和定位地图以及走廊名称一起被张贴在每个十字路口,这样就不会有人走失,也不会忽视了法律。它们体现了一种在永久控制之下关于个人行为的完美的法律条文。标准的数字工具和一支警察巡逻队保证了走廊城市的过渡特性。

自动步行道可以有效地加速人流。行走是唯一正常的行动方式,小跑就显得十分可疑。因此,居民们就和流浪者不同,因为他们永远不会偏离自己的路线,也不可能走失。当人们穿越不同的部分时,不应该停驻,也不能打散人流。在线性建筑里的相遇时间不会很长,因此,社交只能当人们以相同的速度在同一方向上行走时才能发生。在走廊城市中,个人消解在了匿名的人群之中。

城市不再被理解为一个由空间定义的区域结构,而成为一个由间隙空间——走廊——产生的动态系统。这些走廊创造了一种最极端的集合形式,一种有实用潜力空间的积聚和物理流动性的增加。这里的每个人都热衷于从一个地点走到另一个地点,同时可能发现新的商店和服务设施。只要这些人为直线具有一种介于住宅和领地之间的主要功能空间,其空间的灵活性和连续的人类迁移就会创造出一种类似西洋跳棋似的运动。

Gutierrez + Portefaix / Laura Ruggeri
探索香港内部空间

I

《香港实验室2》是对《香港实验室》的拾遗，同时也是遵循其逻辑的延伸。

《香港实验室》三部曲被看作是一种新型的城市自传，是一种回应新颖特殊的都市、经济、社会和政治状况的实验性出版物。它聚焦于城市物质结构和贯穿于其中的各种系统之间，聚焦于现实数据的收集和它们的敏锐解说之间，聚焦于当地的建筑生产和作用于其上的全球影响之间。外部的波动通过一系列现象呈现出来。《香港实验室》通过居住、工作、交通和娱乐等不同的地理中心，探索了很多独特而相互联系的主题。后资本主义的逻辑是分散的，不指向任何整体性。它标志着现代建成环境的一种疏松关系，各种元素和组成部分在某种程度上保持着距离，但产生了处于不断变异中的形式，继而变形成为我们在书中写到的新的地形学。

相应地，现在这部《香港实验室2》将交流更向前推进了一步。编者的手法从城市景观的概念转向都市实践。从宏观的方法转向微观的结构，它将艺术家项目和关于香港地下空间的一系列理论和批评观点结合起来。因此，都市体验和居住的变化本质需要新的评判标准和学科交叉的研究方法。

《香港实验室2》被看作是一本多中心的书籍，不同的主题汇聚到一起，私密-公共、使用-交换、空间-时间、地方-全球、规定-暂时、控制-背离、表面-结构。它们是例证和/或辩证的对立。这些对立多体现为联系/冲突、社会节奏、杂交以及空间和身体的重置。

本书并不试图将秩序强加于反抗分级和超越空间分类学界限的材料，而是一如既往地，力图保持异类集合可以触及的动态和流动性，在本质上与以不可预知的方式做出回应的潜力保持对话。它有意擦除了理论和艺术之间的细微的界限，阐述都市生活曲折迷离和被污染的本质所导致的结果远远不止于简单的新型文化联系。它同时也攻击了思想的纯洁性，如果批评的思想可以接受这种挑战，那么它就被投射到了每日的生活世界和一个完全不同的更加广阔的领域。

我们相信要了解一个城市就必须包含微观和宏观两个方面。它们内部并不存在主次关系，但是人们的共识是无论选取那个视角，没有一个城市——事实上是没有一个"居住"空间——是能够被全面认识的。相对于宏观景象，对于微观的适当的回应因此是一种决断和具有创造性的反抗。

艺术家们关于城市内部空间的项目和想法处理的是当今世界的突变，无论它们是以种极端和壮丽的方式被表达，还是以渐进和潜在的方式被表达。

建筑、装饰和家具占据、改变和表达了室内空间，充满了含蓄的或是明显的意义。这些含义可以使我们了解到房子的创造者、拥有者和使用者；了解到政治的、社会的和家庭的渴望和态度；了解到人和室内环境之间的相互关系。本书所编纂的项目探索了人们通过与其所居住、短期占有或是表现的空间之间的关系来表达这些意义时所应用的策略。

它对于香港有限空间前所未有的表达提供了一次漂流和探寻，为描绘其可能的复杂结构提供了一次检验和尝试。《香港实验室2》的内容由投稿人的空间体验组成，就像所有探寻的行为一样，它固然有失真的成分。但是我们相信，在城市所提供的大量材料中培育一片真正的创造性的土壤，有助于瓦解惯有的思维和观察模式，使一种新的结构从中浮现出来。

这里所倡导的有机结构全面反映了都市实践/体验。沿着由不同实体组成的线索前进，人们可以从中识别出应被追寻的特殊图案。

本书的主要结构由书中的第一个和最后一个故事给出——"走廊城市"和"电梯城市"。每个故事都开启一片研究的特殊领域，即可以被独立看待，又可与书中的其它部分相联系。读者既可以依次阅览，也可以按照自己的喜好阅读，有所取舍。本书的四个范畴——家庭、商业、策略和虚构是贯穿全文线索、有机划分书中内容的最大可能性。

II
追寻《香港实验室2》的线索

内部与外部和公共与私密的区别在不断发生着变化，这是一个模糊而柔和的区域，边界开放、表皮展开，允许发生滑移、渗透、错位和重置。这个柔和区域同时适应于都市环境（硬性空间）和私人领域（柔性空间），硬性空间和柔性空间彼此融合。当代都市主义的复杂要求与都市和个人的要求相结合，导致了人们对通常两分法关系的反思。个人被置于多维的非连续现实当中，各种差异与不稳的网络关系并置和共存，且不能被轻易地调解或是综合。

Ho Siu Kee作为香港最重要的艺术家之一，研究身体与环境之间的空间关系。他从中国民间方言"三月爬、六月坐、九月走"中获得暗示，观察人体根据空间进行调整的方式，以及伴随这种适应过程产生的自然而然的知觉变化。香港看上去是一个对人体提出不断要求的场所，生活在其中的人们都是极具柔韧性的，他们没有固定的尺度，他们异乎寻常的弹性常常可与城市自身的弹性相媲美。在"创造空间，找寻个人空间"中，Leung Kam-ping描述了与父母和亲戚合住在狭小公寓里的单身上班族女性所采用的策略。她们试图通过利用个人物品来界定出"个人领域"或是占用图书馆和餐厅等公共空间的办法来应对空间不足和缺乏私密性的问题。另一位香港著名的艺术家Leung Chi-wo将自己的作品基于对空间的记忆，并且探索观察和展现它的可能性。艺术家通过一系列照片和图画展示了书桌、扶手椅和橱柜等家具下面被遗忘空间的图景，发现了可以进一步用于存储的可能性空间。"看不见的室内"则对家庭主妇（他的母亲）的持家知识和她们压缩和隐藏日常生活用品的能力表示了钦佩。

无论这些文章如何，室内设计树立起了一种引人入胜的符号系统，它可以指示出个人的和集体的心智。无论在物质形式上还是在相互关系上，它都展现了某种"家"的概念——一种所属的和自我的主张。与所有的语言含义一样，事物的符号价值加强了一种区别的逻辑，通过展示和挥霍建立起了一种与众不同的品味、地位和身份层次。事实上，所有的商品都参与了一种独创的"物品的社会话语"，从而呼应了Jean Baudrillard所曾经描述的一种普遍的"歧视和尊重机制"

祖传的房屋曾经被一度认为是结合思想、记忆和梦想的地方。当过去被擦除的时候，人们的感情投资指向了未来，现实也不得不被人工地重新施以魔法。在"建造真实的梦想之家"中，Cecilia Chu和Mishko Hansen研究了香港房地产市场的独特之处以及室内设计的角色：井然有序的样板间在展现理想生活图景的同时，也是人们彼此接触和发挥想象力建造自己家庭不同版本的真实空间。如果说香港的居民已经学会了高密度的生存之道，懂得最大限度

地利用空间的话，那么在湾仔等拥挤的街道从事廉价住宅项目的房地产经纪人也采用了相似的方式。他们小得不能再小的店铺里仅有一台电脑、一张书桌和几把可以在人行道上支起的折叠椅，所占据的进深甚至不到一米。Pierre Larauza将镜头转向这些街道层面的办公室，转向资本主义交换原则和空间利用最大化的结合点，这些经纪人的办公室和他们所租售的房产反映了同样的逻辑。Gutierrez + Portefaix的"货摊城市"和"光的城市"对于这种最大化进行了进一步的探究——香港为了发展商业而创造系统和空间的能力。一群学生对"货摊城市"中的这种小型建筑进行了详细调研，得出这类狭小空间具有用最低成本满足不同配置的惊人能力。图纸和照片记录下了旋转、滑移、折叠的基本运动，表面积扩大，从而整个商业功能展现出来。与此相似，"光的城市"探寻的是一种在密林中的新的商业活动。

消费是香港城市生活的一个重要组成部分，但就像在大多数发达国家一样，购物不仅仅是消费商品，更是建立身份、与他人建立联系、标志社会差异和追求情感及审美快感的一种方式。Kathy Lo的"楼上店铺：反抗世俗"研究了一种新生的现象——处于底层商业和上部公寓之间二到三层的店铺。它们不仅提供了与众不同的、更富冒险性的购物体验，同时也可以被看成一种作为补偿的异位移植。顾客在猫狗主题的咖啡店里可以与别人的宠物玩耍，从而实现在香港高密度居住条件和限制饲养动物的法规下拥有宠物的愿望。零售商店因为提供了一种家的感觉而格外受到欢迎，而这种感觉在个人空间不断受到威胁的拥挤的大商场中已经体验不到了。Rene Chen的"See Fung Choi（私人楼上餐厅）"，或者说家庭烹饪餐厅是一个发生新的消费行为的场所。文章从传统中国饮食文化、社会等级区别、社区、唯一性和生活方式等各个视角分析了这种现象。私人的公寓经过改造后，不同的空间不再有区别，厨房和餐厅被扩大，私人领域被公共领域所侵占。

从楼上到楼下，这是一个透视角度和疆界限定的问题。占有和改造所带来的分配看上去是一种潜在状况的主要逻辑。Maeva Aubert / Gutierrez + Portefaix / Laurent Malone 的"高速公路之下"研究了架空基础设施之下的空间。从肯尼迪城到北角，他们始终如一地建造着一种照片和声音的记录，从而清晰地描述沿线的主要序列。如果元素和功能的并置会导致对文脉和环境的忽略，那么"下面"无疑是一个机会的空间。一种类似的逻辑也适用于"HSBS故事"。这一章由前一作者在图像上做解，由Mary Buneo完成文字部分。菲律宾女佣们每个星期天都在世界著名的银行总部的玻璃敞廊下聚集，她们对这里空间的占用成为一种对抗资本主义的形式。她们会见朋友、吃东西、

做买卖、交换讯息以及无休止地谈天说地。银行总部在这一天里变成了喧嚣的剧场。

Neil Leach的"拖曳空间"将香港看成一个空间配置的精髓之地，一个检验空间行为表演理论的实验室。空间的本质通过一种活化的方式被转换，空间的功能因而被改写和再造。这可以提供一种设定用途和事件之间的交替，会议室可以被转换成结婚礼堂，然后在24小时之内又变回到会议室。又例如两段租期之间的临时商铺，或是建筑之间被小商小贩利用的剩余空间。同样的，Gary Chang的4C理论将连接、选择、变化和共存看作是香港城市空间的主要特征。建筑师通过自己的设计和对于不同现象的解读建议通过灵活性和可逆性对于可能性空间实现不断的探索。

作为以上特殊情况的例证，Chungking大楼是香港最著名的建筑之一，但还很少有人讲述它的故事。与曾经一度被破坏的九龙城成为很多出版物的主题不同，Gutierrez + Portefaix的"大块头城市"将那些被遗忘的建筑转化成丰碑，并最终演变成一种探索复杂室内空间的可能性游戏。他们的另一篇"再-城市"选取产品而非空间最为对象，质询使用之后的物品和香港的回收策略，这部用照片反映的作品敏锐地揭示出我们日常消费背后的阴暗面。

Laura Ruggeri在她的实验性写作"霉变时代"中跟随《香港实验室》的前提，直到得出最极端的结论。她将香港置于显微镜下，观察有机物和无机物彼此的相互作用。她的观察距离越近，得出的结果就越具有隐喻性。徜徉于隐喻的网络联系之间，她通过将意义从熟悉的体验向不熟悉领域的转移和延迟创造出了一种新的联系。她释放出一种类似于真菌繁衍的过程，其中大多数是回收者、"处理工程师"和变化要素。

Eric Howeler的"热度城市"提出了一种特殊气候条件下的多样化空间设计——空调。按照作者的看法，香港反射性立面颇具气氛的投射创造出一种否定外界的内在化状态。

Laura Ruggeri在他的"购物商场的性欲"中进行了进一步的反思。在大型商场中，人们发现自我、欲望和消费的暗影在展示的商品和拥挤的人群中彼此交织。巡游、潜近、恳求、窥视和拜物主义组成了购物体验中一个巨大但却常常被忽视的方面。在后台，在闪光的店面和大理石墙面之后，人们可以找寻到商场柔软的腹地。这里没有安全摄像头，混凝土的地板和

楼梯上方密布着管线。售货员和清洁工在这里聚集，在楼梯上吃饭或是休息。瘾君子们也加入其中抽上几口烟，情侣们在这里慵懒地进行爱抚。

非赢利性组织Ziteng在2004年策划了"我的生活"展览，30名性工作者每人获得一部相机，用来为展览拍摄她们自己及其工作环境，进而颠覆了通常使她们成为男性目光追逐对象的拜物主义和窥淫癖经济。她们为《香港实验室2》所选择的照片表现了她们在自己的工作场所中为创造自我表达空间所做出的努力。1-lau-1是妇女们轮流租借的小型公寓——有人可能在白天上班，而在晚上回家照顾家务，而另一个人在晚上取代她的位置；有人只在周末工作，而另一些人则在旅行签证的有效期内全时工作，试图接触到尽可能多的主顾。1-lau-1的安排避开了取缔多人从事色情服务场所的法律规定，反映了社会中的特殊权力关系。因此香港的大多数性工作者都来自于大陆、泰国、菲律宾和其他亚洲国家也就不足为奇了。

James Law的"2046"指南沿用经典旅游指南的写作手法。背景知识、出行、参观和消遣、住宿和餐饮等组成了一个未来空间/城市的信息。受香港电影导演王家卫之邀，作者为一部小说提供了一个完整的场景。令人惊奇的是，2046被描述成一个具有极高密度的垂直城市，它被巨大的穹顶所覆盖，形成了有史以来最大的室内空间。

作为对于香港的另一种战略观点，同时遵循着从实验的角度接近城市领域的思想，《香港实验室2》探究了中介空间。尽管内部空间的提法在某些论题上可能听起来觉得刺耳和灰暗，但在另一些问题上将会显得十分性感和充满创造性。通过对空间、活动和建筑的特殊关注，本书整体的策略是捕捉动态性，并探究超高密度所引发出的可能性。无论真实或是虚构，这里的故事或文章的目的都是要展示空间（主要是内部空间），而非其中的居民。通过将事物上下倒置、内外相调和宏观微化等，城市变得更有人情味，即使是没有人类居住其中。从疯狂科学家的试管及其机器人创造物那里，一种新的有机生命正在浮现。

Kathy Leung Kam-ping

埃莉的故事
从空间布局到个人强调和家庭关系

剖析香港高密度的生存环境及其对那些与父母同住的未婚女性的压力，本文将讲述这样一个实例，看看女主人公是如何斗争并扩展自己的私人空间的。

埃莉父母的房子——六个家庭成员挤在18.6平方米的公屋里

作为一个34岁的未婚女性，埃莉与她的父亲（65岁）、母亲（60岁）和妹妹（22岁）一同居住。埃莉的哥哥和姐姐在结婚以后都搬了出去。这所18.6平方米的公屋是她有生以来和家人共同居住的地方。"这里有一间厕所和一间厨房，但是厨房同时也是连接厕所的走廊。厕所的前方有一个小阳台。整个单元里没有划分房间，也没有隔墙。"

下面是埃莉父母家的平面图

尽管没有隔断，但是一对父母和四个兄弟姐妹都有理所当然地属于自己的空间。在这间单元里，既没有门也没有锁。个人的物品和衣服都根据习惯被放置；没有一个家庭成员超越自己的或是他人的界限。积习已久，埃莉已经完全掌握了在家中空间使用的规则。

个人化的物品——一种超越个人空间的途径

埃莉1.2 x 1.8米的小床从幼年时代起就是她的领地。这种个人化的物品超越了地理上的距离并形成了一个私人空间，它同时也是建筑埃莉自己的小王国的砖石。

对于这种情形的反思

个人的所属物不仅是对于其主人疆界和唯一性的表达，同时也是内在感情和思想的延伸。我们在相册中记录重要的时刻，用奖品展示成就，留存以前的物品来追思逝去的亲人。在一生的不同阶段中，我们丢弃或者收藏个人的物品，这些物品被赋予了私人的意义。像我们大多数人一样，埃莉与不同的私人物品有着特殊的联系。例如她的藤条篮子、早年的书包、纪念图书、"聪明小孩"、表盒……这不仅是埃莉的珍宝，同时也是一座记录了埃莉个人成长历史的私人博物馆。

与家人保持物理和心理距离

即使埃莉使她的床成为了自己的小王国，但是获得自治感的能力仍然被家庭空间的布置所阻碍。在这样一个小屋子里，家庭成员彼此近距离生活。他们以牺牲个人的身份为代价建立起了亲密无间的家庭关系。用埃莉的话说"房子太小了，家人挤在一起，我的自我感好像在一点一点地消失。"她与母亲的"脐带关系"可能就是这样一个没有隔断的家庭的产物，从幼年时代，她就与母亲有着十分亲密的关系。母亲的话就是埃莉的话，母亲的喜恶就是埃莉的喜恶。埃莉的第一次恋爱之所以失败就是因为母亲认为它的男朋友收入水平低、教育程度不高，配不上埃莉。

埃莉不喜欢母亲评论自己的外表、穿着自己的衣服、花自己的钱并且阅读自己的日记，她发现很难让自己摆脱母亲的教训，来形成自己的精神疆界。出于尽孝心的想法，埃莉容忍着母亲对自己思想的教导、对自己感受的解释、对自己选择和决定的影响，甚至替母亲抱守着自己不想保守的秘密。

埃莉很清楚她的母亲的过分干涉。尽管她决定摆脱这种束缚，但是做起来并不那么容易。这一方面是因为她的母亲不想改变目前的关系，因为"房子太小了，沉默在所难免"。在其他时候，埃莉被母亲不快和孤独的表情所影响。在这样一个没有隔断的狭小空间里，母亲的焦虑和不快很容易感染到埃莉。它们影响到了埃莉的感情，使她不能享受精神的平静。

距离使心灵变得温柔

面对竞争激烈的就业市场，埃莉的确曾经很努力地攻读硕士学位。但是她爱说教的母亲和狭小的住房成了障碍。"我觉得家里没有我的容身之地，我找寻不到自己。除了感觉到拥挤，我没法专心学习。这一点是至关紧要的，我根本不能把精力集中起来。"

当埃莉提出要在工作地点旁边租一套房子的时候，立即招来了父母的反对。她的父亲坚持不许自己的未婚女儿独自住在外面。面对如此之多的打击，埃莉想过要死。由于害怕女儿自杀，父母最终同意了让她搬出去。但是这件事没有让任何亲戚知道，因为埃莉的父母觉得这是一种耻辱。

地理上的疏远反而带来了情感上的接近。埃莉喜欢自己在新家里自由自在的感觉，但同时也更加思念自己的亲人。埃莉的父母很珍视与女儿的感情，并且在她搬出去以后在很多细微之处体现了他们的关切。当他们再次相聚并且互诉衷肠时，以往紧张的情绪已经明显地减弱了。

"我住在原来的家里时，那是一种家庭关系，并不是他们不爱我，但是看上去并不那么好……我不能说这不是一个好的家庭！他们很爱我，在我遇到麻烦的时候，他们和我一起哭泣，他们分担我的焦虑并且支持我……那个家的确很小，小到连站着的地方都没有。因此，当少了一个人以后，就少了一个争夺地方的家伙。他们就有更多的空间转悠了。"

"相见容易相处难"

"相见容易相处难"这句谚语可以准确反映人们的物理和心理空间与家庭的交互作用。一方面，狭小的居住空间培育了亲密的家庭关系。另一方面，它也会有消极的干涉影响，很难维护个人边界的不受侵犯。亲密和自由、空间和联系、自治和关联，这些进退两难的局面都起因于我们和家人共处的居住空间。

我们可以借用公共空间来进行日常活动，例如餐厅、图书馆、快餐店、停车场、商场等；我们可以在公园里修心养性；但是我们需要一个叫做家的地方来停靠我们的身体和灵魂。家的空间布局就像是一面镜子，告诉旁观者在这里居住的人的故事。

乱糟糟的卧室可能显示了一个十来岁孩子的性情；过期的日历可能告诉我们这里的精神病患者缺乏自理的能力；为葬礼准备的大幅遗照面对着儿子的卧室，这可能是老妈妈难以言表的愤怒。关于居住空间和它的居住者心理紧张状态之间的联系还可以列举出一大长串的例子。我们能从中看到它的暗示么？

Cecilia Chu & Mishko Hansen

建造"真实的"梦想之家
香港的室内设计和消费活动

对于那些从来没有到过香港新建楼盘售楼处的人来说，首次光顾必定觉得那是一种奇观。尤其是在开盘那一天，会吸引成千上万的人前来。很多人都是全家出动，扶老携幼，仿佛是一次家庭的外出旅行。人们热情地徘徊于样板间之中，观看、交谈，评论的话题从房间的布局到色彩搭配再到室外景观，并将其与别的样板间相比较，然后得出哪一套他们更喜欢、为什么喜欢的结论。总会有谦恭的销售人员拿着一摞小册子站在出口处，尝试说服一些潜在的买家能为房子交下定金。

人们可能会认为上述描述的现象是房地产市场繁荣的必然结果。但事实是，香港的市场在过去七年间一直处于相对低迷的状态。尽管报道说样板间观众的数量不断创下新高——有时候这种报道几乎成为了每次房地产项目开盘后的例行宣言——大多数参观样板间的人最终并没有买房。在最近一次销售开盘中，一些参观者说自己前来的目的并不是要买房，而是要享受参观样板间的愉悦。甚至有些人承认他们把参观样板间看作是一项日常的休闲活动。当被问及他们为什么喜欢参观时，他们的回答是出于了解"别人"是怎么设计住宅的好奇心。一些人还说他们只是简单地喜欢欣赏那些"设计出色"的家居，并且已经在盼望着下一次的开盘活动了。

当然，以样板间的方式来进行房地产促销并不是什么新鲜事，在世界很多国家都是如此。但是，在香港这样一个房地产在集体意识里尤为突出的城市，样板间的设计和销售就被赋予了特殊的意义。一个特殊的现象是，几乎所有的新楼盘都在建造以前就被出售，这就意味着样板间通常是处于基地以外的某个地方。但是，为了向潜在的购买者传达一种"真实的"感觉，样板间在设计时总是格外用心以使参观者有一种身临其境的感觉。一种方法就是将城市的天际线（通常是在顶层套间里看到的景观）以灯箱的形式投射到样板间的玻璃窗格上。这就使参观者可以"看见"外面的景色，此举可以在很大程度上影响购房者的决定。因为拥有好的景色，尤其是海景，在香港被认为是有身份和有生活品位的表现。

大多数样板间的室内设计都煞费苦心，通常使用不同风格的家居装潢来体现一系列主题，每一种风格都对应着特殊的户型尺度（那些看上去"高端"的装修用于宽敞、昂贵的户型）。但是，当你观察这些户型的平面图时，会发现它们的基本布局只有很小的差别。事实上，大多数新的房地产项目的平面图和建造于十几年前的现有建筑的平面图几乎是完全相同的。很显然，这种相似性的原因之一是与提供新颖的建筑设计相比，开发商可以从中节省大量开销。但更重要的是，在香港限制建造和改造的特殊条款下，这些户型的形状和特征经过计算可以提供最大面积的室内空间。应该注意到这种与现有户型的相似性也是吸引很多参观者的原因之一，这些熟悉的空间使他们可以将其与自己的生活环境相联系，而其室内设计可以使他们想象自己居室的一个"更好"版本。因此参观样板间的激动人心之处在一定程度上与这种想象相关，这种想象力不仅在设计师、而且在每一个样板间参观者的心目中都占据了重要位置。

对于外人来讲，很难理解香港人对于这些样板间所传达的虚拟世界会有如此高的热情，因为组成这些样板间的家具和其他的建造细节毕竟是不随同住宅一起出售的。难怪房地产项目铺天盖地的广告和媒体中的"样板间热"使一些文化评论者总结道样板间是香港狂热消费主义的缩影，制造"更好"生活的梦境助燃了无尽的欲望。但是，尽管样板间作为形象传媒对于消费活动是重要的，但是这个过程却绝不是那么简单。首先，大多数的参观者，包括那些确实的购买者都或多或少地清楚他们所看到的是一种非现实的、理想的描绘，这种景象被建立起来是为了说服人们购买。另外，就像前文提到的，很多参观者并不买房，而是出于个人享受而来此观看设计空间的。这就反映了人们所消费的和开发商所出售的商品之间的矛盾，揭示了这当中复杂、多样的过程。这就使我们不禁发问，这些被设计出来的理想住宅对于香港人意味着什么，同时，作为一种消费活动，参观样板间又起到了什么样的作用？

室内设计在有些时候被认为是追求时尚的雕虫小技，很多关于消费的评论都认为它几乎仅仅被用来促使商品空间的形成。在香港样板间的案例中，开发商的目的是将商品房在尽量短的时间内卖出尽量高的价钱，从而产生最大的利润。作为"理想"居住的标志，这些设计空间可以被看作是关于物品的社会论述的成分，Baudrillard认为这种论述是处于消费核心的歧视和威望机制的一部分。事实上，在香港对于样板间和与室内设计相关的生活方式的宣扬几乎都以引发和强化潜在居住者的地位和身份为目的，他们所设想的"独一无二"与社会的其他部分形成了对比。那么人们就很清楚了，在香港，室内设计的含义在很大程度上被社会威望和成就所包裹。

尽管身份和地位也同时存在于香港以外的世界其他地方，尽管房产无疑是一件最能体现等级差别的"商品"（同时也是最贵的），但是，如果将室内设计等同于对于地位和特权的静态炫耀那就太简单了。设计在这种意义上就被缩减为开发商用于吸引顾客的"工具"，而顾客则被视为被动的主体，他们除了"买进"理想家园的图景而别无选择。正像Penelope Harvey所说的，消费并不是一种自上而下的策略，而是包含了消费者积极参与的动态过程。通过对de Certeau就日常生活的强调，Harvey指出，包含商品价值的消费活动同时也包含一个重估价值的过程，消费者不断从自己的角度对商品的意义和价值做出重新解释。换句话说，样板间的设计无论如何精心设计和布局，也永远不可能指引参观者以同一种"完美的"方式来看待。相反的，它们的意义总是不确定

的，取决于参观者以什么样的方式来进行体验。

如果留心一下样板间参观者的谈话，就不难发现尽管人们热情很高，但并不是所有的评价都是积极的。事实上，很多参观者对于他们所见到的极为挑剔。即使是对室内设计表示赞许，很多人也会说如果他们拥有这套住宅的话，会以独特的方式根据自己的喜好改变房间的布局和装潢。其实，这种体验的一部分快感可能就来源于对这些意见的表达。就这一点来讲，样板间不仅提供了一个想象理想家居的场所，同时也提供了一个人们交流所知所想的场所。

沿着这个思路，我们可以认为重新诠释带来了知识的积累，同时也带来了选择能力的潜在增长，而这些又会反过来影响产品的生产和销售。它同时也揭示了产品——在这里是样板间——总是存在于对话之中的。它们的价值不是固定的，而是受到消费者和生产者之间对话的不断影响。这就从一个侧面解释了为什么房地产开发商不得不积极地提出新的市场策略和新的设计以调动潜在购买者的热情，同一户型的反复出现是肯定是不能让消费者满意的。

在生产过程中意识到消费者的积极参与可以让我们以一种更加积极的方式来理解消费。但是，这并不意味着空间和物品的商品化就不存在问题了。事实上，那种崇尚原子论的市场关系和消费者选择不断扩大的消费至上的反话语是有误导作用的，因为它试图削弱生产者利润最大化的最终目的（通常没有考虑社会和环境影响），以及他们为了实现这一目标而不断进行的重组和调整。还应该指出的是，人们对于他们所消费物品的想象和解释仍然在很大程度上依赖于他们所能触及到的产品信息。在样板间的例子中，开发商无疑很清楚这些过程，它们不断努力提供更加奢侈新颖的室内设计，试图迎合其消费者的兴趣并引发更加强烈的购买此类梦想家园的愿望。

根据Harvey对于世博会参观者的调查，很清楚的一点是人们对于设计环境的评价在很大程度上取决于他们的个人背景。同时，室内设计和消费活动的意义在不同的地方也会有很大差别。这就意味着不能不考虑场所的特殊历史和文化环境细节而做出普遍性的结论。正如Tony Fry所指出的，在设计的产生与消费、教导和领会之间永远存在着一种互反关系——它不可避免地会以某些特殊的方式不断形成感知和期望。换句话说，设计空间不断"设计"人们对于设计的看法以及空间所包含的价值和意义。根据这一理解，我们不妨继续分析一些在香港联系设计、房地产市场以及消费活动的特征。

尽管香港人对于设计的兴趣不断飙升（这点可以从日常对话和流行媒体看出来），但具有讽刺意义的是，室内设计仍然被看作是一种肤浅的包装形式，它或多或少地被认为是"微不足道"的，而不能被归为那些可以"大文化"作贡献的更为严肃的学科之列。这种看法被香港那种认为室内设计是短时潮流的看法所加强。由于快速的人口增长和经济以及土地政策，不断出现更新和改进的推动力，因此香港的建成环境也变

成了暂时性的。不断的摧毁改造已经成为了生存之道，很少室内设计可以持续较长的时间。频繁的房地产投机市场也鼓励了人们的经常搬家。这同样强化了一种观点——室内设计只是临时性的风格，它将会很快过时并为新的不可认知的时尚版本所取代。对于一个有着强烈的从众心理的人群来说，这种一起喜新厌旧的风尚只能进一步强化那种室内设计是装扮性质的、转瞬即逝和可以随意处置的印象。

香港房地产市场的高价和经常性的投机行为在一定程度上归因于当地的政治经济，从而导致了有意限制住房土地占有量的政策，提高了居住的密度和房地产的价值。与香港给国际社会留下的"自由市场"的形象相反，房地产市场被分割成了两个主要部分：政府为大约一半人口提供廉价住房的公共部分，以及由少数大牌人物操纵的私有部分。这些开发商中的一些人同时也涉足其他行业，例如电信、后勤、零售等。他们强大的市场使其地位足以影响政治环境和指挥大规模的销售战以及设计趋势，从而塑造住宅的流行图景和含义。

居住在私人公寓里和居住在政府廉价住宅里人群之间的清晰社会分界对于评价住房设计的意义十分重要。从70年代到90年代中期的房地产热在公众意识中产生了一种通过住宅所有权连接上层灵活性和财富的"神话"。设计被看作是住宅投资的一部分，几乎是完全与私有部分相联系的，因此也包含在对未来的美好憧憬里。Cheng的研究显示，购置住房通常被认为是成家立业的标志，是向更高生活质量迈进的一步。换句话说，一座经过设计的住宅意味着梦想的实现——它可以在很大程度上改善住房拥有者的生活方式和社会地位。

香港房地产市场的特性、政府的政策以及室内设计的角色显然为包含殖民历史、经济转轨和与大陆关系等在内的香港的政治、文化环境更增加了复杂性。不过这篇文章主要讲述的是设计和消费活动的辩证进程，以及它们是如何被当地的政治经济和社会文化环境所塑造的。样板间不仅展示了居住的理想模式，同时它们自己也是真实的空间，人们在当中参与互动并根据想象力来建造自己的家。样板间的多重意义被组合了起来，始终贯穿于广阔的社会和其他价值体系中。参观样板间因此可以被看作是超越"某一"住宅的一种社会仪式。当人们以家庭出游的形式来参与这一仪式的时候，对于现有的社会意义实现了重新配置，并产生了新的意义。这种解说的开放性意味着人们不必"买入"展示的商品。但是从整体的意义上讲，他们确实趋向于"买入"由大的社会环境所塑造的价值和理想。

与住宅相关的消费活动因此在一定程度上既是样板间设计的产物，也是它的决定者。但是在观察室内设计的当前角色和意义时，重要的是意识到所谓的"香港文脉"并不是单一固定的实体，而是动态的和不断变化的，它由物理空间组成，人们在其中不断重新解释和再造意义，是一种在参与的同时施以引导的活动。室内设计可以被看作是个人和群体建造的一个梦境。

每一个住宅、每一次设计都是通往未知未来的脚步。设计作为一种建立意义和新联系的活动在这个过程中坚决地、衍生地、不可避免地扮演着重要角色。

货摊城市

货摊是什么?一个小亭子,一个小铺子,一个小房子……,一个狭小的深绿色结构,一些从水泥上伸出的钢栅栏,一块作为平台的木板。一种不知名的地方形式,一种介于建筑和家具之间的权宜建造物——据一份最近官方的调查大约有10000个。它们通常成群结队,形成一条平行于传统商店的货摊链。他们是政府在上个世纪初的时候设立的,为的是扩大商业活动的范围和空间。在1970年代,50000多个有营业执照和无照的小贩为香港的街道带来了一种独一无二的特色。

无论是政府规定的简易金属结构货亭还是店主自己和木工建造的铺子,造价大约都在7000到10000港币之间。尽管它们轻质、廉价、并且暴露在恶劣的环境之下,但却能轻而易举地维持20年以上。每个部位尽管简单却十分坚固,足以抵抗台风季节的侵袭。货亭可以向帆船一样被驾驭,它可以实现自然通风,下暴雨的时候,店主可以在屋顶的边缘挂上塑料帘子,而木材或是金属板可以形成一把大伞,在夏季屏蔽日光,保证室内凉爽。

店主每天都要花上20到30分钟的时间来开启/关闭他的货亭。良好的封闭性可以保证至少安全。店主往往居住在周围社区中,而他的大部分主顾也是社区中的居民。最近政府正在采取一项清理货亭的行动,大部分货亭都在这次清查中消失,以为开发商和"亚洲世界城市"的美化腾出地方。

调查、采访和测绘图分别由Laurent Gutierrez和Valerie Portefaix与两组学生在2003年进行:
香港技术大学,设计学院一年级学生:
Chau Sau Man, Cheung Hoi Mei, Yeung Lai Sheung, Chan Tsz Wai, Chan Hei Chelsea, Gigi, Kash, Hazel, Jackie, Shun,
香港大学,建筑学院一年级学生:
Chan Kin Cheong, Chan Wing Pui, Cheung Sze Wai, Lau Ying, Leung Lok Kei, Li Ka Man, Mok Wai Ming, Mung Kit Man, Sin Chi Kei, Tse King Tong, Yu Hoi Ting.

光的城市

我们起初以为这一小撮人是拍电影的,他们在丛林中通过计算机和照相机工作,精力充沛地跑前跑后。只有在电影和电视里才能创造出这种气氛,这种不断置于磷粉闪光灯和运动之中的环境。但是一个月以后,他们还在那里,很显然,一些其它事情正在发生着。

香港以具备对新的要求做出反应,从而发展出新行业的能力而著称。这就是其中一个,它开始于来自内地游客所引发的旅游热,并处在一个具有战略意义的地点——一个能够观看到香港天际线的公共厕所。每天从晚上6点到9点,都不断有从山顶驶下的旅游巴士在Stubbs大街这里停靠10分钟左右,最后欣赏一眼"光的城市"。

这里是服务于成千上万游客的公共空间,是一个值得带回家展示给朋友的美丽瞬间,也是6组摄影师赚钱的好机会:他们每晚可以拍摄平均250张照片,每张20港币,大概5000港币就在4个主要角色——"推销者"、"摄影师"、"打印人"和"跑腿人"之间分红。

他们的工作非常简单。"推销者"缠住从巴士里走出的游客并把他们带到观景地点,"摄影师"则等着把一瞬间的景观定格。"我到过这里!"将是游客们在家乡的欢呼。最先进的数码相机和一个小的液晶显示器可以让游客当时就看到效果。付钱以后,"跑腿人"将数据卡拿到100米外的丛林中,这个"基地"装配着一两台强大的笔记本电脑和两到三台彩色打印机,以及包括打印纸和塑膜等在内的用品。照片打印封存好以后,"跑腿人"再跑回景点在大约10000个大陆游客之中找到自己的客户并把照片交给他。

Kathy, Lo Pui-ying

楼上店铺:反抗世俗

Lau sheung pou在香港的历史可以追溯到1970年代。它们通常做的是家庭生意,商店的空间由二层以上的住宅单元改造而来,一部分被用于家庭成员的居住。按照传统,它们所经营的大部分生意是理发店、算命铺子和中草药店。在1990年代,一批新的楼上商店开始出现。由于楼上店面空间的房租要比大商场或是其他临街店面便宜得多,很多年轻人从楼上店铺做起,开始自己经营零售业和服务业的第一步尝试。

这些楼上店铺主要集中在铜锣湾、尖沙咀、湾仔和中环等商业区。新的楼上店铺通常出售在别处很难找到的稀有物品并提供新颖的服务。很多楼上店铺正是通过这些特殊的卖点来吸引顾客。楼上店铺还有一种将零售与餐饮结合起来的趋势,现在,越来越多的楼上店铺也同时提供咖啡。年轻人和十来岁的学生是这些店铺的主要顾客。

通过在楼上店铺消费,当地的年轻人积极地建造自己的特色,以与别人发生联系或和另一些人相区分。根据Chi-wai Cheung的看法,香港年轻一代所体现出的反抗本质就是有个性、不随众和消费主义。(Cheung, 2002, p.562)尽管还算不上激进,但是年轻人在和楼上店铺相关的消费活动中体现了他们反抗世俗的不同方式。

"购物已经成为了我们创造价值的首要策略...购物定义了作为个人的我们。"
- Sharon Zukin, Point of Purchase, 2004, p.8

在这个消费者的社会里,人们不仅消费日常生活用品的使用价值,更重要的是消费它们作为社会等级标志的符号价值。正如Jean Baudrillard所说的,一件商品"消费的从来不是它的物质性,而是他的差别性"。(Baudrillard, 1988, p.22)在楼上店铺里消费的通常是那些不满足于大型市场里的主流选择,而希望购买到不同和特殊商品的人。

稀有的物品除了款式上的独一无二以外也会产生附加价值。Georg Simmel关于商品价值的论述生动描绘了存在于楼上店铺消费者和稀有商品之间的这种紧张状态,他写道,"获取的艰难和在交换中做出的牺牲都是价值的独特组成元素,稀有性只是外在的表现,是数量形式物化表现。"(quoted in Appadurai, 1986, p.4)

"冒险,就它的特殊本质和魅力来说是一种体验的形式。体验的内容并不构成冒险。只有通过设想实现目标的某种体验紧张状态时,冒险才被形成。"
- Georg Simmel, On Individuality and Social Forms, 1971, p.97

没有人可以否认逛商场是香港人生活的组成部分之一。在Tai-lok Lui看来,"商场文化"自从35年前"香港市场化"起就在不断发展。今天,香港人对于购物的体验在很大程度上被巨型商业中心所塑造。商场不仅成为了家庭在周末和假日外出的主要目的地,同时也成为了人们东张西望打发时间的场所。

事实上,这是因为商场如此紧密地与香港人的生活相结合,以至于它们已经成为了日常生活中的惯例性场所。因此,年轻一代反而不认为商场有什么意思。那些标新立异的年轻人开始转向其他地方来满足自己的消费需要。当他们前往那些定位在年轻人的商业中心时(例如铜锣湾的巴特利购物中心),把光顾楼上店铺作为一种冒险。"我觉得商场里人太多而且没有意思。都是同样的商家和同样的品牌,感觉差不多",26岁的Jessie Chung说到"如果有时间的话,我宁愿到楼上店铺去买一些特别的东西,或是在那里喝咖啡。"

Jessie最喜欢的楼上店铺是位于铜锣湾的猫店。这是一家装饰成复古风格、结合咖啡和零售的商店。这里有丰富的商品,包括本地设计的服装、佩饰、礼品甚至是古董家具。在以猫为主题的咖啡馆里养着15只小猫,还会有不定期的音乐表演。Jessie是一年以前第一次来到这家商店的,当时只是为了逗逗这里的猫,同时品尝一下此处的招牌菜——"喵喵吐司"(用巧克力酱在吐司上面做成猫脸的形状)。Jessie说"它和一般的商店或是咖啡厅十分不同"。当被问及有什么不同时,Jessie解释说,"室内设计、音乐、猫、商品……我觉得这里就是所有这些的组合。我很高兴能找到这么一个特别的商店。"从此以后,Jessie就形成了光顾楼上商店和咖啡店的习惯,希望能不时发现特殊的商品和服务项目。

Turo-Kimmo Lehtonen和Pasi Maenpaa关于购物者有像旅行者一样心态的论述最好地描绘了像Jessie这样"楼上店铺冒险者"的心理。他们写道,"令人着魔的……是对于新的和不可预知事物的不期而遇,以及那种'身处异处'的体验……购物者对于开放性十分警觉和适应,他们总是期待能遇到新鲜的东西。这种期待就好像在玩随机游戏,希望有所发生。"(Lehtonen and Maenpaa, 1997, p.146, p.159)

光顾楼上店铺有时侯会有一种撞运气和发现的元素——这很像"寻宝"的过程。在更大的范围上来讲,其中的乐趣来自于发现意料之外的有价值的商品。Turo-Kimmo Lehtonen和Pasi Maenpaa关于依赖于运气的购物"偶然性游戏"描述了这些"寻宝者"所感受到的快乐。他们的兴奋来自于可能偶然遇到称心商品的期待所带来的愉悦。当他们遇到曾经期待或可望的事物时就会激动不已,尽管他们在之以前对于这个事物只有很模糊的意向。(Lehtonen and Maenpaa, 1997, p.158)

27岁的Anthony Yeung有逛楼上玩具商店的习惯。作为一个玩具日本机器人的收集者,他是玩具地带——一座地处铜锣湾的2500平方英尺的楼上二手货玩具商店——的常客。"我每个月都去那里,经常一逛就是两个多小时。我花时间仔细查找商品,就好像在寻宝。"店主Raymond Wong深谙消费者心理,故意将店中的商品散乱地放置。他说,"我故意将玩具摆放的乱七八糟,这样顾客在挑选自己喜爱的玩具时就能从中感受到'寻宝'的乐趣。"

顾客之所以感到兴奋有趣是在有特殊风格的不同寻常环境中探寻和偶然发现有价值商品的结果,楼上店铺为都市中的冒险提供了不少好去处。这种冒险的本质更多的在于其方式而非结果,消费者们津津乐道的是发现的过程。冒险的核心在于找寻的实验价值和与心仪物品的不期而遇。

"古希腊的时候有人知道通往地下世界的暗道。我们的现实生活在某些隐藏的地方也能通往地下世界——一个不为人所知的梦想升起的地方。我们每天都浑然不觉地从它们旁边经过。"
Walter Benjamin, The Arcades Project, 1999, p.875

在香港,高密度的人口为零售和服务业的需求带来了压力。除了最大限度地利用店面空间,零售商店和餐馆还不得不采取措施来加速客流。例如匆忙地完成与尽量多的顾客的交易,零售商店的销售人员对顾客应接不暇甚至是忽视的情况常有发生。在一些情况下,餐馆为了尽快腾出桌子要求顾客提前结账,这经常在顾客中导致紧张情绪和不愉快的摩擦。

与这些状况相反,楼上店铺总是精心设计以使顾客能停留尽量长的时间。很多店都配备有咖啡座。在顾客看来,空间也是同样重要的消费元素,他们十分珍视楼上店铺随意放松的环境。与普通的商店和咖啡店相比,这些楼上咖啡店别出心裁的装饰会使顾客有置身异域的感觉。楼上咖啡店被看作是商店和家庭之间的交叉地带。沙发和靠垫成为了楼上店铺"语汇"的一部分。由于它们是代表放松和舒适的符号,因此成为了营造舒适温暖居家感觉的必不可少的小道具。

媒体经常形容楼上店铺为年轻人的Dau(广东俚语,意指"隐匿处"或更准确的说是"秘密的聚会地点")。由于坐落在底层上方,这些店铺很难被过路人发现。与拥挤和喧嚣的酒吧和咖啡厅相比,楼上店铺是年轻人聚会闲聊更好的选择(在开销比较经济的地点中)。它们同时也适于让购物者从拥挤的街道中得到一些喘息和逗留的机会。顾客们经常是完全融入到放松的环境中,浑然不知时间的流逝,不知不觉中在楼上店铺度过了整个下午的时光。

尽管楼上店铺是营业场所,但对于很多顾客来讲,它们也扮演了临时避难所的角色,可以帮助放松和以往外界部愉快的现实。"别处"是相对于熟悉的地点被定义的。(Hebdige, 1979, p.79)年轻人通过在楼上店铺中游荡对现实世界中的实际问题予以一种消极的反抗。楼上店铺作为"别处",可以让年轻人暂时躲避熟悉的工作和学习环境中的责任和问题。猫店的店主Yan-yan Hui想到了将零售、咖啡、宠物和地下音乐

在楼上店铺空间中结合起来的点子。谈到开这家店的最初想法,她说到,"古董、猫和礼品是我的最爱。我还喜欢喝酒和听地下音乐。我希望能结合所有这些我最喜欢的东西,开一家跳蚤市场一样的商店。这就是我为什么将自己的商店做成混合型的。"猫店是8年前她仅22岁的时候开设的。她出奇的想法获得了难以预料的成功。由于顾客的需求越来越大,Yan-yan不得不两度搬家来满足不断增长的顾客需要。

Ellie Tsui是一个23岁的秘书,她每个月喜欢与朋友在乡村猫咖啡店打发两三个晚上的时光,这是一间位于铜锣湾出售手工饰品和猫主题咖啡的楼上店铺。Ellie就在附近工作,她有时到那里去吃午饭。她很欣赏那里的食物、安静的气氛、乡村风格的室内设计和音乐。"整个商店就好像是在一个完全不同的世界里,每次当我踏入其中时,就会暂时忘记自己的烦恼,"Ellie说,"事实上当我上楼的时候,我能够意识到自己正在进入一个完全不同的地方。"

对于楼上商铺的光顾者而言,上楼的过程可以被解释为一种跨越世俗和幻境的仪式,它将人们从日常生活地点的熟稔转移到"别处"的生疏。这个过程同时也是建立"寻宝"概念的实验元素的一部分。通往楼上店铺的楼梯通常被加以布置以调动顾客的情绪。这就可以解释为什么时尚商店楼梯两侧的墙面上会经常出现雕刻图案。

楼上店铺之所以吸引年轻人是因为它们是出售梦想的地方。这些梦想通过在楼上店铺消费商品和服务以两种方式体现出来。

首先,由于楼上店铺的生存依赖于特殊的卖点,因此他们所提供的商品和服务通常在主流市场提供的商品和消费者不能满足的意愿之间。换句话说,他们暂时地满足了消费者未能实现的愿望。这也是楼上宠物咖啡盛行的主要原因之一。那些由于住房限制或是父母反对而不能饲养宠物的年轻人通过光顾楼上宠物咖啡店获得了很多的乐趣。

Ada Lo是一个20岁的大学生,她是尖沙咀一家狗主题咖啡和用品商店——好狗——的常客。她希望能在家里养狗,但是遭到了父母的反对。在发现这家楼上咖啡店以前,她只能通过宠物店的橱窗瞥一眼小狗并想象和它们玩耍。现在,她几乎每个星期都要去好狗与邻居家的小狗玩耍。除了对每只狗的名字和习性了如指掌,她与那里的店主也成了朋友,他们交谈很多关于训练和饲养小狗窍门的话题。有时她路过的时候也要停下来看看店主和他的小狗们在干什么。

Candy Wu也是一个20岁的大学生,她一直梦想能有自己的房间。但是因为她与父母和两个姐妹住在仅有380平方英尺的公房里,这个梦想变得遥不可及。"我希望有自己的房间是因为我觉得自己已经长大了,我需要一些隐私," Candy说,"如果我有自己的房间的话,我要把它装饰成复古风格的,里面放满五颜六色的家具。"半年前,她开始养成了逛古风咖啡的习惯,这家楼上咖啡屋同时也出售复古家居装饰。"我之所以

喜欢这家商店是因为他们把商店装扮得就像我梦想中的房间。"在闲暇之余,Candy总是独自或和朋友一起来这家咖啡店。她说"这比好在拥挤的家里好多了。"尽管看上去Candy并不会很快拥有自己的房间,但她已经买了这家店里一幅珠子门帘以为将来做准备。

Ada和Candy的例子都揭示出当年轻人在反抗现实中超出其控制能力的失意之处时,常常通过消费来寻找替代品。这是一种拒绝完全向现实投降的方式。这些年轻人对楼上店铺的钟爱通过在一定程度上实现了他们的梦想而形成了一座连接现实和理想的桥梁。

Joey Wong是中环一家出售时尚手工灯具的楼上店铺——Wow因素——的店主和设计师。在开店以前,Joey曾经是舞台灯光设计师。她相信通过营造室内空间的气氛,灯光具有影响人们情绪的魔力。为了使更多的人体验到这种魔力并拥有更广阔的设计自由,她辞掉自己的工作开设了Wow因素。店里出售的每一件物品都是由她本人设计和手工制作的。她十分善于用不同颜色、材料和大小的珠子来做灯。产品包括各种各样的用塑料、玻璃或是水晶珠子做成的灯具和帘子。与制作现成的灯具不同,Joey更喜欢根据顾客的要求量身定做独一无二的装饰灯具。由于Wow因素店里只有Joey一个人,她要承受十分繁重的工作。但她根本不在乎,因为分享她创造性灯具的快乐要比闲暇时光和金钱收入更加重要。

云9是Anthia Lee和Iris Chan开设的一家创意照相馆。他们为自己设定的目标是创造"一种新的结婚照文化"。"可以在任何时间、任何地点、以任何方式、和任何人拍摄结婚照,谁说你必须在结婚之前拍结婚照?" Anthia和Iris认为结婚照应该是个人的、艺术的和时髦的。由于每一个顾客都有不同的个性和不同的故事,他们的任务就是通过创意性的照片来反映独特的风格。他们运用不同的元素来使每个顾客的照片体现个性。手绘插图、刺绣图案和有趣的小道具只是他们众多诀窍中的几个。

Rene Chen

从See-fong Choi到香港新的消费观念及其他……

本文试图阐述在香港突然兴起的"See-fong Choi"(私人楼上餐厅)及其与新的消费观念的联系。通过间接的手段,作者观察、记录和解释了为什么"See-fong Choi"现象可以被用作研究香港中层到高层社会消费新"需求"的指示器。文中的大部分资料和数据收集于当地的报纸和杂志。本文将通篇使用"See-fong Choi"的中文发音,且单复数拼写相同。

中国人相信良好的关系是围绕着餐桌建立起来的。因此和家人、朋友和同事一起吃饭在中国文化中是十分重要的事情。

中国人认为如果要了解经济状况的好坏,只要看看人们吃饭的方式就行了。如果经济状况好,消费能力就强,人们就愿意把钱花在食物上面。换句话说,饮食文化可以反映和预测任何对与社会的经济变化。

中国人还认为饮食文化反映了一个社会的整体文化。

在1922年左右,香港的餐厅开始把"演唱"作为餐饮服务的一部分。由于当时的人们只有很少的娱乐项目可供选择,因此"唱歌吃饭"就变得十分流行,直到1950年代。

"大排挡"(街道上的露天食摊)在1960年代是大多数香港人的"饮食广场",不仅因为那里的食物便宜,还因为在当时大多数人的收入都很少,生活质量普遍很低。

"See-fong Choi"
"私人楼上餐厅"
"特色家宴"

起源
关于"See-fong Choi"的起源有很多解释。其一是说在20世纪早期到20世纪中叶,在香港较为富裕的华人社区里,满足各种形式私人聚会的私人俱乐部十分流行。这些私人俱乐部由一群朋友建立,并成为他们私人聚会的固定场所。

这一群朋友或会员有着相似的爱好,私人俱乐部成了他们打麻将、抽烟喝酒和吃饭等活动的地方。这里都雇有私人厨师来打理俱乐部的厨房,可见"吃"对于这些私人俱乐部成员的重要性。这种"私人俱乐部"的想法可能就是现代"See-fong Choi"的前身。

背景
香港最早的一家较为知名的"See-fong Choi"是由艺术家Wang Hai 和他的妻子、艺术评论家Lau

Kin Wai在1998年开设的。Wang的妻子的厨艺在他们的朋友圈子里是有口皆碑的。Lau曾经是一家酒吧的老板,他最先打起了把Wang的妻子的手艺商业化的主意,并把在自己酒吧里喝完酒的客人带到Wang的"餐馆"里吃饭。(与一般餐馆不同,"See-fong Choi"是在人们的家里就餐,有时可能并没有营业执照。因此"See-fong Choi"不能被归入餐馆之列。)这个讯息在朋友中快速传递,并很快传到了媒体的耳朵里。从此,"See-fong Choi"就变得越来越流行,越来越多的人开始从事这一行业。"See-fong Choi"的很多店主都是艺术家和设计师,他们利用自己的"餐厅"同时作为展示个人作品的画廊。Wang的妻子甚至还会在席间在客人面前唱歌助兴。1998年以后"See-fong Choi"的突然兴起可能也是当时香港经济危机造成的结果。很多"See-fong Choi"都是由那些失业的大厨们开设的,这对于他们来说可能是一条生路。直到今天,"See-fong Choi"不仅拥有众说纷纭的起源,同时也是一种边缘"产业",是营业执照可有可无的商业性"私人聚餐"。

尽管预订一桌晚宴可能需要等上长达一个月的时间,而且价格不菲,通常是每人250到400港币,但还是有很多"See-fong Choi"生意兴隆。"See-fong Choi"的数量不断攀升,并吸引着越来越多的新的客人。

大多数的"See-fong Choi"坐落在中环和上环。(湾仔和铜锣湾最近也成为"See-fong Choi"的流行地带)在20世纪初期,比较知名的餐馆主要集中在中环和上环。因此这两处以美食著称。还有一个重要的因素是兰桂坊——香港都市化消费的标志——就坐落在中环的核心。上环附近沿着Staunton和Elgin的SOHO地区在这些年也成为了第二个兰桂坊。来自于世界各个角落的很多独特和新颖的烹饪聚集在兰桂坊和SOHO地区。作为一种新的饮食风格,"See-fong Choi"当然有足够的理由选择这两个地方落脚。

"See-fong Choi"用的是"家庭/私人秘方"。因此这里的食物本身就自成一体。由于"See-fong Choi"是一种"家庭产业",因此它没有一般饭店那种"菜谱"。相反,"今夜菜"根据市场上新鲜时菜的种类不断发生着变化。除了知道他们将要品尝到特殊的烹饪,客人对具体的菜谱一无所知,也没有任何选择的余地,因为这全取决于厨师根据市场上最好质料的判断来决定。但这反而为消费者带来了一种神秘感,期盼的感觉使"See-fong Choi"变得更加神秘和诱人。

大多数的"See-fong Choi"是中国北方菜,例如四川菜和上海菜。("融合"的食物以及越南菜、意大利菜、印度菜和日本菜等也变得越来越流行)香港人一直觉得中国北方菜异域风味十足,并且要比广东菜"高一个档次"。原因之一可能要追溯到20世纪早期,那时香港的饮食文化十分保守。由于大多数香港人都曾经是来自于广州的广东人,因此饭馆以广东风味为主。广东菜很讲实际,只注重食物的口感。直到1949年新中国成立,很多上海人南迁并定居在香港,才使香港的饮

食文化发生了改变。上海菜与广东菜形成鲜明对比,除了食物的口感,它更重视菜肴细节的体现以及就餐环境。从此以后,香港本地人也开始追求食物自身以外的就餐质量。

"See-fong Choi",私人楼上餐厅,从字面上讲就是在家里的"餐馆"。"See-fong Choi"的室内设计就好像是现代的家居设计。与香港典型的中餐馆那种装饰无度、灯光耀眼、桌子挤在一起的室内状况不同,"See-fong Choi"为顾客提供了一种更加放松、私密、舒适和有家般温暖感觉的就餐环境

"See-fong Choi"每晚只开两桌宴席。限于就餐环境的面积,每桌宴席只能容纳少量的顾客。与大的餐馆相比,主人和顾客之间的关系在"See-fong Choi"里要更加紧密和亲切。主人同时也是侍者和厨师,会亲自逐一照料每一桌宾客。厨师会在席间与客人面对面的交谈。顾客就好像是厨师的朋友在被对待。两者的关系在"See-fong Choi"里要比在以大多数大规模餐厅里深厚的多。

1970年代标志着香港受美国文化影响所进入的"快餐和自助"饮食文化阶段。Coral咖啡、麦当劳和肯德基在那时十分流行。(这种饮食文化直到今天也十分流行)。同时,Cha-chan tang(港式西餐厅)也在70年代开始流行。

香港人的生活质量在1980年代大幅度提高,消费能力不断增强。很多人第一次有了"有钱"的感觉。中式海鲜馆变得流行,吃海鲜成了一种"富裕"的标志。"喧嚣的"和"宽敞的"就餐环境被那时的人看作是豪华和奢侈。

中环的兰桂坊和上环的SOHO有着与众不同的特性,那里聚集着穿着入时、饮食考究、品位高雅、多是中产阶级以上的雅皮士、艺术家和电影明星。这两个街区自己成为了一个独特的社区。任何在这个"社区"内的任何一家商店或是餐厅消费的人都会被看作是这个特殊社会阶层中的一员。

由于大多数的"See-fong Choi"位于这两个"雅皮士"街区,人们很容易找到地点、"See-fong Choi"和中产阶级以上的目标消费者之间的联系。这些"See-fong Choi"的常客——香港的中上层人士——是高消费的一族。他们乐于为高质量的产品花钱,但是当买下食物同时也意味着买下社会地位和进入特殊群体的入场券时,社会地位和进入这个圈子就变得更加值钱了。香港人对与社会地位的差异十分敏感。如果去"See-fong Choi"在别人看来是"高级"的标志,那么食物本身就很容易的成为了社会等级的副产品。

"See-fong Choi"的菜谱之所以独一无二是因为它们是"秘方"。独一无二的概念对于消费者来说很有吸引力。他们认为吃了独一无二的饮食,自己也就变得与众不同了。"与众不同"是人们趋之若鹜的东西,使他们感觉到价值,从而证明了自己的存在。这里的食物于是再一次成为了"独一无二"的心理因素的副产品。

"See-fong Choi"不提供菜谱,有限的选择意味着更少的余地。人们喜爱这种"有限",因为在今天,选择越少就意味着价值越高。这就好像G2000大众服装大量的选择余地与Prada或是Gucci等名牌服装有限的选择形成的对比。在过去,多意味着价值,自助餐厅是高级的。但是这种概念正在过时,取而代之的是选择越少就越值钱的理论。少的选择面可以被联系为独一无二的概念,独一无二为产品增加了价值。因此又一次证明了"See-fong Choi"的客人们并没有太在意食物,而是从中提炼出的附加价值——独一无二的价值。

"See-fong Choi"的顾客同时购买的是他们提供的原始价值。"See-fong Choi"强调家庭烹饪,这就意味着天然的配方和原创的烹饪技巧。当人们意识到健康饮食的概念时,家庭烹饪就成为了他们的选择。去"See-fong Choi"吃饭就意味着追求原始,因为那里的食物都是家庭制作的。家庭烹饪是最"回归本色"的饮食体验。因此,去"See-fong Choi"可以被等同为购买一种"回归本色"的体验。

需要领会的重要一点是这种个性化以及对于地位和社会等级的追求都是以符号为基础的。也就是说,它们并不是基于事物或商品本身,而是基于差别性。只有以这种方式我们才能理解"潜在消费"或"隐藏消费"这种矛盾对立观点。例如,声望的高度区别性不再体现为风头主义,而是体现为一种判断力、清晰性和自我谦逊。但这只是体现了一种更高程度的奢侈、一种风头主义的附加元素,它走向了自己的反面并因此产生了一种更为微妙的差异。

在过去的几年中,"生活风格"的概念一直是通过不同的渠道施加给人们的。像Ikea、G.O.D.和MUJI这样的商店和很多室内设计杂志就是推广和销售这些"生活风格"的一些渠道。这些媒体试图传达的"完美的生活方式"依赖于创造温暖舒适家庭环境的概念。任何有"家的感觉"的环境都被设计成时尚的、现代的和有品位的。甚至连办公室和商店也把这种"居家感觉"的设计风格带到自己的室内设计和家具装饰上来。"See-fong Choi"一切尽是"家居风格"的实质恰好完全符合这种"生活风格"。因此,去"See-fong Choi"的人可以同时体验到自己身处高雅品位和质量的生活方式之中。当大多数香港人由于家庭空间有限而不能轻易实现这种"生活风格"的时候,"See-fong Choi"让他们可以付钱借用到这种"生活风格"的体验。

典型中餐馆的服务方式通常是冷漠的和疏远的。"See-fong Choi"打破了这一惯例。在就餐的几个小时里,主人和顾客的关系就像朋友那样亲密和友好。这种亲密不仅可以为顾客带来受到尊崇和优待的感觉,更重要的是,可以带来私人接触的感觉。再一次的,"See-fong Choi"的顾客买下的不仅是食物,同时也买下了几个小时的人际关系。

工业化经济的重点是批量生产。批量生产之下的产品是毫无特色的同一模型的拷贝。就好像在香港建造的大多数千篇一律的大型房地产项目一样。很多典型的中餐馆的运作方式与这种批量生产的概念近似。顾客很难区分A餐厅和B餐厅在风味、菜谱甚至是室内装修上的差别。今天的消费者,尤其是那些中产阶级以上的消费者,已经厌倦了批量生产的"拷贝"。他们需要像"See-fong Choi"这样量身定做的产品。他们需要的产品和服务可以满足他们"与众不同"的愿望,可以将他们与社会上的其他人区分开来。他们渴望商品能给他们带来的独一无二的特性,因此通过购买商品,他们感觉到自己也变得独一无二了。他们相信独一无二使他们变得特别和稀有,而这使他们感觉到了声望和"高级"。

例如,当中产阶级不断挥霍无度的时候,那些精英们可能只是进行一些不引人注意的新的形式的消费活动,并以此来建立他们与社会中其他人之间新的、更加微妙的差别。

Baudrillard, Jean. The Consumer Society. Sage Publications Ltd., 1998, p.6.

消费者开始认同你们公司的产品或者服务,并将其结合入个人意识当中。这变成了他与世界相区分的途径之一。

Rifkin, Jeremy. The Age of Access. Penguin Putnam Inc., 2001, p.109.

就像世界上的其他大城市一样,香港同样经历着信息科技的爆炸。高科技随处可见。尽管高科技使生活在很多方面变得更加便利,但它绝对是一件人工"产品",冷酷而没有人情味。当人们被暴露在过多的人为体验中时,他们就会转回头去寻找最基本的事物。这也就是为什么今天的很多消费者都追求自然、原始、手工和家庭制作(就像"See-fong Choi")的商品。今天的消费者更加赞赏和珍视产品背后的原创性和创造性。

香港是一座速度的城市。人们永远都匆匆忙忙,生活节奏十分紧张。在经历了太多的紧张以后,人们会丧失自己的敏感。人际关系变得冷漠而疏远。从"See-fong Choi"现象,我们可以看到一种亲近的人际关系有很大的"需求量"。消费者希望得到的不止于商品和服务本身。他们希望得到商品之上的个人接触和人际关系。即使人际关系是在像"See-fong Choi"这种地方"买"到的,人们也乐于为这种体验花钱。

超越所有其他因素,到达的时代是由人类体验的不断商品化而被定义的……

物品和服务的商品化已经变得次于人际关系的商品化。

Rifkin, Jeremy. The Age of Access. Penguin Putnam Inc., 2001, p.97.

消费观念的变化在香港的中上阶层人群中尤为明显。顾客在消费时有更多的需求需要被满足。人们购买的已经不仅是物品和服务,例如"See-fong Choi"的菜肴。事实上,商品和服务已经变得次于随之而来的符号价值和人际敏感性。这些符号价值是那些能为顾客带来"回归自然"、特殊的生活风格和"我与众不同"等概念的潜在信息。人际敏感性则是可以建立于商品和服务之上的人际关系,例如在"See-fong Choi"中主人和顾客的友谊。

香港的经济正在面临着一段变幻无常的时期。了解香港人的消费概念对于了解香港的经济是十分重要的。由于香港中上阶层是具有消费能力的主要群体,因此其消费概念可以被用作未来香港消费模式的指示器。我认为"小群体"和"小生意"将成为香港接下来的消费模式。形成小的群体可以使这部分人满足区别于社会其他人群、追求属于特定人群商品的愿望。在特定群体中,"成员们"可以建立人际关系和分享共同的爱好、知识和他们的"社会名望"。为了满足这些"小群体"的需要,"小生意"具有重视个人的特点和原创性的概念。因此,大的连锁商店和批量生产的操作方式将逐渐让位于为"小群体"量身定做的"小生意"。事实上,它的结果将十分接近关于"See-fong Choi"起源的解释之一,将成为供私人聚会的私人俱乐部。

香港是东西方文化的融汇之地。传统的中国文化十分注重家庭和朋友之间的"爱"和分享。这种"爱"同时也意味着存在与家人和朋友之间的人际关系。西方文化强调个人主义和私人生活。(根据一些学者的看法,隐私的概念出现于19世纪的英国,它与当时"中产阶级"文化的建立有直接的联系。)这种存在于中西方文化中对于"人际关系"解释的显著差异可能会在香港人当中造成困惑。一方面,香港人追求"个人主义"的理想,另一方面,他们又有中国情结,不能抗拒对和谐人际关系的渴望。怎样才能最好地满足这两种对立的文化价值观呢?也许就是"小群体"的概念——它的内向性使它既可以培养人际关系,同时也可以延续对"个人主义"的追求……

Gutierrez + Portefaix / Laurent Malone

高速公路下

穿行于高层建筑之间的高速交通体现了一种香港所独有的动态性。在这些蜿蜒的水泥长龙上以70公里/小时的速度行驶,眼前呈现出一个国际化都市,高效和连通创造出了一种迷一样的中介空间,几乎没有任何私密性可言。冲突是香港文化中的重要元素,它包含着一种断裂、一个外来元素入侵和破坏都市肌理的瞬间。但是高速公路之下正在发生着什么?

《之下》泛指那些不愿被暴露的区域,它们同时也体现了不同于暴露空间的精神世界的特性。无论是在床下、桌子下、中环香港和上海银行的中庭下还是在高速公路下,《之下》在香港是可以支配的宝贵空间。它们有多种形式,被用作逃避上部高速城市严酷环境的庇护所、游乐场和栖身之处。

Neil Leach

拖曳空间

"我们都正在被拖曳"-Ackbar Abbas.

香港是空间配置的精髓之地。城市肌理的缝隙以一种极高的强度被利用和再利用。形形色色的货摊在一夜间出现,蜷富在城市被遗忘空间的角落里,但又以同样的速度在一夜间消失得无影无踪。室内空间——住宅——甚至是在公共领域的边缘上被建造的。街道成为了庆典和事件发生的场所。这些空间——大多数是通过性的——只拥有短时的身份,它们的特性根据其被配置的方式而发生着改变。

每个星期天,菲律宾工人聚集在中环的人行道上、香港上海银行的大楼下,铜锣湾的维多利亚公园和很多其他公共空间和街道上。他们在这里安营扎寨一整天,进行着各式各样的"私密"的活动,比如理发、交换信息、修剪指甲和聚餐。对于他们中的大多数人来说,这是一个放松休闲的好机会。他们不喜欢那些专门进行这些活动的私密空间,而单单青睐公共场所。

在其他地方,小商小贩在能够找到的空地上设立违规的露天咖啡店——或者用当地人说法"糖水店",向打工仔、清洁工和大陆行出售食物。同时房地产经纪人虏去了沿街的边线空间——通常不超过50厘米的进深——作为他们的店面。他们的全部工作展示在墙上,多则不过一桌、一椅、一台笔记本和一部手机,这些经纪人遍布了整个街道,将街道变成了一个权宜之下的办公室。更大一些的空间被租赁给短期的商户,他们与更为长久一些的房主之间维持着短期的合约。这些空间通常被用来出售来自大陆的便宜商品——主要是塑料厨具等烹饪器具,它们被包在纸盒子里,外面用手写的商标来标记。尽管有时前一个房客使用的室内装饰会被揭除,但是这些临时性的商铺就像是一个易装癖者,总是通过遗留下的标记和装饰隐隐约约地诉说着它前一个特性的蛛丝马迹。

在香港,空间成为了一种总是在被重新商议的日用品。它们总是处于合法性的边缘。空间的配置也同样成为了香港主流商业社会里的统治逻辑。这里我所讲的并不是香港典型的室内空间混合配置,例如酒吧坐落在游泳池的上方、停车场的上方和商业拱廊的上方,这种状态已经使Rem Koolhaas那著名的市中心运动俱乐部模型显得平淡无奇。我所讲指的是短时空间配置的逻辑,即同样的商业空间可以变成会议中心,再变成婚礼大厅,再变成展厅、酒吧甚至是妓院,然后再在一夜之间变回会议中心。香港——这片曾经是殖民地的土地——已经变成了剧烈的商业配置的场所。

Bernard Tschumi曾十分推崇空间的交叉利用。在空间被反复利用的今天,现代主义"形式追随功能"的古老宣言连同空间决定论的梦想已经被质疑。住宅可以是警察站也可以是妓院。屠宰场变成了艺术画廊。

居住的模式更多的是被发生在其中的事件,而非建筑形式本身所限制。空间成为了"事件空间"。这种交叉利用存在于世界的很多地方,甚至可以体现为空间的多层利用模式。例如在拉斯韦加斯,赌场同时也是饭店、会议中心、度假村、商店和色情场所等。但是在香港,我们很难发现空间配置的复杂舞蹈所体现出的丰富而多样化的迹象,从这点上说,香港在根本上是一个"匀质空间"。

空间交叉利用这个过程常常带来公共和私人之间界限的模糊。通常意义上的公共空间经常被配置给某种特定的半私密活动。Walter Benjamin曾经评论过那不勒斯拥挤街道上公共和私密空间的多孔性,但他自己也没想到公共和私密的强烈重叠会发生在香港这样的城市。确实,当我们处理此类空间时,可能应该放弃所有公共和私人之间固定的差异,反之将其看作空间配置的临时性策略,一种总是处于设定边界和消解边界之中的动态景观。

但是,我们如何将这些空间配置理论化?我们怎样来理解这些空间获得其暂时的和策略上的方式?我希望提出"拖曳空间"的概念,并作为一种描述方式来解释这些发生在香港的复杂空间配置如何才能以一种暂时的特性渗透进室内空间。因此,我需要通过外推朱迪思-巴特勒在解释交叉人格时使用的"行为活动"的概念来探究身份的概念,并将其作为一种拖曳的形式。通过调整和运用这个概念,我希望可以提供一种可行的理论框架,用以理解这些"拖曳空间"。

巴特勒和行为表演

朱迪思-巴特勒曾经描述过一种基于"行为表演"的身份特性。这使她可以以一种相比于传统方式更为流畅和动态的方式来审视特性。此外,这种方式还将身份政治学看作是一种赋予个人权利的领域。

巴特勒是一位研究性别政治学——更准确地说是女同性恋政治学——的理论家。她所关心的是阐明一种身份的概念,这种概念不为传统的异性恋模式所束缚,并且是一种对于精炼思考模式的根本批判。按照她的看法,是我们的行为和举止——而不是生物特征——准确地造就了我们的特性,性别在她看来不是一种预设的本体论状况,而是由行为活动造就的。这是"一种隐藏了起源的建造过程",也就是说,存在于行为、生成和维持离散和分级性别之间的默许一致被最终结果的可信度模糊了。

我们可以通过我们的行为活动来有效地重新描述我们的身份和重新塑造自己。重要的一点是记住特性是行为表演的效果,反之亦然。行为表演不是通过单一的行为(因为行为表演不能被简化为行为),而是通过对于特定活动的反复实践积累实现自己目标的。它建立在一种对于整理和复制的形式引用之上。就像巴特勒解释的:"行为活动不是一种单一的'行动',因为它总是对于一种或者一套规范的重复阐述,但在表象上它需要一种类似于行动的状态,它隐藏和掩饰了其作为重复的惯例。"

巴特勒认为特性不是一种内在的东西——一种本质的"赋予",而是某种外部的东西,一种散漫的外部效应。它产生于行为表演所反复进行的"行动、举止和表演"。更重要的事,它不仅与女同性恋的性特征有关,而是与所有的性特征有关,异性恋本身也是作为一种基于"表现出来"的行为模式随社会传播而出现的。就是从这里,性别和"模仿"之间的联系就开始浮现出来。事实上,巴特勒的整个论述看上去都是基于广义上的模仿和特殊意义上的拟态。所有的行为都是某种模仿,包括标准化的异性恋行为也是通过重复的力量"移植"和例示的结果:"所有的性别都是某种扮演和模拟……异性恋性别的自然主义行为是通过模仿的策略产生的;它们所模仿的是一种通过模仿产生的异性恋身份的幻影理想。

文化实践被支配权所统治。它们例示了某种规则,鼓励对于规则的默许。它们通过建立一致的愿望得以传播。这点在性别实践中极为明显。标准化的性别实践通过伪装的逻辑被控制。顺从于统治性的文化准则就是避免冲突,并根从一种移植的、支配式的行为系统。作为一种伪装,性别可以被理解为一种"有效的"文化实践。

性别,在这个意义上接近于拖曳的概念。它处于一种"假定的"地位,显示出来的逻辑与某种被接受的规范一致。巴特勒因此动摇了异性恋的传统权威性:"认为所有的性别都像是拖曳,或者就是拖曳,这就意味着'模仿'是异性恋和它的性别双变主义的核心,拖曳不是一种预定了优先和原初性别的次要模仿,处于支配地位的异性恋本身是一种对于自身理想状态的不断反复模仿。

这是对于文化实践机制在文化生活的各个方面一种根本意义上的重估,无需将特征、阶级、种族和信仰划归在同一范畴,所有类型的特性都可以被解释为依赖于某种表述性的结构。尽管它们在各自的范畴中运作,但其大致框架是相同的。每个都依赖于行为表演,每个在特性上都是引用的,并且每一个都是"有效的"。这并不意味着忽视物理特性的重要性,而是对于那种认为这些特点是由特性单独决定看法的挑战。

根据这样的观念,基于行为活动的个人身份组成超越了表象,而深入到行为特征和感觉与表达的模式。以种族为例,我们都了解为某些事物分类或者是"被分类"的过程。由于行为活动同样作用于知觉的模式,例如"凝视"不仅为我们对于世界的视野着色和构图,更重要的是,它也是构成部分之一。"黑色"意味着用"黑色的"凝视来审视世界。这种方式也同样适用于凝视之外的其他感知表达方式。

巴特勒将行为活动作为今天我们文化特性的核心。根据Marc Augé的观察,在这个"虚拟世界"的殖民时代,幻想使身份可以像时装配饰一样被占有和放弃,自我意识通常与从好莱坞得到的模型相一致,这种概念相对于对于自我组成的传统理解提供了一种更加有效的概念。整个身份的概念和很多固定的状况在这个角色扮演和身份政治学的时代需要被重新审定,身份必须

要被看成是多重的,并且经常是看上去与个人表达相悖的。但这也并不一定是被动的,事实上这种策略可以被解释为是一种个人在当代文化环境中"生存"的防御机制。就像Sherry Turkle在"显示器人格"泛滥的环境中所说的那样,多重人格紊乱在这个不稳定和无深度的时代可能并不是一种问题的症状,它更是一种生存的策略,一种文化伪装,使人们可以在复杂斑驳的世界中富有成果地行动。

巴特勒对于行为表演的强调并没有破坏潜在的形式的价值。事实上这正是她在其著作《举足轻重的身体》中传达的主要思想。她的理论是对于身份的一种本质的有形哲学。巴特勒的论述同时也对那种认为"形式仍是普遍深入"的积极理论的修正。在她看来,物质不存在于话语之外。就像Mariam Fraser观察到的"物质不存在于自身之内或是话语之外,而是通过行为活动反复创造的,从而'带来了它的存在或者扮演了它的名称'。

空间政治学

这些观察与空间政治学的讨论有明显的联系。巴特勒的深刻见解,即身份不是由生物学特征,而是由行为活动"扮演"的评论可以被移植到物理空间。巴特勒的逻辑暗示着某一空间是通过发生在那里的活动而获得意义。在这个意义上,统治个人身份的机制也同样统治着空间的身份。如果个人身份的组成可以被定义为"拖曳"形式的行为活动体现,那么空间自身的身份也可以用相同的方式来理解。因为如果身份被表演出来,那么发生这种行为活动的空间就可以被看作一个舞台。在一系列的表演之后,这个舞台就不再是中性的了。在那些目睹了这些活动的人看来,它将与发生在那里的活动充满联系。如果身份是表演性的行为,如果它像电影剧本一样被表现出来,那么建筑就可以被理解为一种"电影布景"。但是作为一种"电影布景",它从发生在其中的活动那里获得自身的意义。彼此联系的活动的记忆仿佛幽灵一样徘徊在物理空间中。

巴特勒的思想在此处可以被借用,用来解决存在于空间政治学之中的很多疑惑。人们经常将某种政治意识形态简单地附着在一种特定的形式之上,仿佛政治理想可以和审美理想合并。这不仅存在于性别政治学,也存在于大多数的政治学中。根据这个逻辑,特定形式的自身渗透在某种内容之中。正像看上去有某种"民主化"的形式,同样也存在着"女性的"形式。Fredric Jameson想挑战的正是这种思想。对于Jameson来说,形式在本质上是"惰性的",无论什么样的内容嫁接于其上,它的特性都是寓言式的。任何形式都不存在内在含义或是政治潜力。同时,可能确实有某种形式将自己"借给"民主的目的而非集权的目的。同样的,也必定有某种形式可以"体现"一种女性的敏感。尽管某些行为是由这些形式导致的,但将特定的活动投射于特定的形式必定是错误的。

空间是不会因为联系而产生政治性的。某种联系被"投射"到空间中,但是这些联系并不是被空间的材料特性——而是通过发生在那里的活动——所限定

的。此外,它们依赖于对于联系保持生机的记忆。在这个意义上,一个被用作某种目的的空间将会在一段时间后自然出现某种特性,但是随着新的活动将其取代,随着对于前一活动记忆的消退,这个空间将会具有新的特性。一个"男性化"的空间可能会转变为"女性化"的空间;一个"法西斯"空间可能会转化为"民主化"的空间。拓展一下,一个"殖民地"的空间可以转化为一个"后殖民地"的空间。通常这种过程伴随着一种战略上的重新配置,并与前一种联系相在。而在其他时候,它们可能会将那种联系以前空间的记忆忘却或是压制。

此时我们就可以认识到这样一种可能性,即运用巴特勒关于"行为表演"的论述来理解香港的城市空间是如何充满了短时性的身份。空间成为了"拖曳空间",它们从在那里上演的行为活动获得其身份。它们已经不再被某种本质上的"赋予"所定义,而将会根据其所容纳的每一个新的活动而被有效地被重新定义。

表皮效果

但我们仍要检验拖曳的特殊实践,从而引导出行为表演文化。例如拖曳文化的主要特征之一,就是它依靠于效果。表皮展示提供了一种强调行为意图的机制。一些小道具作为索引标记增加了含义。行为表演因此变得夸张,以强调原本不属于形式本身的实践。因此拖曳以伪装的形式运作,这种伪装将重点放在表皮和表皮的效果,通常伴随着对于意图的有意扭曲和夸张。拖曳的女王要更加女性化。它们提供了一种对于女性行为表演的模仿,一种对于强调姿态的表现和夸张的道具——例如假睫毛、高跟鞋、假发和垫起的胸罩。

这种视觉展示在香港的"拖曳"空间里找了其回应,短暂的和飞逝的道具在各种各样的仪式庆典上被尊为神圣,就像公众节日里的舞龙一样。一旦场景本身不再为发生的活动提供某种特性时,注意力就被转移到了效果上。因此效果需要补偿在某种场景中身份特性的缺乏。

也许有人要批评这种"拖曳"文化,说它是一种提升短时视觉效果的肤浅做法。但是我们还是应该认识到表面文化的积极价值。不同于Guy Debord 和Jean Baudrillard等人将表面文化作为奇观和超现实的评论,我们应该将图像的角色看作是所有身份形式的组成部分。例如,Debord首先认为图像使人类远离自我,这明显地与心理分析学的方法不符,心理分析学认为表演在自我定义的所有形式中起到了重要作用,这是身份的特殊本质。事实上,我们是通过对自己的再现来获得身份的,也并不存在某种外表之下被遗忘的本质"真实"。根据Lacanian的观察,至少我们认为是真实的事物事实上是想象的。我们从来没有接近过"真理的硬壳",除了短时的阵痛。身份总是某种形式的伪装。"化妆品"这个简单的例子就可以说明表面操纵和提高是如何或多或少地拓展了现代身份的定义的。

相似地,可能也会有人批评这种表面效果的"拖曳文化",说它是虚假的文化。但是它的逻辑可能就是挑战

真实性的文化本身。行为表演的概念帮助揭示了所有获得支配权的标准化文化实践(它们因此被看作是"真实的")都依赖于行为表演。这种行为表演是作为对于整个真实性话语的批判出现的。它并不像Fredric Jameson 等作家简单总结的那样,认为我们这个时代自相矛盾的事物之一就是真实性倒塌成为非真实的,因此真实性在Quinlan Terry 和他人的作品中被非真实地再现,并且就像拉斯韦加斯那样,非真实在某种程度上被当作真实接受。事实上,整个关于真实性的论述都是有缺陷的,并且建立在一种试图维持某种传统的说教之上。"真实性"常常被守旧者在建筑的话语中作为反抗"非真实"的新鲜事物的武器。一旦这种论述被认出是将"真实性"简单地定义为所谓的"非真实性"的反面,它的薄弱之处就显而易见了,这种论证很快就会陷入自我循环的逻辑中。所谓的"真实性"仅仅是通过对于这种特性反复的引用文化。换句话说,真实性就是将某种价值投射到世界,这种价值是不存在于某个特定事物之中的,而是在一段时间以后嫁接于其上。我们认识到所有的文化实践都基于行为表演,行为表演是作为一种潜在的解放概念出现的,这种概念认为无论何种被认为有原始支配权形式的实践都是可以被其他的实践形式所替代的。

香港和真实性

相比于其他地方,香港更是一个挑战真实性概念的地方,某种形式被看作自身就是"真实的"。评价"真实性"的标准从来就没有被清晰地描述过。例如,什么才是香港"真实的"的空间?我们是否在通过古董和地方形式来对抗新的"冒牌",从而表扬传统的延续?换句话说,我们是不是在表彰过去时代语言的恢复,尽管传统是一种被固定在过去的东西?还是我们将传统自身看作是一个不断排斥和更新的动态过程?

Rem Koolhaas和Jameson认为这种对于地域性和传统的表扬可能会导致一种"迪斯尼化",城市历史的肌理通常被作为为城市提供个性"身份"的手段,但是它已经丧失了其原有的内容,缩减成了一种游览景观。比这更糟的是,这种试图通过恢复传统和地域来超越资本主义强权空间的手段也有可能恰恰支持了它要反抗的文化。结果不是反击了后起的资本主义文化,而可能是通过为文化市场提供了传统和地域性的延伸"产品"而在事实上滋养了资本主义文化。

这并不是挑战对于过去怀旧的空间配置(无论是以中国化的方式还是以其他的表面方式)是作为后现代文化中建筑形式普遍性的产品而非对抗的想法。而是说要意识到普遍性的形式和对于传统以及乡土空间的重新配置都是对于一种后现代文化的体现。

一种更加有益的探索路线可能是,认识到普遍性总是与个性交织在一起的,就像是个性总是交织在普遍性中一样。个性通过普遍性蔓延,反之亦然,这是一个互惠假设的过程。对某一事物的复制越频繁,它就越显示为个性的差异。在香港的环境中,我们可以通过普遍性的塔楼通过当地人的活动成为"生活"传统认识到这一原则。这里我们可以再一次借用行为表演的理论来理

解这个过程。行为表演的逻辑认为不是形式自身,而是行为在特定社会活动中的痕迹赋予了身份。香港特定的身份是通过在这些塔楼里的特殊的行为表演而被遗忘。同样的塔楼可能会出现在香港、南美或是东欧,是它在香港(或说是在香港某一地区)被利用的特殊方式保证了它会一直保持一种特殊的身份。

在这个角度上,香港的室内"拖曳"空间是作为后现代的典型空间出现的。如果我们可以将现代性归结于固定的规则和深层次的含义,那么后现代性的特点就是被表面迷惑。后现代性是一种取样的、冲浪式的和临时的文化。它同时也是一种朝生暮死的文化,固定的规则让位于动态的系统。它是一种激变的文化,对于生长和适应的生物学隐喻最好地抓住了同化作用的过程。

因此,我们可以在香港的"拖曳空间"里意识到一个十分现代的时刻。这些空间暴露了新的文化实践形式,而这些文化形式是为了应对变化的文化而出现的。它们概述了一种能够同时在世界其他地方的多功能商业空间里被感受到的适应性策略,尽管不是以同样的强度。赋予香港极端文化身份的特殊环境暗示着我们可以从它创新性的文化实践中学习到很多东西。香港可以被看作一个充满了各式各样试验行为的地方。这些行为无疑也可以在世界的其他地方落脚,"拖曳空间"当然也可以在其他地方扩散。

Rem Koolhaas引入了"垃圾空间"的概念来形容20世纪的很多建筑生产。最近,他又为21世纪的"新世界"加上了另一些类别,包括:纳米空间、空间空间、倾倒空间、隆起空间、声音空间、布什空间、边界空间、紧张空间、拥挤空间、博客空间、机器人空间、DNA空间、监狱空间和性空间等。作为21世纪典型的行为表演空间,我建议将"拖曳空间"加入到这个名单里。

解读香港- 新城市动力学:变化的文化- 选择- 连接- 共生

条件:城市如何强化
强度描述了事物的状态,一种非实质性的强度作为一种普遍性的文化渗透于城市中。它虽然强势,但却不一定具有物理形态,另一方面,城市强度的极端形式体现为大量事件(或是事件之间)的迅速发生。这尤指那些大规模到来,之后又悄然消失的事件。

密度一词常被人用来形容香港。尽管这也不假,但是人们对于这个城市常常忽视的一点是它的强度。从地理和政治的角度上讲,香港都有自己的疆界。只是没有水平拓展的空间。因此,当被施加如此的限制时,强度的程度在这种环境中被进一步加强了。

回顾一下今天中国大城市的历史,可以发现它们的发展总是或多或少地在水平和垂直方向上同时进行的。作为在过去二十年出现的新兴城市的典范,深圳从来没有停止过向外部蔓延。北京、上海等传统城市除了在旧城区的快速发展,也同时在郊区以前所未有的规模扩张。在另一方面,香港在自身的强度之上一直保持繁荣,作为一种独一无二情形,它很值得被作为个案来研究。

下面我们将建议用4个概念——变化、选择、概念和共存——作为解读框架,来进一步看看香港详细描述强化城市的概念。它们并没有先后次序,也没有等级关系。相反,它们彼此以一种非线性的方式紧密关联。

每一个概念都不是下文某一现象的严格起因或结果。这些概念被讨论的目的是为当地的现象提供某种参考的相关点。

变化
力是变化的非物质起因。城市景观是无数各种各样的外力在同一时刻作用的产物。社会、经济、政治、文化或是历史等外力从各个方向施加作用,但导致的变化是有方向性的,它指向某种关于城市空间的理想。总之,变化是社会的生存之道。

变化总是与时间交织着。时间是一种独特的维度,它拥有自己关于空间的内在逻辑:这种空间不是以物理单位度量的,而是以非物质的标准——持续时间——度量的。就像物理空间提供了一个放置物体的媒介,时间提供了一种发生变化的媒介。但是不像物体会撑满空间,时间是永远不会饱和的。变化的强度可以是无限的,总是伴随着不同规模和持续时间的进一步强化的可能。

外力产生于时间进程中变化的关注和理想。虽然它们是外部因素,但是却可以导致系统内部的爆发。我们有可能找到外力的起源,但是将变化的起因归结到一个外力就是过分简单化了。变化没有最终的形式,而是变型过程中的中间产物。尽管变化不一定带来成长或是无方向的进步,但是外力的变化和伴随的系统转变却可以做到这一点。

以旧街区铜锣湾的转变为例,这是一个在一段时间内不同外力(已知的和未知的)在不同方向转变,从而带来变化的典型案例。当香港时代广场建成以后,这个街区立即变成了铜锣湾的第二个中心。从而使此处地价飞升,破旧的出租房屋被开发商改造成了五星级的写字楼。但这一切恰恰伴随着亚洲金融危机,因此本打算做办公室的空间不得不被改造成发廊、美容院和餐馆等流动的商业区,但是,当所有这些被堆积成40层那么高时,其结果就是一个垂直的娱乐/购物商场拥有了办公楼的外形。

连接
连接是指在系统之间建立关系。系统的规模和性质不尽相同,在两极之间的谱系中呈现,无论是物理的或是虚拟的,微观的或是宏观的。高峰时间地铁发出的嘟嘟声会导致人们找寻自己的手机。无线通讯系统就这样作用于公共空间系统。尽管这样的场景反映了拥塞、大规模移置、群体行为和生存方式。这里,连接是一种联系一系列参照物的手段。

连接确认了界限的存在,各种关系就在各异的实体之间建立起来。换句话说,边界在分割的同时也在连接。边界的流动性发生转换、溶解,并与远距离的元素或现象发生联系,从而创造出强化的空间蒙太奇。

连接是通过界面实现的。它为相互作用搭建了一个平台。平面外围的本身就是连接的策略。它引发了不可预见的空间体验,并且颠覆了视觉信息的联系,从而使本来静止的公共空间变的活跃起来。建筑的立面可以被纯商业的视觉效果所包裹。妓院的灯光显示了街道和建筑之间一个特殊的层面,从而形成了一种非正式的(可以说是非法的)城市指南的新系统。

连接引发了一种联系网络。空间以一种液态的方式流动,而不为独立的建筑所限制。它导致了一个尽管与其它已知系统杂交但却独立的系统。

连接最粗野的方式是通过重叠和渗透体现的。表面通过增加层次和实体而增殖。每个表面都被最大化以提高视觉联系,最重要的是,通过视觉联系数量的增加来提升商业价值。

连接性可以在乘坐地铁时观察到,一系列投影广告与火车的速度是一致的。每隔10秒钟,只要转向窗外,乘客就可以欣赏到一则简短有趣的广告短片。所有这些是通过视觉在时间和地点上发生的重叠和渗透实现的,从而造成了主动和被动之间的连接。

选择
选择是一种个人和集体意愿的体现。选择是一种响应性的行动。它可以识别存在的潜力并为重新设定可能的结果提供了空间。这经常导致通过对常规方法的背离来反抗规范。

选择可以被调整,但是不能被完全控制。选择是通过对各种因素的全盘考虑得到的,包括现有的条件和所施加的外力。

选择体现了公众实现目标的创造性能力,而这些成绩往往被误认为是给予的。在选择的过程中,个人的见解片断可以被重组和阐述。通过对于个人选择的解读,外部的和内部的限制可以被体现出来,同时,最大限度的可能性也可以通过在同样条件下创造灵活性而被获得。

正如前文所说的,选择可以通过香港铜锣湾旧街区的变迁感受到。新的商业繁荣是人们创新力量作用的结果——无论是雄心壮志的成功实现,还是经济利益驱使的决定所带的不可预期的失败。

共存
共存激发了混合,从而形成了一个完整的系统。香港的大致印象就像是从一个单独的巨大城市建筑中雕刻出来的。放大看,它是由事件和实体的片断组成的。我们称其为都市片断(城市字节)。通常,它们数量庞大、规模各异、周期不同。它们无时无刻不在自我发展。城市字节的丰富性产生于集体的创造性。它们渗透入城市的每个角落,改造了空间的原本利用方式,同时使城市的废弃地区重获生机。它们有时候可以完全有条不紊。

作为一种方法,共生选择适应而非强制、回收而非消灭、多样而非单一。因此,城市字节由于产生于特殊的都市环境而具有很高的适应性。它们尊重现状并且寻求现状中被忽视的潜力。它们将过于精心安排的城市打碎,为城市的自我发生注入新的活力。无论从目标上还是经济上,共生都是一种可行的发展策略。

共生是一种开放系统,并以一种都市可持续发展的方式运作。与限于实体内部转化的进化过程不同,可持续性与一系列相关系统一起发生变化,是一种截然不同的策略。

结论
上述讨论试图阐明在城市运作的逻辑中,有效性和强度更多地来自于临时作用,而非规划好的模型。尽管三维的都市景观雄伟壮丽,但却是通过其后部不以视觉效果为基础的实用主义来实现的。这种4-C方法可以避免任何对于都市景观有妨碍的呈现,它可以使人们最终脱离对于理想城市的任何虚假目标。

Gutierrez + Portefaix

Laura Ruggeri

再-城市

再-城市指的是固体废物及其处理。

再-城市指的时香港成千上万的把时间花在收集和回收我们所产生废物上的人和地点。

再-城市指的是我们的疯狂消费所代谢出的纸张、塑料、金属、非金属、玻璃、木材、橡胶轮胎和织物。

再-城市指的是香港在2003用掩埋法处理的大约17 760 000公斤的垃圾。

再-城市指的是香港每天用掉的2400万个塑料袋,平均每人3.6个。

再-城市指的是香港在2003年回收的大约238万吨固体废物。

再-城市指的是一卡车旧纸板换取的几个美元。

再-城市指的是能把碎料挤压成方方正正盒子的机器。

再-城市指的是能在垃圾堆中找到一手提箱钞票或者至少是还能工作的电脑零件的梦想。

再-城市指的是拆成小块的机器和电器元件。

最终,再-城市指的是那些我们无需处理就可以发送走的废品。

霉变时代

你离开香港已经有几天了,你关了空调,在你离开这段日子,油漆脱落了,屋顶发了霉,墙上出现了潮印,书本和杂志乱七八糟,你的书包和皮裙上出现一块块霉斑。你的新鞋上长出了白毛。真菌在一把不知是谁留在你房间的吉他上蔓延。

"在这种热带气候下东西会很快变质"Alain Robbe-Grillet提醒《约会的房子》的读者,你回到的地方已经不是你离开的地方了。

就好像重庆快报中的663号巡警,你开始捉摸为什么在你离开这段时间房子会有如此大的变化,难道它变得多愁善感了么?
时间被这种变化重新校正,随着锈迹的加厚,几天感觉就像是几年。

霉菌生长得要比城市快得多。

香港一直在与霉菌和……时间进行着斗争。时间留下的任何痕迹都被迅速清除掉了。塑料表面要比那些容易被污染、老化和生锈的表面更受欢迎。时间在这里站不住脚,它一下子滑过,以加速通往未来,到达"别处",那里没有时间的钳制,没有沉重的历史和记忆。任何事物都不容许老化。商品在刚刚出现时间积聚迹象的时候就被丢弃了。对于新事物快速而狂热的追求伴随着对于旧事物的遗弃。

时间在这里是固定不动的,人们可以走出历史,退守到一个受到控制的、有空调的和一尘不染的环境中,它不能被时间触及,永远重新创造着自己。

在消费和处理的加速循环中,老化是不能被容忍的。

但时间是一个狡猾的对手,在转变的空间中,它变形为"气候"。Temps, tempo, tiempo…在罗马语中,时间和天气有着共同的词根。

在变为气候的过程中,时间获得了一种经验上的尺度,它避免了被分为可以计量的单位,使持续时间成为主体和它们环境之间的连续统一体。

真菌可以分解棉布和纸张当中的纤维素,从而使材料解体。这个过程在热带地区这种湿热条件下尤为迅速。在二次世界大战的时候,在东南亚地区战斗的国家就因此丧失了大量的设备。
涂刷的墙面可以使真菌大量繁殖,墙纸内的砒霜染料也可以成为一些菌类的营养源。
皮革的主要成分是蛋白质,为霉菌提供了便利的食物源。还有一些皮肤真菌会侵害人体的表皮。
一些看似完全不可能提供真菌生长环境的物质实际上是积聚了大量的此类微生物。例如聚乙烯醇的糖浆溶液中。

锈:
由于气候变化产生的化学反应而在人造物品表面形成
的污点或附着的硬皮。
生锈不见得意味着物品经历了很长的时间。

我不知道是不是天气的原因,但是我发现东西变质得
很快。
巡警663, 重庆快报

就像时间一样,霉菌顺着潮湿的缝隙和裂痕蔓延……扩
散到所有密封性不好的地方。
作为时间的铭文,霉菌就像是一部索引,它是自己存活
周期留下的痕迹。

疑惑和入侵必须要不惜代价的避免。
保卫边界变成是强制性的。
霉菌的繁衍被视为是对身体、建筑和所有物品健康的
进攻。

Eric Howeler

室内18度:香港的热空间

香港特别行政区
气候:亚热带
七月份平均气温:32
起月份平均湿度:87%
每平方米平均空气污染:120

香港的城市形态描绘出了一幅精确的几何和光学轮
廓,这是房地产投机、商业产权租售标准和气候控制
交叉作用的结果:退台的塔楼形象、可以出租的底层
空间、电梯服务空间的间隔、以及外部反射的玻璃幕
墙。从经典建筑学的角度来讲,香港城市环境的决定
因素是地缘政治学、地形学、人口统计学和气候的混
合。气候可能是与建筑形式关系最小的一个决定因
素,但它却是香港决定性的特色之一。香港高密度的居
住环境使它成为了人造物的中心;维多利亚港的土地被
不断改造,新的居住塔楼形成了建筑地理景观,机械调
节的和光学控制的建筑创造出了大量新颖的建筑外皮
和室内氛围。

香港的室内环境模仿跨国商业标准所规定的热舒适条
件,在输出商品和服务的同时也输送标准的环境。通用
室内环境的历史可以追溯到国际式的建筑风格,这种风
格的建筑被认为可以满足任何地方的特殊气候条件。
Le Corbusier在1930年说道,"每个国家都建造适应
自己气候的住宅。在这个科学技术国际通用的时代,我
建议一种适用于所有国家和气候的建筑,它具备精确的
呼吸功能……空气可以保持在18摄氏度,湿度与气候条
件相协调。" Le Corbusier的这种恒温通用建筑的梦
想是一种乌托邦式的理想——一种人造的优化环境。
关于气候的讨论和关于全球化的讨论不可避免地联系
了起来。

表面
香港的两种建筑表皮原型显示了它的气候学需要:随处
可见的办公楼反射玻璃幕墙和嵌满空调机的居民楼立
面。这两种表皮揭示了两种对于热环境的主要策略:光
学上的和机械上的。玻璃幕墙通过光学性能反射热带
阳光的强烈光线,而机械系统通过热交换来创造和调节
室内的热环境。

先决条件
虽然钢框架、电梯和摩天楼的结合是都市生活神话的
核心,但空调的作用是绝对不可忽视的。在空调出现以
前,办公楼依赖于开窗来采光和换气。空调的发明使建
筑的平面尺寸和红线边界更加接近,将建筑体量从自
然采光和通风的限制中解放出来。空调对于香港来说
是个先决条件。密布的办公塔楼就是一个个被楼板分
割、被玻璃包裹的冷却塔,而大型商场就是宽敞的冷却
房,在这里,空气被监控、过滤、除湿和调节。空调使
香港超高密度的都市生活成为可能。

元件

机械系统是建筑内看不见的元件,它被隐藏在百叶之后,占据了建筑隐藏的内部空间。无论是头顶还是脚下,建筑都配备着大量的机械和信息设施。在香港寸土寸金的房地产市场,租售面积争夺着每一平方厘米的管道空间,设备布置规划被精准地计算着。香港的上海银行是这种隐藏元件规则的一个例外,它有意地把建造系统展示在建筑外部,机械设备被提升到了标志物的地位。

过滤

香港的交通污染和大陆边境的重工业使香港成为世界上空气污染最严重的城市之一,危害性空气质量等级的频率达到了惊人的程度。无所不在的玻璃幕墙将室内空间密封起来,以避免外部有毒气体的侵害。百叶和机械设备形成了室内外的条件界限,两者之间的空气流通被调节和过滤。

解剖

玻璃幕墙是香港商业建筑的普遍立面——它分格的反射表面形成了城市的物质DNA——幕墙单元是香港建筑基本的建筑构件和不可或缺的模块。将玻璃幕墙系统解剖,可以发现它的组成层次:铝、硅和玻璃。

挤压成型的轻质铝材具有中空的断面,它内部轮廓的设计使其可以具备像墙体一样的强度,并可以结合成整体的框架。硅胶集强度和韧性于一体,可以将玻璃和铝框紧密粘接而无需任何机械扣件。硅结构的幕墙使香港的玻璃地景成为可能。幕墙的最外层表面是玻璃装配单元:夹层的、中空的、镀膜的......使其具有不同的特性——热工性能、隔声性能、防暴性能、防尘性能,还能调节视角。一个典型的玻璃装配单元包括两块玻璃和一个铝制间隔,里面密封了少量的空气或是氩气。反射层使玻璃具有反射或过滤阳光的光学性能,低辐射镀膜可以使可见光透过,而屏蔽掉热能。

反射

香港的垂直玻璃地景创造了一种多棱镜和万花筒般的都市主义。中国银行整齐的玻璃表面形成了一种多面有角的形式,反射膜创造了一种选择性的光学外壳,在镜面的折叠中将其周围环境增殖。

由于有大量的色彩可供选择,香港的玻璃塔楼形成了色彩斑斓的天际线。彩色玻璃增加了反光系数,过滤掉了日光辐射。彩色玻璃还会引发大量的联想。远东金融中心金色玻璃的立面就是一个比喻:银行就是一根金条。北角的AIA总部运用多彩的玻璃表面作为香港的绘画隐喻。随意布置的玻璃条带使香港多彩的天际线内在化,将建筑立面变成一幅抽象的拼贴画。

玻璃的光谱特性和机械通风的方式被One Peking Road利用得淋漓尽致,香港的第一座双层玻璃幕墙就出现在这里。幕墙的两层玻璃之间、铝框的宽度内夹着薄薄一层空气,这个空腔在每一层进行流通,使热空气在向办公空间散热以前就被排除掉。双层玻璃幕墙在提高透光率的同时无需增加整体的传热系数(OTTV)。机械性能的提高使这种玻璃幕墙可以具有香港其他玻璃幕墙所不具备的优势:透明。

网络

商场为了经济目的而普遍营造室内气氛。中环的高架步行道零售网络连接着各种各样的建筑,将王子大楼、亚历山大大厦和查特大楼等地标建筑联结成一个知名的零售环境。不同商业设施结合成天衣无缝的零售氛围,凭借的是对于所有天桥统一的美学设计,以及创造了机械调节的稳定小气候——一个密封的空调空间。从中庭到步行桥再到零售商店,消费者拥有连续的恒温密封空间,从而保证了顾客至上的持续气氛和无间断的销售周期。中环将它的零售环境拓展到了热工品牌。

室内溜冰场

九龙的节日大道的娱乐消费网络在一个建筑体量之内,形成了一种连续空间内和可控气候下的消费体验。继Chep Lap Kok机场之后,节日大道拥有香港最大的空调调节的连续建筑单体。这个商场的特色是拥有一个室内溜冰场,在亚热带气候的香港提供了一种冬日的娱乐。节日大道使消费体验的乐趣成为了一种热工乐趣。

山

更接近于完全建筑气候营造的是"雪世界"——一个为Ma Wan设计的冬日主题公园。这个公园将容纳旅馆和温泉设施,它巨大的室内空间将有人造山体和人造气候。参观者将可以一年的任何时候在冰雪覆盖的山坡上滑雪。与香港的迪斯尼乐园不同,雪世界主题公园并不是对于已有主题环境的进口。雪世界是完完全全产于本地的,它是香港气候下的主题公园,只不过是反向的:是其气候特征的对立面。雪世界提供了脱离香港气候而享受一种平行世界的机会。雪世界是一种热工旅游。

边界

在香港,气候只是另一个需要被克服、调节和消费的现象。香港的建筑限定了外部环境和巨大而崭新的内部环境之间的边界。它仅25毫米厚的可调节玻璃表皮界定了香港的使用空间。外部环境是不可预知的:热浪、城市微气候、热岛效应以及空气污染。而内部环境是严格调控的恒温恒湿的世界。同时,作为热工空想主义,在建筑创造天气条件下的旅行提供了一个遥远气候环境里的梦想世界。

Laura Ruggeri

商场对于不同的人意味着很多不同的东西。对我来说,它首先的也是最重要的意义就是交流。

由于个人在城市空间中的行动越来越被限制和引导,城市变成了一个经济和商业的伺服系统,通常我除了跟随人群进入金光闪闪的大堂几乎没有别的选择。大型商场坐落在地铁站出口、机动车道上的步行天桥、汽车站和出租车站,它们就像办公楼里的大堂一样,是平行网络中的一部分,这种平行网络为香港这种高密度的城市提供了成倍的空间。

由于分割室内与室外、公共和私密的边界变得具有渗透性,我会在漫不经心中或在忙乱中踏入商场。节省时间和躲避燥热——而不是购物——可能是我进入商场的唯一理由。

进来,可能是因为买了一双新高跟凉鞋的原因,我开始更加注意从架高的步行道进入商场时发生的事情。混凝土地面变成了光亮的大理石地板,每天都被一大群廉价的清洁工擦拭。在这里,我的高跟鞋发出不一样的声响,突然变得有自我意识了:我脚步的节奏发生了变化,变得短促、轻盈。这种不同寻常的声响使我成为了新的体验的主体,同时也成为了被关注的客体。

当我自己在注视时,我同时也是一幅图案,我也在被注视。

这三英寸的变化建立了一种新的步态,也进一步创造了一个新的空间。

现在,我身体感受的特殊之处形成了我的视角。穿高跟鞋走路将焦点重新转移回我的身体,从平凡的穿越转变成诗意的巡游。

新的步调影响到我观察他人的方式——一种新的视角被建立起来——使我获得了一种与该空间一致的理解。

在明亮的迷宫中,我失去了自己的影子,得到的是自己多重影像的碎片。

我的身体反射在商店的橱窗里——玻璃放大了展现和表演——也反射在磨光的不锈钢柱上和天花板上,我的身体融入了表面。空间开始回顾。在卷曲的镜面上,身体的距离被消除了。

通过自身身体的运用和描述,尽管受其自发性的局限,商场也变成了一个充满承诺的地方。

当地的同性恋群体对于大型商场的色欲承诺是了如指掌的。香港最著名的三个巡游场所都是高档的商业中心(太平洋中心、节日大道和国际金融中心)。它们的所在地可以通过大多数街区的公共交通便利到达,它们的建筑造型是某种有选择性的极少主义,有光鲜的产品和充满诱惑力的光滑彩页杂志。这是一个为时尚梦幻所搭建的舞台,用来崇尚那些被认为是奢华和经典的倍受青睐的场所。

在公众场合选取某人并与其发生性关系决不仅限于同性恋者,妓女们从19世纪出现开始就选择商业拱廊作为活动的场所。

在商场里,身体和商品都成为了布景展示的一部分:它们都在同时成为了观众。眼神的交换补充了商品的展示。

镜子就好像剧院空间里的透视布景,使视觉优先,它成为了香港商场里普遍存在的特色。即使是在很少使用镜子的地方,商店的橱窗、打磨光的大理石表面和不锈

居住在喇嘛岛上,我在城里的一天通常是从坐落在国际金融中心里的商店开始的,这里同时还容纳着机场块线的中转站,以及入境登记处等。几座步行桥将它与汽车中转站和偏远岛屿的码头相连。乘坐电梯可以达到低下停车场。

我每日从中环4号码头到巴特利大街的路线在地图上是找不到的:在距街道上方及英尺的地方,我在各种商店、办公楼和私人步行桥间穿梭。

慵散的楼梯的合唱

例如,漫步/书写"间距",对于空间和时间的阐述,时间的空间化和空间的时间化。

2003年9月16-20日 下午4点

4号码头—国际金融中心:335级台阶
国际金融中心:520级台阶
港岛步行道:272级台阶
聊天室:86 级台阶
步行道:40级台阶
亚历山大大街建筑:130级台阶
步行道:30级台阶
皇后大道建筑:52级台阶
步行道:70级台阶
标准特许建筑:94级台阶
通往巴特利大街的步行道:26级台阶

1655级台阶,25分钟,穿着舒适鞋子。不接电话,不东张西望,不停,好的体力。

我们对于空间的理解产生于行动,事实上空间应该被定义为"世界被身体所占有的某种形式"。
Maurice Merleau-Ponty,感知的现象学

Michel de Certeau, The Practice of Everyday Life
故事叙述不仅通过推理和想象串联起了不同的元素,从而连接起来了空间,它同时也通过赋予含义、描述体验形成了新的分支,从而创造了新的空间。
Michel de Certeau,日常生活实践

女人的行走更多地被认为是一种表演而非交通,它暗示着女人行走不是为了看,而是为了被看,不是为了自我的体验而是为了某个男性观众。
Rebecca Solnit, 旅行

尽管欲望是不受限制的,但是它只是在可靠的环境中是自由的。任何意识都是与身体保持在一个安全的距离外被宣读的,此时视觉先于语言。
Eric Laurier, Glas-z城市, 博士论文, 威尔士大学.

我相信在乌托邦和异位移植的其他地方之间,可能存在着一种混合的、联系的体验,也许是镜子。由于镜子是一个无空间的空间,因此它是一个乌托邦。在镜子中,我在我不在的地方看到了自己,那是一个在表面中展开的虚幻空间;我就在那里,但是那里没有我,一种影像使我看到自己,使我能够看到我在我所缺席的场合:这就是镜子的乌托邦。但是只要镜子存在于现实中,它就同时也是一种异位移植,它对于我所属于的位置施加一种反抗。站在镜子的角度,因为我是在那里,所以我发觉自己从我所在的场所的缺席。镜子使这个我在镜中审视自己时所占据的空间变得立刻绝对真实起来,同时与它周围的空间连接起来时,又变得绝对不真实,因

钢面板也都可以保证随时反射出身体。

反射表面的空间布局使人们彼此对视而不会尴尬,视线被调节了,通常是反射后又被反射,往复不停。被看只有在观察自己时才能被发觉。窥视癖者和自恋者在同时满足二者的商业空间中被并合了。镜子就像商场一样,开拓出一片游荡于室内和室外、现实和非现实之间的空间。

市场商人试图将快感原则用于可以预测的商业渠道,从而带来升华的意愿。商业恋情的诱人标志出现在商店橱窗里、模特和身体的不同部位上——通常是女性的——使商品变得充满性欲。

人们可以虚构占有的可能性,呈现或者丢弃与物品相关的整个身份。

人们可以将自己理解成虚拟物之外的另一件物体。但是就像盗窃癖所证实的那样,商品所带来的拜物的力量可以超越商品本身的经济价值。

如果本该使购物者围绕固定商品流动的意愿变成了购物者之间流动的意愿呢?

当注意力从理性的经济活动中分散时,人们将利用这个机会来进行更加复杂的社会行为,加入到更多的角色中,甚至是挑战行为本身的合理化原则。

走路对我来说类似于巡游。其中充满了窥探的乐趣,这同时也是一种终结于性目的的炫耀,我通过观察别人来分析他们的表情,判断他们是否愿意和我再一次交换眼神。

19世纪被视为异常的浪荡子在21世纪这个充满镜面的时代里找到了自己安身立命的地方。人们可以说在以视觉为主导的商场秩序井然的空间里,男性目光物化的特点使浪荡子的概念变得几乎不可能。这种说法没有考虑目前的性别关系,也没有考虑个人的潜能——这些人看上去被规则所控制,但是他们却发明了一套技巧来颠覆商业的空间理性。

通过在无性空间秩序里对于情欲和愿望的描述或强调,巡游扮演着对半公共空间配置的角色。它并没有创造出一种边缘地带,使异性恋者和同性恋者明确划分地域,事实上,巡游是脱离于空间之外的。这是一种短暂的体验,有时看得见,但在大多数时候是看不见的。它的神出鬼没不仅是因为它周旋于可见/不可见之间,还因为它向我们展示了欲望和身份——这些从社会角度和空间角度被排除在半公共商业空间创造之外的概念。

巡游暗示着建筑中盲点的存在,退格可以保证一定程度的私密性。

"进入镜子"或是"穿越镜面"意味着越过一条界限进入另一个世界。这是一个超越于图像之上的世界。在"那里",世界体验的原则和原型状况都将被发现。

内脏空间

商场是一个消费的领域,它将生产领域从视线中有效地排除。它是对于维修管理技术的"假想工程",使运输途径或是辅助系统都变得不可见。

这种对于纯粹追求的必然结果是使商业中心背后的地下和肮脏的"功能"都被掩藏。

在Mary Douglas对于"场所之外的污垢"的著名论述中,纯洁是相对于污垢被建立起来的。这一点与建筑的建造尤为相关,因为是图纸和边界限制形成了被限定的纯洁的建筑。

为如果要被看到,就必须穿越这虚幻的界限
Michel Foucault,关于别处

如果我的身体可以被认为是包含了某种抽象和具体的生存原则的话,那么镜子的表面将其解码,使这种原则变得不可见了,镜子揭露了我和我自己、以及我的身体和我的身体意识之间的关系,这并不是因为映像组成了作为主体的我,就像很多心理分析学者所认为的那样,而是因为它将我自身转变成了我的符号。这光滑的屏障,它自己无非是一种惰性的光辉,却在一个想象的但却很真实的虚球里复制和展现了我自己——或者说表现了我自身——。这是一个抽象的过程——但却是一个迷人的抽象。为了了解我自己,我必须将自己从自身中脱离。

游手好闲的人在商场里扮演着侦探的角色。因此,他同时也是人群中的发现者。在那些将自我放逐于其中的人来讲,人群激发了一种陶醉的感觉,伴随着特殊的幻想:这些人引以为骄傲的是,当路人擦肩而过的时候,他们可以准确地将其分类,仅从外表就可以把他看透到骨子里。
Walter Benjamin, 拱廊项目

我们每日都与他人擦肩而过,我们可能彼此并不认识,但我们可能在某一天成为朋友。
Wong Kar-wai, 重庆快报 1994

巡游于香港 - 从同性恋指南到香港

最好的时间是在晚上8.30以后一直到关门。

太平洋购物中心,地铁站出口
地标:中环地铁站
海港终点站购物中心,3层,尖沙咀地铁站
国际金融中心商场,底层,1层,中环地铁站

节日大道,九龙,2003年6月24日,下午6:30
当我乘坐通往山顶的扶梯时,发现有几个男人斜倚在楼上的栏杆旁,正在向下看。与此相对的是,站在我旁边的中年男人也正在朝上看。他的目光定格在头顶的扶梯不锈钢面板上。我原本以为看不到的前方的景象反射在头顶,那是一位站在我前面的妇女。

窥视癖一词是由两个希腊词组成的,scopos,指的是看或者观察,philia指的是喜爱、乐于某事。窥视癖因此形容的是从观看中得到的乐趣。

欲望的元素。感性的体验。从太平洋广场发觉欲望的动力。让灵感成为你的向导 。太平洋百货,必到之地。(广告语)

太平洋广场,就像是传统的巴黎商业拱廊的变身,提供了发觉更多情欲愿望的可能性。乘坐电梯可以从商场到达服务式公寓和两座饭店。在晚6:30后关闭男厕所的最新决定使太平洋广场作为顶级巡游地点的声誉受到了损害,同时将那些漫不经心游荡的活动也被推向了其他没有此类时间规定的商场。

现代的购物商场暗示了同时存在于展示商品和人群之中的自我、欲望和消费。
Rob Shields, 购物生活方式

被定义为"污垢"的区域,在字面上理解就是开始获取污垢的和收集那些不合适的事物。

在商场里,可到达区域和后部服务区域的界限不仅被清晰地标示出来,同时也被不同的建筑材料界定出来。光亮的表面被粗糙的表面所取代,大理石地面被廉价的瓷砖所取代。

暴露的管道、水管、通风口、电缆、服务楼梯和喷淋器……所有这些仅仅当你推开防火疏散门或是顺着标识找寻厕所的时候才能看到,走道越变越窄,楼梯间变成了后台。

这些空间就像是巴特利大街的内脏,既拒人千里之外又充满了诱惑,它们同时也是一个假想的地带:是一个身体界限扩充和渗透的地带。

在这些利用率很低的边缘地带,充满情欲的活动自然发生。

未受控制的空间吸引了那些边缘的、被认为是不正常的、或是违法的行为。但它们的存在同样指向了一种辩证的运动:禁令作为一种权力创造了空间,空间作为一种禁令,又产生了权力。空间决不是一种被动的布景,而是暗示了新的、不曾被预料到的用途。

后台变成了另外一种表演的中央舞台。在防火疏散门后,你可以发现一个可以吸烟但不会被监视器或保安发现的地方,还可以吃便当、调情、藏匿偷来的物品、非法交易、偷懒或是睡觉。作为功能的边缘,这个空间创造并且迎合了不少需要和意愿。它通过对系统进行微分使这些需要和意愿超越了特殊地点的限制。

在商店的橱窗前,一身黑衣的年轻女子的眼神与玻璃镜面中的眼神相遇。她慢慢地转过身来,继续用同一步调走开。

年轻女子穿着着低胸的紧身衣,肩膀和胳膊全部裸露着。

明天,她说。或许是后天。
精巧的高跟凉鞋,每一只上都由皮带儿形成三个镀金的交叉装饰。在迈出每一步时,紧身的裙子都会在胯部和小腹部呈现随之摇摆的轻微皱褶。
Alain Robbe-Grillet, 约会地点

空间或者概念本身都不是情欲的,但二者的结合却是。
Bernard Tschumi, 建筑的愉悦

女人是商家们竞争的原因,通过用展示的商品打动她们,商家把女人反复拉入他们销售的圈套。他们总是唤醒女人新的欲望,这是一种巨大的诱惑,使她们彻底屈服,开始是为了成为一个好的家庭主妇,接着是为了取悦于男人,最终是为了挥霍。
Emile Zola, 女爵士的幸福

快感的原则交织于一系列的决定之中,甚至与购物者在商品前进行经济决定的强度是相同的。情欲节省除了字面意思,也有隐喻的成分,在两者之间没有明确的分解。
Eric Laurier, Glas-z城市

这是一个奇怪的空间、一个暂时的空间,它没有固定的形状和地点,但却总是潜入每日的生活,将其转变为一个充满可能性欲望的幻想世界。
Aaron Betsky, 建造性欲

人们知道在古希腊有一些通往黑社会的地方。同样,我们的现实在某些隐秘的地方也可以通往黑社会——一些不显眼的地方,梦想从那里升起。
Walter Benjamin, 拱廊项目

即使是最具条纹的空间也要让位于平滑的空间……运动、速度和迟缓在有些时候已经足够重新建造一个平滑空间。当然,平滑空间自身并不是释放的。但是斗争在那里被改变和替代,生命重新组份,对抗新的障碍、创造新的步法,转换新的对手。
Gilles Deleuze and Felix Guattari, 千座高原

只要整理包含着排斥不适当元素的概念,污垢就是系统整理和事物分级的副产品。在有污垢的地方就有系统。
Mary Douglas, 纯洁性和危险性

国际金融中心购物商场,2003年10月15日,下午6:00
在一层的台阶上,我看到了售货员和清洁工正在抽烟、聊天和吃便当。他们的周围是废弃的包装材料、拖把以及装满清洁工具、厕纸和肥皂水的手推车。

地标商场,2003年11月23日,下午6:45
在和别人在商场里见面之前,我溜出来抽了根烟。一对年轻夫妇(购物助理?)正在二层和三层的楼梯之间调情。当他们看见我时,我微笑着晃了晃香烟,以此作为一种借口并退回到楼下。

真正的色情开始并终结于个人的想象。性感的效果可以通过模糊常规环境的定义来获得。

空间要想表现出一种色情,就不可避免地要结合某种矛盾,无论是含义上的还是功能上的。

如果在公共空间发生了某种亲密事件,场所本身保留着对此的感受,这个事件将永远成为场所的一部分。

空间是动态的和活跃的:将权力、身份和含义的很多捕捉点组合、展现、包容、模糊、隐藏、限定、分离、划界和命名。
Steve Pile, 身体和城市

我的生活- 性工作者的照相作品

"我的生活- 性工作者的照相作品"是Ziteng的新项目。它的目的是增进性工作者之间、以及和整个社会之间的交流。这个项目以性工作者照片的形式在香港巡回展出,最终将被整理成"性工作者相册"。

在这个项目中,照相机成为了性工作者的一双眼睛,通过它,人们有机会近距离接触一直以来被视为对抗主流和统治性话语的性工作者的世界。这些人由于社会对于该行业根深蒂固的偏见和歧视而被剥夺了自我。他们曾经没有自己的声音,借助照相机和胶卷他们将开始自己的言语,我们将可以通过他们的眼睛来阅读他们是如何理解这个世界的、他们的感受、他们的日日夜夜、以及由他们的直接讲述自己究竟是谁。

建立于1996年,Ziteng是一个关注性工作者的团体。它通过支持和组织各种活动来提高和促进公众对于性工作者边缘状态的理解。它与性工作者们协同工作,来提高他们的工作条件和包括医疗保障在内的基本权益。这个项目旨在帮助改变公众对于性工作者的态度,并最终消除对他们的歧视。

为什么选择照相?
照相是一种强有力的表达手段。随着技术的发展,它已经成为了记录信息最流行和友好的媒介之一,是一种跨越边界、种族、文化和语言的世界话语。人们通过这种视觉工具彼此直接交流。我们观看、感受、被震惊和感动。照相机捕捉到了我们观察的瞬间,只需轻按快门,胶卷就会纪录你的眼睛所记录的东西。照片继而会成为其他人的纪录,它们铭刻在我们的脑海中、留存并且塑造着我们的世界。

这就是为什么我们选择照片。再加上它是在众多记录和表达方式中最流行、直接和简单的媒介,这个过程可能为其使用者带来自尊和自信。

为什么选择性工作者?
性工作是世界上持续时间最长的行业之一。它们一直以来都被歧视。人们对从事性工作的人有强烈的偏见:"他们是坏人、无耻的、肮脏的、道德败坏的、邪恶的、异端的,他们不知道如何去爱,没有'正常'的感情……。"

但是Ziteng的工作经历却讲述了另外一个故事。香港的大约10,000名性工作者大都在自己的公寓里工作。其中大多数是单身母亲,并且是家庭收入主要来源的依靠者。她们之所以从事性工作是因为她们想照顾家庭,但又不愿成为社会的负担。就像其他香港人一样,她们十分坚强,工作也很卖力。她们也是社会中的一员,为它的发展做着贡献,因为分担着同样的职责,因此她们也应当享受到与他人一样等的权利和社会地位。但是,歧视和偏见掠夺了她们本该有的声音。整个社会在很大程度上不能了解性工作者的真实生活,因此我们希望为性工作者办一个影展,通过照片来表达他们自己,并让人们用自己的眼睛去了解他们的生活!一个包容的社会在困难的时候将尤其能使我们奋进,来创建一个坚强、和谐和有爱心的群体。

影展:香港的40名性工作者参与到这项活动中来,每个参与者都得到一部照相机并独立工作。他们可以拍摄自己想拍摄的一切,只要是能最好地记录他们日常生活中的喜恶和感受的。在这个过程中曾经有一些交流会,让参与者来回顾和反思他们所拍摄的照片。其中的30名参与者还选出了一部分作品参加巡展。展览开幕式于2004年1月28号在香港文化中心举行。

这些照片于2004年分别在香港文化中心、香港艺术中心、香港中文大学、Yan Oi社区中心、国际援助大会和咖啡厅等地展出。我们同时还组织了公共论坛和研究小组来让公众参与反思这些照片,讨论性工作和性工作者的社会问题。

性工作者相册:我们希望能在2005年出版一本记录性工作者图片和反思的相册,并借此来增进性工作者和社会中其他人的相互理解。

关于Ziteng
Zi Teng于1996年由当地的妇女活动家们建立,她们共同的目标是通过直接服务、法律援助和提升公共意识等手段来帮助和扶持香港的性工作者。她们的目的是为香港和大陆的性工作者提供服务。

性工作是世界上流传时间最久的一个行业,但长期以来却受到人们的歧视和厌恶。我们相信所有的妇女,无论她们的职业、社会等级、宗教信仰、种族、年龄和性取向,都应该享有同样的基本人权。

在很多国家,性工作者都是一些最边缘的群体,面对着政治、法律和社会等各种形式的压迫。香港的性工作者也面临着同样的问题。她们在法律和社会阶层上的边缘状态使她们在很大程度上没有法律保护,并且很难得到其他行业员工所享有的社会福利、医疗保健和法律信息等权益。这个问题在香港已经变得迫在眉睫,因为只有很少的团体注意到她们的需求,也没有任何组织站出来为她们说话并为她们争取权益。

Zi Teng相信,无论性别、性取向、阶层、种族、年龄或是职业,任何人都应该享有同样的基本人权,同时还应该享有生活和工作的尊严。这就为什么我们一直反对歧视、疏远和中伤香港的性工作和性工作者。我们还坚信性工作者处于伸张自我需求和保护自己权益的最有利位置,Zi Teng因此通过教育、行业网络和法律协助等强化的方式来帮助这些妇女。

在香港工作的性工作者有200,000多人。目前我们联系到的有10,000多人。我们通过直接救助和热线服务为她们提供服务和支持。并且通过组织培训和各种活动来强化这些性工作者并为她们提供与社会中的其他人对话的机会。我们同时还组织了不同的公共教育项目,例如志愿者训练、交谈、研讨会和性教育项目等,来消除公众对性工作者的歧视,并改变对她们的看法。例如在2002年,我们就出版了两本书:《性是面包和黄油》和《亚洲性空间》。

就像它的名字"紫藤"一样,Zi Teng将继续发挥它的力量和活力。我们将尤其在公共教育方面强化我们的工作,为人们提供对于性工作更好的理解,并增强性工作者和整个社会之间的交流。

"2046"

James Law

历史

在2046的街道上游荡过的人都知道,这个城市建筑悠久的历史可以回溯到16世纪。2046是作为鸦片、糖和丝绸的贸易港口而兴起的,但在19世纪成为了一个工业基地,世界上任何地方的移民都可以在这里打工,并获得免费的公民身份和工作机会。在20世纪,经济的发展带来了政治的动荡,周边地区对2046发起了一场贸易战。出于自卫,2046开始建造围墙,限制移民和旅行。20世纪末期,2046成为了一个神秘的地方,它既像香格里拉——一个难以到达的梦想之城,又像是一个无人之境,历史开始被渐渐遗忘。

地理

2046有一系列环绕的河道水系,它们曾经是工业船舶运输的通道,现在却随着水位的降低变得空旷和寂静。随着城市在19世纪的发展,2046渐渐地失去了它所有的郊野地区,城市化不断蔓延扩张。今天,这里已经没有任何开敞空间遗留下来。作为城中城的一个范例,2046成为了一个分层的城市,旧城的下面是一个新城。绘制2046的地图并非易事,因为传统的笛卡尔坐标地图已经不能充分反映2046分层的实质。

2046的复杂性几乎是有机的,少数民族聚居区不断出现,不同种族的社会群体混合在一起。就像是社会风潮的一个大熔炉,即使是这些聚居区也是一层层叠和着,将不同群体的人们混合起来。

这个城市自身是黑暗而幽闭的,令人生畏的巨型结构和古老的建筑以及新建的建筑交织在一起。在城市的深处,自然光线几乎从未到达,这些内部的深处对于游览者来说是诡异不安的。而在城市的上部,高耸的塔楼为人们提供了俯瞰2046的全景视野。

气候

与一般城市不同,2046因其高密度而遭受着自身产生的微气候。2046深处通风不畅,这就意味着那里终年空气潮湿,气温维持在寒冷的19摄氏度。

在城市的上部,阳光炙烤的城市可达35摄氏度,同时大量的人口产生很多的二氧化碳。

我们建议你不要低估了2046气候的严酷,请带上应付不同环境的不同厚度的衣服。

生态和环境

就像世界上其他发达城市一样,2046的经济繁荣是以空气污染、水土流失、植被减少、物种灭绝和工业废料为代价的。2046庞大的人口再加上地理因素使其环境问题要比世界上的其他地区严重得多。

一些专家预测一场环境大灾难正在逼近,并警告说2046面临的最大挑战是来自于生态的。

不幸的是,这里没有任何防治环境恶化的严格标准,也没有采取任何措施来避免灾难。可能人们所能做的已经太少了,也太晚了。

动植物

18世纪的2046有丰富的自然植被和动物。但在今天的2046,城市的扩张已经使很多动植物灭绝了。

到19世纪,2046实际上已经成为世界的"烟草"种植中心,大片的土地高密度地种植着出口到全球市场的烟草。很多自然动植物栖息地被砍伐,而被用来种植烟草。

到了21世纪,在全球20世纪的普遍禁烟令的作用之下,2046的烟草种植地成了那些瘾君子的地下供给仓库。

今天,烟草已经成为了2046的国家植物象征,只要提起2046,人们就会自然联想起烟草。

政府和政治

2046在历史上经历了一系列的政治变革。可以概括为马克思主义、社会主义、资本主义和法西斯主义。2046已经成为了一个政治的大熔炉,世界上没有任何地方的人类政体要比这里更奇怪、更不稳定的了。

今天,很少有人知道2046的政府内部是如何运转的,但有一点是确定的,在这个巨大而独立的机构里,从基层的行业单位到最上层的政治权力都是由万能的2046国会控制的。

国会包含着一个由2046常任理事组成的理事会,其中的13人被选入中央理事会,来监督常务理事会的工作。

政治结构的基层是一系列遍布于社会不同部门的控制机关,包括军队、大学以及军队、警察和工业企业的行政部门。

在这个等级系统中,2046每日的监管由理事会的成员来负责,他们是中央理事会决议的执行者。

政府是一个巨大的官僚机构。有数不胜数的复杂规章系统,政府体系的发展与2046作为一个国家和城市的发展思路一脉相承。重重叠叠的规则导致了一个政府过度控制的社会,但这些规则又太过复杂,以至于它们不能以任何有序的方式来被执行。

326
327

从理论上讲,2046的每个公民都是某一系统的一个成员,因而是整个系统的一分子。但是,这种乌托邦式的系统并不是那么完美,很多人钻了2046规则的空子,逃脱了社会管制。不少人在2046的法则之外进行着活动,私人交易、自主营业或者脱离系统独立游荡。

2046试图通过以下途径来建立完美的社会制度:赞同结婚、离婚和生育;分配住宅;制定工资;控制邮政通讯;征募公务员;为每个公民留档;安排工作调动;控制移民和控制国内外旅行等。所有这些延伸进了2046每个个人的生活。

对于那些反对这些制度的人和那些持不同政见者,安全警察会将他们严厉而迅速地解决掉。2046监狱里关押的犯人几乎都是政治犯和反政府的人。

这里不存在有组织的或是被公认的反对派,也没有党派制度。

经济

在现在的2046国会中,经济是一个独立的部门,当地货币的解体在20世纪末就已经完成。就像回到原始社会那样,2046所实行的是一种物物交换的经济体制。

因此2046的工业领域通过材料和服务的交换来进行贸易——无论是大量集中购置还是个人在街道上的买卖。

传言说最接近于货币的东西就是烟草,虽然它在世界其他国家已经被禁止了。在2046,烟草以小袋出售,每一小袋就相当于黄金。

还有传言说这里存在一个向外部世界走私的巨大的地下烟草市场。

人口和民族

2046的人口中,90%是本土人,其他的少数民族占据了5%。

另一个少数民族是机器人种群,占据了剩下的5%。

到21世纪初期,这里的人口已经超过了10亿,但目前还没有关于人口数量的确切数字。

两个少数民族和机器人种族主要集中在2046的中心,他们在这里共同生活和工作。在2046拥挤的城市中心地带,这两个民族形成了难以计数的聚居区和街区,其独有的文化在这里混合到一起。

其余的族人在2046平均分布。

不断增长的人口数量和不断缩减的粮食生产能力促使2046从1950年代就开始实行控制生育制度,但这一制度在新千年到来的时候被废弃了,因为老龄化的人口已经不能支撑起社会的经济,从而导致了社会的动荡。机器人因此被引入整个人群来作为补偿。

2046是世界上唯一一个承认机器人公民的国家。

教育

2046的社会分裂为学者和工人两大阵营。

学者在出生时通过遗传监控被认定,之后在年轻时被安置在巨大的学术机构接受整体教育。

学院里那种机械式的学习和开放式讨论的缺乏形成了一种有局限性的教育模式。

由于本土语言(主要的写作语言)十分艰深,一些学术机构认为2046的教育结构太过苛刻和古板,因此英语、法语和俄语也被同时教授。

工人所接受的教育是应用在工业领域的技能教育,尤其是重复性的工作部门。

2046的政府颁布了两者之间的严格界限,以减少社会冲突,一方面应付着工人,另一方面对学者进行洗脑。

2046里受过教育的人仅为70%,这个数字在发达国家的标准看来是很低的。

较低的教育水平意味着大多数的公民在毕业之后就被国家安排了工作。这点对于工人尤其如此。学者有较多的选择余地,尽管工作的机会并不是那么充裕。

艺术

有些人说2046本身就是一件艺术作品,是一张长时间以来被反复绘制的画布——一个有多层历史和建筑的城市。即使是今天,你仍可以在城市深处发现18世纪的建筑,它们的上面是19和20世纪的建筑,在往上的顶端是21世纪的巨型建筑。2046就像一个时空胶囊,是建筑遗迹的一个活的储藏柜。

关于2046的艺术舞台的另一个有趣之处是,这里存在着丰富的地下艺术文化,它们颠覆了那些被生产的、被展示的和被交易的艺术品。任何被视为批评国家的作品创作都是违法的,因此评判社会的强烈愿望就转化成了地下活动。颠覆性的绘画、剧场表演、写作、音乐和电影等在2046深处的艺术家聚落被生产出来。

社会和行为
传统文化

与世界的其他地区相比,2046文化因其独立于世界文化的神秘感而变得独树一帜。尽管它在很大程度上和中国文化相似,但它发展了属于自己的人与人之间的文化和规则。

面子被定义为个人的基本"身份",或是自我,或是其在社会中的地位。在2046的所有对话和谈判中,交换的规则都基于"面子",因此对抗可以被避免。个人的社会地位在很大程度上通过"面子"的表达和接受来体现。

算命

迷信是2046世界的一个主要组成部分,命数是大众思想中的一个关键信仰。因此很多年以来,在很多街角不断有"算命先生"的流动小摊子,提供具有个人特色的算命服务,例如"看掌"、"看面"、"看兆头"、"看家谱"和"DNA推断"等。算命很便宜,但是2046著名的算命先生都是开价数百万的名人。同时,随着这些年社会中机器人的增长,它们也开始寻找自己的生存意义,因此就出现了"计算机算命先生",他们通过解读机器人的操作系统来预测事件。

应该的和不应该的

诚实坦率地讲话 2046的人很少诚实坦率地讲话。例如,当你向某人问路时,他可能会把你带到别的地方,而不是准确地告诉你路线。这当然是为了在众人面前保住"面子"。你必须要学会十分确切地描述你的问题来应对这样的问题。

微笑 微笑很少是愉快的表情,事实上,它是2046的很多人用来掩饰在这个孤立的国家里日复一日的乏味的面具。所以当你等待对方抱歉、愤怒或者悲伤的表情,而看到的却是微笑的时候,请不要惊奇。

性别主义 以国际标准看着,2046是一个典型的男性至上主义的国家,直到今天,社会结构中还有很多20世纪前的性别偏见。在2046,国家依然被男性所统治,无论是商业还是政治,男性都是唯一的统治者。但在这个倾斜的世界里,女性却在地下扮演着说服者的重要角色。因此你会发现在公众场合,一对夫妇里女方沉默,男方发言,而在自己的家里,女人的话却要比男人多得多。

性别政策 在这个社会的限制范围之内,婚姻有严格和保守的传统,性别的角色在居民之间的权力平衡中十分重要。你能给某人的最大好处就是慎对他的轻举妄动,他对你也是这样。如果你们之间有这种协议,就是有友谊的协议。这通常被用作外交的手段。因此当你需要朋友的时候,就给他找个女人,然后告诉他这没问题!

协商 如果你打算在2046干一番事业的话,要是能带上一些烟草(在2046已被禁止)或是其他形式的非法物来和潜在的合作者分享,事情就会变得容易得多。这是一种信任的标志,同时也是在2046体现街头信誉的一种手段。

烟草政策 尤其是在你第一次来到2046与某人见面的时候,不要忘记给他敬一根烟。如果他们做出接受的姿态,你就算被应允了。如果他们作出拒绝的姿态,你就必须更加努力地以某种方式使他们接受你,例如利用他们的性喜好。当你为某人敬烟时,必须拿出整盒香烟同时使其中一只向外伸出——从自己的烟盒里拿出一根递给他会被视为不礼貌的。你的香烟必须要外国牌子,这样才能显示你作为一个旅行者和外宾的身份。如果你想巴结你的主人或者客人时,就告诉他们留下整盒香烟,同时还要告诉他们下次你来的时候会带来给他们。2046的人们着迷于香烟,因为这种走私货对于他们来讲很难得。记住当你把它们带进2046的海关时必须十分小心。如果被抓住,你将不得不无限期地延长你在2046的停留时间。当地人会在任何时候点燃香烟,尤其是在吃饭的时候,因此你也可以这么做。如果你不吸烟,最好开始学。

送礼 当首次拜访当地人的家里时,送上某种形式的礼品是一种习俗。外国货是最受欢迎的的礼品,鲜花、食品和酒也不错。由于香烟和烟草是秘密的和最需要的,因此这些物品由于其非法特性而从来不被作为礼品送出。送礼时,要把它给夫妻当中比较强势的那一方,比如说妻子。但是永远不用给机器人,因为它们没有社会等级。你要学会如何区分机器人和人。

信仰
2046是一个没有信仰的地方。信仰的根源存在于个人。尽管2046有很多人希望成为他们信仰的传教士,但是这里的人没有听从他人的习惯。2046是孤独和内向世界的原型,这里没有对于信仰的普遍认同。

语言
由于这里有来自世界各个角落的移民,因此2046是一个多语言的地方。这里的语言是如此的混杂以至于有时人们的交流都成了困难,同时还有一种迹象,就是操同一语言的人群聚居在一起。为了克服这个障碍,机器人的程序都被设为多种语言的,进而来扮演人类种群的媒介和翻译员的角色。

参观者事宜
何时出发
在过去的50年里,到2046旅行的人越来越多。如此大的人流就意味着在各个旅游季节都会有大批的游客等待申请有限的签证。这里几乎总是处在旅游高峰,因此根本没有所谓的淡季,但是冬天因其严酷的气候有时候可能会有较少的游客。主要的公众假日应该尽量避免。新年对于2046来说是个糟糕的旅游季节,还有2046的国庆日。

边境每天开放两次,一次是在中午,另一次是在午夜。当你在当地的2046大使馆申请签证时,他们会安排你进入的时间。如果你打算在这两个时间之外进入2046,可以申请加急签证,这不仅昂贵,而且不易获得,你也可以向边境警察行贿来获取进入的机会。但要记住,无论以什么方式,你都需要一张合法签证。

定位
被陆地所包围的2046有四个主要进入点。北面的一点是作为外交入口,很少对公众开放。南侧的一点作为物资供给。西侧和东侧的两点是为个人旅游者开放的。进入2046以后,所有的铁道和交通线路都可以进入2046城市中心的中央火车站。从这里你可以计划你通向各个不同街区和聚居点的行程。所有的游览者都要接受移民检查,注意这可能要花上一些时间。

地图
由于这座城市敏感的本质,地图在2046从官方意义上是禁止的。除非你能从街头小贩那里买到非官方的地图。城市地图的准确性不敢恭维,因此建议你在当地再买另外一张地图,以校正你的方位。

在2046旅行最流行的做法是雇佣一个当地的向导,它可以把你带到你的目的地或是带你在城里旅游。当地的导游喜欢聚集在中央火车站的从它们外衣上的红色条带辨认出他们。导游一天收费从30美元到100美元不等,不包括交通。他们有时也会要烟草来替代部分的支付。如果你有兴趣研究和发现2046,一个好的向导对于你的旅程和人身安全是十分重要的,那些老练的向导还会向你讲述2046的各个方面。你会发现他们也很有兴趣发现外面的世界。提防一些向导也会是机器人,尽管你可能不能轻易区分出它们。

旅游办事处
旅游办事处散布在城市的各个角落,最大的一家坐落在中央火车站。他们将要求登记你的姓名和旅行证件号码,并和你一起预测游览路线,之后可以给你推荐一个向导。你可以在人类和机器人当中做出选择。

证件
A. 护照
你必须要保证随身携带护照。这是参观者身份的基本证件。证件必须要是合法的和有效期之内的。他们经常对参观者进行抽查,如果他们从你的证件发现问题,你就要被拘留直到事情被澄清。如果你丢失了原始证件,带上复制的证件也不失为一个好办法,也可以是其他形式的身份证件,例如驾驶执照(尽管游览者不允许在2046开车)。

如果你遗失护照,请立即通知2046的公共安全局或是大使馆。

千万不要把你的护照带到任何聚会上去,因为你的护照很有可能作为假的护照和身份证被复制和销售。

签证
所有到2046的参观者都需要签证。中转旅客不需要签证,但是只能在中央火车站停留最多24小时的时间,并且出于安全考虑不允许独自参观2046的城市。

如果你希望停留最多3个月的时间,你就要在到达以前提前向当地的大使馆或领事馆提出申请。你要提供在此就业和家庭成员在本国的证明,同时还要阐明你希望在2046停留如此长时间的理由。签证费是100美金。

如果你要将签证延期,就必须返回到中央火车站移民中心来处理此事。

如果你打算移民到2046,要提前12个月提出申请。申请的程序十分繁琐,同时需要的还有健康检查和心理测试。同时你还需要向2046提出你打算从自己国家向2046转移的资产。

旅行许可
在2046的某些区域需要旅行许可才能进入。旅行许可由公共安全局发放,需要在进入2046以后提出申请。

敏感的军事区当然是排除在旅游范围以外的,一些聚居区和不同种族混杂的少数民族区域也因其微妙的社会混杂而受到限制。

旅游限制在2046的晚上也是强制执行的,因此游客不得不在晚上留在屋里看电视或是收听国家电视台的广播来避免被捕。

为了避免误解,旅行者应该在最近的游客办事处登记个人细节,以防你被发现没有必要的旅行许可。

总的来说,你需要在2046聪明而迅速地旅行,不要绕不必要的弯子,并且为了避免与当地聚居区起口角,要对状况时刻保持警惕。

旅行保险
目前还没有银行或者保险公司愿意为2046提供旅行保险。你必须要自己承担风险。

驾驶执照
在2046旅行者不允许开车,因此驾驶执照也没有用处。如果你需要车的话,你可以座出租车或者雇人开车。

居民许可证
如果你打算移民到2046,或者在这里停留3个月以上的时间,你就需要申请并随身携带居民许可证。

许可证将决定你可以进入的区域,并且每12个月就要更新一次,同时要再进行一次严格的身体和精神检查。

即使是机器人居民也要求许可证。

大使馆和领事馆

本国的使馆
2046不存在大使馆。进入2046就意味着你放弃了自己的国籍和公民身份,大使馆的角色就是不存在的你所属国家的代表。

海关
2046的海关十分严格,除了随身携带的食品和衣物,所有物品都不许带入。这是2046保持自身文化纯洁性、使其不受外界影响的一种政策。

货币
你不需要货币,为什么需要?在2046,你只需要带上脑子。在这里你必须通过交易来生存。交易违禁品、交易点子、交易时间、交易服务、交易性。这是你在2046所需要的生存技巧。

邮政和通讯
在2046没有邮政和通讯。没有电话、没有互联网、什么都没有。因此在你离开自己的国家之前要把想说的话都告诉你的亲人!

网络资源
网络在2046的边界就被掐断了。没有数据传播可以进入2046的边界。2046有一个内部网,但是大多数的资源都局限于官方使用,而不是供公众使用。黑客确实有机会侵入,但是有被抓进监狱的危险。

图书
2046在大多数的国际指南上都有提及,但是由于没有来自于游览者的反馈,因此也没有关于它的细节。有传言说这部2046的指南是到目前为止最完善的一部,因为我们可以接触到唯一一个从2046回来的人。但是本书的出版商否认这个人的存在。

报纸和杂志
新闻发布主要由2046的官方报纸——2046时报——来负责。它们张贴在主要的布告栏里,同时也有杂志版本的。报纸在晚上会被回收,因此它们是被租借而非出售给读者的。人们必须要在每天傍晚把报纸和杂志归还到官方的报纸回收站。

电影
2046有很多的好莱坞大片,尽管对于这个神秘地域的涉及首先出现在2004年王家卫执导的电影当中。在这部影片中,一个作家在思想上经历了深刻的个人情感旅程,并虚构了暗指一个叫做2046的科幻世界的故事。

光盘
这本2046指南的配套光盘可以在Ebay等知名零售商店找到,尽管亚马逊图书网站因为某种不可告人的原因拒绝这些产品。

广播和电视
2046有世界上所有的广播和电视,但是在时间上却落后50年。它播放的还是老式收音机和黑白电视机播出的节目。显然,无论哪种方式,都只有一个频道。

视频系统
2046主要使用的是旧式录像带,但是老式的塑料胶片也被广泛使用。

照相和录影
因为照相和录影需要获得允许,因此很少人会这么做。回忆在2046并不能很好地保存,数据也会很快被破坏。相片退色、录影失真。人们试图用2046周围存在着很强的磁场来解释这些现象。

时间
2046并不适合世界的时区结构。因为到达那里的行程很长,同时与外界接触很少,因此时间在2046并不那么重要。

电气
2046使用的是240伏的电压。电池几乎在每个街道拐角都能买到,上发条的电气用具在这里很流行,大多数家电都是这一类。

度量衡
米制和传统单位在这里共同使用,因此记住你的换算系数!

洗衣房
几乎每个街角都有公共洗衣房。你也可以把衣服捐献给当地的救济委员会,并以此换得新的衣服。于是就省去了洗衣的麻烦。

厕所
在2046公共厕所并不普遍。如果你友善请求的话,可以使用家里、办公室或是商店里的私人厕所。但是记住要自带厕纸。

健康
大多数的医疗保险在2046都不提供。你应该考虑在到达时就在当地火车站购买医疗保险。他将承担你的所有不测,并使你从2046的任意一个医生那里获得医疗帮助。

女性旅行者
对于女性旅行者来说最重要的一件事就是要知道2046的大多数女性都是机器人而非人类。她们向男性提供性服务;因此要确认自己不要把机器人搞混。

同性恋旅行者
在2046,同性恋活动十分活跃。同性恋和异性恋完全没有区别。

残疾旅行者
残疾旅行者会发现2046有他们旅行所需的所有物品。

高龄旅行者
年长的旅行者会发现2046是一个退休后很好的修养之地。很多高龄旅行者把到2046看作是自己的最后一次旅行。

2046对于孩子
不是一个孩子们该去的地方。建议到2046的旅行仅限于成年人。大多数国家都禁止17岁以下的孩子到那里去。

有用的组织
2046的中心散布着很多游客中心。从那里你将得到最多的去2046旅行所需要的信息,例如安排住宿。这些游客中心同是也是签证中心,因此你需要在到2046的48小时内找到一家去申报你的到达。此时,他们会请你出示你以前从自己国家旅游的证件记录。

其他有用的组织是2046的地理局,他们很欢迎人们把旅行的照片寄存在他们的档案里,同时也是2046的记忆库里,你可以在此接入数据库下载你的记忆,并和机器人们一起分享。

图书馆
图书馆通常包括两部分的信息。第一部分的图书是外面人带到2046并上缴给游客中心的。这些书介绍了外部世界的知识,但是只有在2046生活超过10年的人才能看到这些书,以防它们会激起人们离开2046的愿望。

另一部分的图书包括基于下载知识和2046初到之人记忆的机器人信息。

你可以在2046的游客中心或者是图书馆的入口处申请图书卡。期限是27天。

大学
2046有连续的高等教育。唯一的一项课程就是艺术史,它的重点是"自身的艺术"。不同年龄的学生被召收入这个6年的课程,做为学习的一部分,他们要做一份作为自我展示的艺术作品集。毕业时,你将被赋予自我硕士学位——MOO,这是2046的一个奖项。

文化中心
主要的文化中心坐落在2046的中心,你将在这里看到2046的纪念堂。那里记录着2046以前公民们的信息。纪念堂每逢周二、周四开放。但是如果有从外面世界开来的火车的话,他们有时也会为新的到达者特意在周日开放。

危险和麻烦
2046是一个平静的地方,但是平静也会被新的到来者推翻自己世界的思想斗争所打乱。这有时表现为压抑、暴力、酗酒和纵欲。因此,人们要在幼年与游览者保持距离,而紧紧地围绕在当地民众的圈子里,以防激化矛盾。很快地找一个机器人情人总是一个比较好的办法。

法律事件
2046是一种无阶级的体系,法律事件由你的所属国在2046的中央法院处理。不需要出庭也不需要陪审团。要获得更多信息,请记住在到达时向游客中心查询。

营业时间
通常是一天24小时,由人类和机器人倒班。为了避免让机器人来为你服务,把你的业务集中在早上3点到下午3点33分之间,这是机器人们充电的标准时间。

公共假日和特殊事件
在2046没有公共假日和特殊事件。

做生意
物物交换是2046的主要交易方式。香烟和雪茄十分流行,通常被用作货币。

虽然2046没有明显的商业活动,但是却有供性和毒品交易的活跃的地下市场。尽管卖淫已经合法化20年了,但它只有在人类和机器人之间才是合法的。真正的女孩只有通过地下妓院网络才能找到。

移民到2046
在过去50年中,有无以计数对世界不再痴迷的人们前往2046。随着世界的现代化和人类关系的模糊,2046的人口也急速增长。

作为一个避难所,2046被传奇化了,移居2046既是人们所期盼的,也是一种缓解外部世界压力的方式。

尽管没有官方的移民局或旅行社允许组织向2046的正规移民,但还是有办法的。

在每个市镇,都有移民可以进出的大门和通往2046的火车。它们通常是隐蔽的和在城市的边缘,你所面临的挑战就是找到这些大门并将自己带上火车。这里没有固定的时间表,上车唯一的票证取决于你对于这种旅行的适宜性。其他的方式还有乘坐飞机、汽车、火车或是轮船。

电梯城市:垂直旅行

"满怀希望的旅行要胜于到达目的地" Robert Louis Stevenson

我经常做同一个噩梦。进入一部电梯,按下按钮,然后感觉不是向上,而是向下,或者是一直向上、无止境的向上。电梯是一个可以允许垂直运动的封闭胶囊——一种沿着垂直指针运输的方式。当我们思考它时,它就是一条神秘的空间切片,一种挑战重力法则和直击长空的机会。

电梯赋予了我们城市的形状并使建造高层建筑成为可能。作为最安全的运送系统之一,它使得地面可以变得复合化,同时可以使人们感受到从一个场所飞跃到另一个场所的惊心动魄。更高更光滑,这个胶囊带你带入在同一建筑体量中旅行的奇妙感觉,电梯城市就是一个垂直的体量。

"比子弹的速度还要快!"广告词中是这么说的。现在,垂直旅行的速度仅受到人类适应气压快速变化的能力限制。8米/秒是我们能够安全接受的最大速度。

没有人可以对城市的高度给予一个客观的估计:我们也同样不善于捕捉垂直的尺度。事实上,电梯城市仅仅是被我们的技术能力所局限。

在电梯城市中,封闭的、独立的房间是唯一面向世界的窗口:无论是新闻、股票交易还是天气。这是在电梯厅或是胶囊里播放的3个电视频道。它们都是简短的节目,但却提供了你所需要的足够信息。

独自在胶囊里的时候常常会反省,在一个无限复制自己影像的光亮反射空间里独处难道不是一件很有意思的事情么?但是在拥挤的时候,自省是很难做到的,因为为了避免尴尬,你被迫盯着没有反射性的表面。这时,鞋子就变成了一个回避的吸引点。

电梯城市是一个个人前提的堆栈,可以允许行为和活动的连续变化。由于完全没有规定,电梯的每一站都向一个新的世界开敞。因此每一个按钮都与一幅特殊的场景相对应:泰国餐厅、寿司吧、游戏中心、卡拉OK包间、夜总会、办公室、饭店大堂、健身中心、电影院、书店、仓库、桌球厅......

今天,你的路线可以被归纳为:212 - 78 - 25 - 69 - 111 - 57 - 212,就像是一个个性化的垂直抽奖。但是不要搞错了,这里没有什么是随机的,每种顺序都以某种方式解释了你的个性、能力、行为、性取向和信仰,使你很清晰地成为了你打算成为的人。

电梯城市是一个独一无二的按时间顺序分割空间的时间城市。等待的时间——平均15秒、挤满电梯的时间、运送的时间——到目前为止最多是220秒。在尽可能有效的同时,它创造出了一种短时的高密度,为居民提供了更高的、更省力的体验。因此,每次垂直旅行都是在摸索未来时暂停歇息的机会。

Lift city: travel on vertical motion

To travel hopefully is a better thing than to arrive." Robert Louis Stevenson

used to experience the same nightmare. Entering a lift, pressing a button and either having the feeling of going down instead of up or going up, too far up, indefinitely. The lift is this enclosed capsule allowing a vertical mobility - a means of transportation along a vertical cursor. A curious slice of space when we think about it. A chance to challenge the laws of gravity and scrape the sky.

The mechanical elevator have given shape to our cities and made possible the construction of high-rise buildings. As one of the safest transportation systems, it has allowed the multiplication of grounds, along with the sensation of flying from one place to another. Higher and smoother, the capsule exposes you to the magic of travelling while staying in the same block. *Lift city* is this vertical block.

"Faster than a speeding bullet!" they used to advertise. At present, vertical travel speed is only limited by the human capacity to adapt to fast changes in the air pressure. 8m/s is the maximum speed we can tolerate safely.

Nobody can give a realistic estimate of the city's height: w
are not that good at capturing the vertical dimension. As
matter of fact, *Lift city* is only limited by our own technologica
capabilities.

In *Lift city*, the enclosed, isolated room is the only window o
the world: world news, world stock exchange rates, and worl
weather. These are the 3 TV programs played in the lift lobb
or inside the capsule. They are short programs, just giving yo
enough for what you need.

A self-introspection happens when alone in the capsule. Isn'
t delightful to be finally alone within an infinite reproductio
of yourself in the shiny reflective surface? The introspectio
s different when crowded, as you are force to stare at a non
responsive surface in order to avoid any embarrassment
Therefore your shoes become an attractive focus point t
escape.

Lift city is a stack of individual premises, allowing a continuou
change of activities and lived programs. With a total absence o

rticulation, each stop of the lift is opening onto another world. o to each button corresponds a different scenario: a Thai estaurant, sushi bar, game centre, karaoke box, nightclub, ffice headquarters, hotel lobby, fitness centre, cinema, ookstore, warehouse, snooker room...

oday your daily route can be resumed as follow: 212 - 78 - 25 69 - 111 - 57 - 212. Like a personal vertical lottery. But don't et it wrong: nothing is random here. Each sequence decrypts our personality, your competence, your behaviour, your sexual ptitude, and your religion in a way that you clearly become vhat you plan to be.

ift city is a time city with a unique chronological division f space. Time to wait - an average of 15 seconds, time to ill the shuttle, time to be transported - so far 220 seconds naximum. As efficient as it can be, it has produced a emporal density (vs. solar time), offering the inhabitants a hance to experience greater heights effortlessly. Therefore, each vertical journey is an occasion to take a pause while navigating your future.